POLICING CONTROVERSY

IAN BLAIR

PROFILE BOOKS

First published in Great Britain in 2009 by
PROFILE BOOKS LTD
3A Exmouth House
Pine Street
London EC1R 0JH
www.profilebooks.com

Copyright © Ian Blair, 2009

1 3 5 7 9 10 8 6 4 2

Typeset in Garamond by MacGuru Ltd
info@macguru.org.uk

Printed and bound in Great Britain by
Clays, Bungay, Suffolk

The moral right of the author has been asserted.

A CIP catalogue record for this book is available from the British Library.

ISBN 978 1 84668 304 5
eISBN 978 1 84765 247 8

The paper this book is printed on is certified by the © 1996 Forest Stewardship Council A.C. (FSC). It is ancient-forest friendly. The printer holds FSC chain of custody SGS-COC-2061

FSC
Mixed Sources
Product group from well-managed
forests and other controlled sources
Cert no. SGS-COC-2061
www.fsc.org
© 1996 Forest Stewardship Council

Contents

'The romance of police activity keeps in some sense before the mind the fact that civilisation itself is the most sensational of departures and the most romantic of rebellions. By dealing with the unsleeping sentinels who guard the outposts of society, it tends to remind us that we live in an armed camp, making war with a chaotic world, and that the criminals, the children of chaos, are nothing but the traitors within our gates ... The romance of the police force is thus the whole romance of man. It is based on the fact that morality is the most dark and daring of conspiracies. It reminds us that the whole noiseless and unnoticeable police management by which we are ruled and protected is only a successful knight-errantry.'

G. K. Chesterton, 'The Defendant'
Quoted in Edwin Delattre, Character and Cops

'They were killed because of their colour, which was neither black nor white, but blue.' Elegy for two murdered police officers, one black and one white, New York City, 1972.

Quoted in Robert Mark, In the Office of Constable

'Circumstantial evidence is a very tricky thing', answered Holmes thoughtfully; 'it may seem to point very straight to one thing, but if you shift your own point of view a little, you may find it pointing in an equally uncompromising manner to something entirely different.'

Arthur Conan Doyle, 'The Boscombe Valley Mystery' in
The Adventures of Sherlock Holmes

Acknowledgements

My first acknowledgement has to be to the innumerable police officers and police staff from whom I have learned so much over more than thirty-four years. I also need to thank those many colleagues, past and present, within and outside policing, who assisted me in the preparation of this book. They are too numerous to be named but they know who they are and every suggestion was valuable.

I am most grateful to Andrew Franklin, my publisher at Profile, for all his encouragement and advice, together with his colleagues, Penny Daniel, Kate Griffin, Ruth Killick and Stephen Brough. My literary agent, Felicity Bryan, should be declared a national treasure. I would also like to thank my PA, Philippa Boston, and Oli and Jake from Computer Medicine, more magicians than medics, without whose combined help this book would have been in a very different shape indeed.

Beth Loftus from the Oxford Centre for Criminology supplied invaluable research support during the early stages of the book's composition and I would like to thank both her and the Director of the Centre, Professor Ian Loader. I also received generous support from Larry Sherman, Wolfson Professor of Criminology at Cambridge, whose private library has been inestimable. Thank you.

I want once again to acknowledge those unsung friends from my private office while Commissioner, Rebecca, Tom, Steve, Dave, Stuart, Mark, Joy, Felicity and Michael, without whom and many more I could not have done the job at all.

I drew great comfort from the community at my church, St Margaret's, and I will always be grateful for that. My final and most important thanks, however, go to my family: to my brother Sandy, who has supported me for years through many vicissitudes and who took the trouble to read and comment on an early version of the manuscript; to my children, Amelia and Josh, and above all, to my wife Felicity. Without their forebearance, support and love, the pressures of office could not have been borne and this book would never have been written.

Foreword

A few minutes after noon on Wednesday 1 October 2008 I went into the City Hall office of the Mayor of London, Boris Johnson. I had been the Metropolitan Police Commissioner for nearly four years. After defeating Ken Livingstone at the beginning of the previous May, Boris had been Mayor for five months. I had met him many times since but, on that morning, our relationship had formally changed. New legislation had come into force that day which provided Boris with a power which Ken had not possessed. As Mayor, Boris was now also empowered to decide whether he would also wish to be the Chair of the Metropolitan Police Authority, the body by which the Commissioner is most publicly and visibly held accountable. Boris had decided that he would.

Despite what had been expected and was often reported, I seemed to get on well with Boris. He is a likeable and witty man. With the exception that he had not been the Chair before, that morning's meeting should have been a standard one. The Commissioner would normally meet the Chairman of the Authority to discuss the agenda for a forthcoming MPA meeting. The next one was scheduled for the following Monday and, of course, Boris would now be chairing it for the first time.

As I arrived I felt good about the Met. Crime was falling at an unprecedented rate, down nearly 20 per cent since I had taken office: violent crime was down by double digits, the alarming increase in murders by teenagers of teenagers in London which had begun in 2007 was now slowing as the result of a number of Met initiatives, public confidence in London's police was up and a series of terrorist trials was clearly reducing – but not eliminating – the terrorist threat to the capital. There were troubles around: there always were. The current ones were a very public spat with one of my senior Asian officers, Tarique Ghaffur, and a spurious but also public set of allegations about the letting of a contract by the Met to one of my friends. I was thinking, as I went into the Mayor's office, that despite an overwhelmingly hostile and disbelieving press – a normal situation for a Met Commissioner – I would have a good account to give of my stewardship to the Authority, whose members were largely new after the same recent elections which had brought Boris to office.

There were four of us in the room: Boris and me, Catherine Crawford, Chief Executive of the Metropolitan Police Authority and a good friend, and Kit Malthouse, who led for the London Tories on policing and was already being seen as Boris's right-hand man on matters to do with the Met. I began the meeting by telling the three of them about an injured officer I had just visited in hospital but Boris suddenly changed the course of the conversation. Without warning he made clear his determination to force my resignation and indeed I did announce my resignation the next day, although, in law, I could have chosen not to, as the power to appoint or remove me lay not with the Mayor but with the Home Secretary. I explain in Chapter 9 what happened, why I took the decision I did and who said what to whom, but my personal experiences are not the only reason for this book.

For nine years, from the beginning of 2000 to the end of 2008, I held the two most senior operational positions in the British police service: Deputy Commissioner and then Commissioner of the Metropolitan Police. This book is my account of those years: of what it felt like to be the Commissioner during July 2005, when the bombs went off in London and fifty-two people died in the largest act of mass murder in recent English history, of what happened in the case of Jean Charles de Menezes, of how was it that the most liberal Commissioner in the Met's history became a leading advocate of the most draconian powers for which it had ever asked in peacetime, of the arguments over policing and race, of how the Commissioner accused of being too close to New Labour was in charge of the force which investigated the New Labour Prime Minister.

These years coincided with two specific developments: first, the way in which crime and terror became issues of increasingly rancorous political debate and, secondly, the resurgence of the Conservative Party, from bewilderment at the triumph of New Labour through furious impotence to rising influence and eventually power (at least in London). Throughout this period the Tories were obsessed at every level – from Michael Howard through David Davis to Boris Johnson – with the example of the reduction in crime that had been achieved in the 1990s in New York, with the doctrine of 'zero tolerance' and with the charismatic figure of my friend of long standing, the one-time Commissioner of the New York Police Department, Bill Bratton. Bill was an enormously successful Commissioner but he made the mistake of appearing on the front of *Time* magazine as the man who had saved New York. The mayor who had appointed him, Rudolph Giuliani, thought that this accolade ought to be his and promptly sacked him. A week after I went to City Hall I was due to go to an *Evening Standard* reception that would announce the 1,000 most influential people in London. The top five were highlighted in the newspaper. Boris was number one. I was number three.

Boris has never chosen to give me a coherent reason as to why I should step down. He made clear that, in his words, I was 'more sinned against than sinning'. Given the Met's successful performance in recent years, the most likely explanation for his action would seem to be that he had made a political decision that he did not want competition in either the achievement of crime reduction in London, which he had placed at the heart of his manifesto, or in the manner in which it should be done. I stand for a model of policing intensely concerned about, as a namesake once said, the causes as well as the actuality of crime, particularly where these concern issues of race and gender. I believe that senior police officers, like other experts in other fields, have the right and the duty to speak out about what should be done. There are others who see the police service as a body of street butlers, to be called on when required and invisible for the rest of the time.

The Conservatives have long been gripped by the power of the US model of policing, where police chiefs come and go at the behest of mayors. In New York, for instance, there have been forty-one Commissioners of the NYPD. In London I was the twenty-fourth Commissioner. Bill Bratton has just retired from being the fifty-fourth Chief of the Los Angeles Police Department, founded in 1853, more than twenty years after the Met. The American system is a viable model but it is heavily politicised and connected to a different judicial system and Federal structure.

The system of police accountability in the United Kingdom balances power, in a classically British style, between the Home Secretary, Police Authorities and chief officers. What Boris and his advisers did on that day was to crash through that balance and politicise the position of the most senior police officer in the country, an act subsequently described by Charles Clarke, the former Home Secretary, as rendering them 'not fit to hold high office'. My concern for the future is that this politicisation may be repeated elsewhere, as the various political parties make different proposals about accountability: either Police Authorities which consist only of directly elected members or directly elected, single police commissioners to replace those authorities, or simply the bolting of executive mayors on to the current system.

Policing is a very significant function in any country: its police service is the principal organisation empowered to use force against a state's own citizens. Together with the absence of the rule of law, the absence of a properly functioning police force is part of the definition of a failed state. A police service that serves one political party or individual is an emblem of dictatorship. Mature democracies across the world have all developed methods of safely controlling the police function. Such systems have many similarities but there are also many differences. The British system which began to evolve in the nineteenth century has a number of features which are in balance with this country's particular legal and constitutional arrangements. This is made more acute by the fact that the Metropolitan Police is not only the police of London but also leads and coordinates the national police response to terrorism, a situation apparently not to the liking of Boris and his London supporters.

The argument is not about me or whether any politician should have sought to do what Boris did. The argument is that the constitutional and legislative position of the police in Britain is a carefully constructed balance of competing and overlapping powers. Three coequal partners deliver policing: the Home Secretary, the local Police Authority and the Chief Officer of Police, who in London is called the Commissioner. All have different roles and none is entirely independent of the others. The system has grown up over nearly 200 years and is completely different from that of, for instance, France, where the police are almost entirely subordinate to central government, or the United States, where local police can be characterised as subordinate to local politicians, although the Federal police, in the shape of the FBI, have more independence. In much of Europe, the police work more directly to the requirements of prosecutors.

In Britain, however, the individual constable and the chief officer are independent office holders under the Crown. No senior officer can order a subordinate to make an arrest: that is a decision for that officer. The police in Britain have a far more significant role in the criminal justice system than their counterparts in continental Europe and are far freer to act independently within that system than officers in America. Similarly, in a manner different from other jurisdictions, chief officers in Britain have increasingly felt it incumbent on them to develop policy, within the rule of law, independently of the wishes of local or central government. That may be wrong and it may need changing, but not by one politician on a political whim.

The story of policing in Britain is the story of the struggle to develop that kind of system. It began with the Metropolitan Police, the headquarters of which were in a central London sidestreet called Scotland Yard. The Met was founded in 1829 by Robert Peel, then Home Secretary and later Prime Minister. There had been years of often acrimonious debate about what should be done about the rising levels of crime in London. For some the very idea of a police force was anathema, an affront to the rights of freeborn Englishmen. Many pointed to the despotism of the French police system under Napoleon.

The British already knew how to run police forces: they had them, mounted, armed and in barracks in their colonies. What Peel created, together with his first twin Commissioners, Charles Rowan, a soldier, and Richard Mayne, a barrister, was neither French nor Irish: it was something completely different, unmilitarised, preventative rather than detective, dressed as civilians, unarmed, a police for the people, not for the state. What began in London spread across Britain and then, with variations, across the common-law, English-speaking world (including New York in 1845).

And far beyond the English-speaking world. David Triesman was at one time a Minister of State at the Foreign Office. He told me that, on a visit to Darfur during the humanitarian crisis there earlier in this decade, hundreds of miles from the sea, he met a group of women in a refugee camp. When they found out he was from Britain they did not ask him for aid just in the form of shelter, water or education for their children. What they asked him for were British Bobbies. Which illustrates why what was said and done on 1 October 2008, whether I was a good or a poor Commissioner, is so important and so disturbing. Some eleven months later, on 3 September 2009, the events were still reverberating. 'We have seized control of Scotland Yard,' read the front-page headline of the *Guardian*, 'Johnson aide says Home Office "elbowed out" as Mayor tightens his grip on the Met.' (It is also interesting to note how the language changes over time: immediately after I had resigned, Boris repeatedly refused to say he had sacked me, insisting it was my decision. By September 2009, his official spokesperson referred quite openly to the 'sacking of Ian Blair'.)

A political approach like that to some functions in government seems to me to be inherently dangerous. The Opposition and the press that supported them criticised me for seemingly to support some aspects of government policy: the same combination praised Richard Dannatt, the recently retired head of the British Army, for apparently criticising the government. The party in government seemed to take the opposite view in both cases. It is interesting to surmise what would happen to both views were the roles of the two political parties switched after an election. For whatever reasons and with whatever caveats, the appointment of the former First Sea Lord, Alan West, as a minister by Labour and of Richard Dannatt as an advisor by the opposition, so soon after they left office, indicates that a potentially seismic shift is taking place in relationships. It may be impossible to return to a period in which such positions were not politicised in this way but, if so, then those that hold them will need ever greater support and skill to discharge their duties.

I fully accept that I am a controversial figure. I certainly made mistakes during my time in office. And perhaps there was some justification for the same Kit Malthouse to announce that Boris and he wanted the next Commissioner to be boring (although this is not at all a fair reflection on Paul Stephenson, who was selected to succeed me). Much of that is because of the tensions I have just outlined, together with the events which happened on my watch, whether the bombings of July 2005, the death of Jean Charles de Menezes, the 'cash for honours' investigation, the campaign for increased powers of detention or the manner of my departure. What follows recounts those years and those events, together with some of the less well-known things of which I am proud: the reintroduction of community policing in London, the fall in crime there and the significant rise in both public confidence and minority recruitment to the Met.

The political controversy which surrounded my tenure needs to be seen in the light of the political controversy in which Britain's police service was born. The argument with Boris Johnson and the uneasy relationship between his City Hall office and that of the Home Secretary echo the arguments between the first Commissioners and the Home Secretary and the emerging metropolitan councils in nineteenth-century London. The arguments about extended detention repeat the arguments between utilitarians and libertarians in the eighteenth and nineteenth centuries, as the response to international terrorism echoes recent responses to the IRA and to Anarchists and Fenians at the end of the nineteenth century. The rows over race and gender are a continuation of similar concerns from the second half of the last century.

Perhaps only the rise of the twenty-four-hour global media takes what I experienced into a place not visited before, although the unrestrained newspapers and cartoonists of the early nineteenth century would recognise their successors as heirs.

This book shows how politics and policing have mixed for centuries in London and how the Met, while occasionally engulfed in scandal at home, made 'Scotland Yard' one of the most enduring brands in the world. It was no surprise that, in 2007, the government of Pakistan asked Scotland Yard to assist in their investigation into the death of Benazir Bhutto.

Shortly before my resignation, an article in the *Observer* suggested the Commissioner's post might be the most difficult job in Britain, bar none; after I resigned, Bill Bratton said that I had held the most challenging police job in the world. As the main political parties now consider different options for police accountability, I end with an examination of what lies ahead for policing in England and Wales.

I am very proud to have been a police officer. I am very proud to have been the Commissioner of the Metropolitan Police. I am very proud of the men and women whom I had the honour to command. I think they are extraordinary. Britain has in common with only New Zealand, as far as I know, a police force which is largely unarmed. And, with all respect to Auckland and Christchurch and Wellington, they are not Hackney or Lambeth or Moss Side or St Paul's or Croxteth. British police officers are the heirs of Peel, who said of them that they 'are only members of the public that are paid to give full-time attention to the duties which are incumbent on every citizen'. And sometimes they pay for that with their lives. The arrangements by which they are held to account, commanded and supported are worthy of close attention.

Politics and terrorism have been the context in which its Commissioners have worked almost since the very beginning of the Met: over the years corruption, race and an ever more intrusive media have joined as other pressures. I will tell something of the story of how other Commissioners fared after 1829 but the book begins with one day in the summer of 2005.

1

7 July

Graham Cross is a Metropolitan Police sergeant who, on 7 July 2005, was based at Albany Street Police Station, in the Borough of Camden, just north of central London. He had a small team of neighbourhood officers doing 'early turn', the shift which runs from early morning to early afternoon. Around 9am on that warm summer morning Graham was told that there had been a train crash at nearby King's Cross Underground Station. He volunteered his team to close Euston Road, a major thoroughfare which runs past King's Cross, in order to provide a clear route in for emergency vehicles. It was towards the end of the rush hour but still very busy.

Inspector Mark Perry of the traffic division worked at the Met's Euston garage. He was informed of a developing major incident at Edgware Road Underground Station, about a mile from King's Cross, which was believed to be the result of an electrical power surge. Mark was making his way towards Edgware Road on his motorcycle when he was redirected to Aldgate Underground Station in the City of London. However, he found he could not go far in that direction because the road was closed near another Underground station, Russell Square, because of an incident there. Something much worse than a power surge was going on, he realised, so he radioed his concern to the Met's traffic control unit. It was nearly 9.40am.

Graham Cross and his colleagues had the road closure under control. A number 30 red London bus came past the team and they sent it south down Woburn Place towards Tavistock Square, about 150 yards away. Mark Perry was some 300 yards further south and east.

At that moment I was in my office at Scotland Yard, four miles away. I had been Commissioner of the Met for a little over five months out of what was expected to be a five-year term. I knew neither Graham Cross nor Mark Perry, although I would meet both of them in the months that followed, when I awarded them and many others with High Commendations for the outstanding leadership and bravery they displayed on that day.

I had already been made aware that there had been an incident on the underground, more often known in London as the tube. The first report to reach me was the same as Mark had received, of a power surge, though I had been told that it was in Edgware in north-west London. This made sense because I knew that a part of the electrical supply to the tube came from near there. I was very busy as a meeting had been scheduled for two hours later that morning with my 200 or so most senior staff. I had spoken to this group on my first morning as Commissioner, on 1 February, and outlined to them my intentions for the service. The meeting this morning was my first chance to bring most of them back together to assess how things were going. I always write my own speeches and invariably leave myself a bit short of time, probably because I know I work best under pressure. That day, however, I had really cut it short. Very unusually, I asked not to be disturbed unless it was something very important.

I never finished the speech. The meeting didn't happen. Graham Cross and Mark Perry had one of those moments which define policing, when, without warning, an incident unfolds in front of a police officer which he or she has to deal with then and there. And they both had it in spades because what was unfolding was the beginning of probably the most challenging three weeks in peacetime in the long and often tumultuous history of Scotland Yard.

Neither officer actually saw the bus explode at 9.47 but both heard it. Graham only had to look up to see the smoke. The roof was torn back so savagely that at first he thought it was an open-topped tour bus as he and his colleagues ran down Woburn Place. Mark radioed in that there had been another explosion and rode his motorbike to the scene. It was horrific: the dead, parts of the dead and the desperately injured lay in and out of the bus. Long experience had drummed it into all the officers there that they should fear secondary explosive devices (and despite the blast a large cardboard box – actually a microwave oven - was still perched on the downstairs luggage rack); experience also warned them not to interfere with a scene of crime. Nevertheless, without hesitation most of them climbed into the bus to do what they could. Mark and Graham took command, desperate to get stuck in but knowing it was their job to call for assistance, ambulances, explosives officers and dogs, to set up cordons and casualty reception points and to provide a commentary to the control at Scotland Yard. Thirteen people, including the bomber, died at Tavistock Square and many more were dreadfully injured: Mark Perry and Graham Cross were now in charge of the most dramatically visible part of the worst terrorist atrocity in English history. The picture of that wrecked bus became one of the iconic images of what would be known simply as 7/7.

A few minutes later Caroline Murdoch, my chief of staff, knocked on the door and came in. Caroline was the first non-police officer to hold this position and she was to be one of my closest confidants in the years ahead. 'There are reports of a bus blowing up,' she said. There were two large television screens in my office, one connected to network TV and one capable of capturing images from the police and traffic cameras across London. While I called for more information, the screens were switched on. I can't remember now which screen first caught the image of that number 30 bus but I remember how instantly it was obvious that what we were looking at was not the result of a power surge. And I had another problem.

My sixteen-year-old son Joshua was staying with me in London because he was doing work experience with the *Sun* newspaper, whose editor, Rebekah Wade, my wife and I had grown to know. Just the day before he and a fellow reporter had covered the announcement from Trafalgar Square that London was to host the 2012 Olympics. On 7 July, I had gone to work before Josh and he was to travel a bit later on by tube to the paper's offices in Wapping. He had rung my mobile phone a minute or two before Caroline had come in. He had said that his train had only got to Victoria, had stopped there for ages and then there had been an announcement that the line was closed because of a power problem. I told him to get on a bus and which one I thought it would be. As soon as I saw the bus at Tavistock Square, I went cold. I knew Josh wasn't on it, but how many more buses would be attacked? At the very moment when I had just begun to realise that I was facing the greatest policing challenge of my life, I did not know where my son was and I might have just sent him to his death. I rang his mobile phone. It took a long time before it rang. When he answered, as calmly as I could, I told him to get off the bus and walk straight to the Yard. That moment remained with me, as did the call from my wife, Felicity, who rang me as news began to break of the scale of what was happening. Of course, she had only one question and her relief was immense when I told her that Josh was sitting in a room along the corridor from my office. Those brief moments of concern have always stayed with me and later gave me some tiny insight into the nightmare that was now to engulf so many families. In fact it was one of the things that made me so insistent that we should do everything to get as much information out to people as we could as soon as we could.

We needed to: in addition to the explosion on the bus at Tavistock Square, carnage had occurred in three tube tunnels under the streets of London. Liz Kenworthy was a police officer, based at Haringey, who was travelling into central London to attend a training course. She was in the third carriage of a train when the first carriage exploded, an hour before I saw that bus. Almost everyone else streamed away as fast as they could: alone, not in uniform and with no means of communication, Liz struggled forwards into the carriage where the explosion had occurred and found the dead and the dying, people missing limbs and with their clothes blown off. She used her own clothing to make tourniquets and did her best to comfort and reassure those who were still conscious. Liz saved lives that day and was later awarded the MBE for her bravery: in the darkness, she also knew about secondary devices and was conscious that the tunnel might be about to collapse.

I have used Graham, Mark and Liz's stories to illustrate what was going on that terrible morning. The police use the phrase 'the golden hours' to describe the first period of response to a catastrophic incident. If the policing in those hours is not got as right as possible, the days and weeks that follow will be much more difficult. This was the period when these three officers and many other brave men and women, some from the emergency services (including colleagues from the City of London and British Transport police forces), but many others who were not but happened to be there, chose not to flee but to stay and fight in the filth, the blood and the chaos to save lives and give some comfort to the dying. Without what they all chose to do, the eventual toll of fifty-two innocent lives would have been much worse.

But at the strategic level there are also golden hours in the handling of such an incident. Difficult decisions have to be taken which are capable of affecting the outcome of an attack carried out on such a scale. In the longer term the response is a matter for government but, during those golden hours, the responsibility lies above all with the police because, by long-established convention, they coordinate the work of the fire brigade and ambulance service at incidents of this nature. And this one was on my watch.

The Met's most senior decision-making body is known as the Management Board and at that time this consisted of seven police officers and four non-police colleagues, looking after finance, human resources, IT and public affairs. Over the years we had prepared for this moment and by 10.15 we were meeting in emergency mode. I was very well supported by Paul Stephenson, who had taken over from me as Deputy Commissioner, later to be my successor, and on whose loyalty and judgement I would increasingly come to rely. Others who would be particularly involved that day were Andy Hayman, the counter-terrorism chief, an Assistant Commissioner; Alan Brown, another Assistant Commissioner, then carrying out the internal review of the Met which I had announced on my first day; and Dick Fedorcio, the head of press. For the moment the key players were the operational cops but everyone had a role to play and had delegated every other task.

I had appointed Andy Hayman as head of counter-terrorism. In this position he had to follow a long-standing and famous predecessor, David Veness, and this incident was a huge first test for Andy. I was confident he would be fine. We were friends and had passed together through some very choppy operational waters. Later he and I would part company but this was his finest hour and he richly deserved the CBE he was awarded for his part in this investigation.

For now, the crucial issues were to try to get the best picture we could of what had happened, to devise a plan for these first few hours and to determine whether we should be making any public announcements. Each member of the meeting reported on what was known. Our approach that morning was based on the system then in use in COBR – rather prosaically, the acronym stands for the Cabinet Office Briefing Room, the location of the government's first response mechanism to an emergency – as this was what we had practised.

Of course, it was still very unclear what had happened. The bus was obvious but it seemed there might have been five other incidents, not only at Edgware Road but also at King's Cross and Russell Square and Liverpool Street and Aldgate because casualties were emerging from both pairs of adjacent tube stations after bombs had gone off in the tunnels between them. We didn't know that. What was clear was that this was a massive and coordinated attack on the capital. Loss of life was going to be very high. It was almost certain that this would turn out to be an Al-Qaida-inspired attack. The effect on intercommunal tensions was potentially very serious. A number of things had to be done. Andy would be throwing all his detectives into the scenes but they needed coordinated uniform command. Resources would have to be drafted in from outer London. We had to prepare for further attacks.

In the half-hour before the 10.15 meeting I had been in touch with both No 10 and the Home Office. A COBR meeting had been arranged for 11am with Charles Clarke, the Home Secretary, in the chair, which Andy was to attend. The Home Secretary was chairing the meeting because the Prime Minister was at the G8 summit at Gleneagles, from where he later rang me. It is probable that the 7 July bombings were designed to coincide with G8, possibly as a message to the West, possibly because the bombers and those who had schooled them thought that security would be lowered in London because we were lending security support to police at Gleneagles in the face of the determined demonstrations there. (I was often asked subsequently if the bombs were a response to London winning the Olympics. My answer was always that this would have required optimism about London's chances of winning of an unimaginable order.) In fact one of the few mercies of that day was that the Met had deployed additional officers into central London already, in case secondary demonstrations against the G8 summit occurred in the capital, and as a result there were far more officers for immediate deployment than usual. This explains why some of the first officers to reach the scenes were from outer London, something which surprised me very much when I visited the locations later that day and met first responders from as far away as Sutton, on the city's southern edge.

As we ran through what we knew, who was in command of what, what had already been done and what were the next priorities, I began to reflect on the time that was slipping past. The news channels were already making clear that this was a very serious attack but no official confirmation or announcement had been made. A COBR meeting would put something out but getting ministerial agreement to a statement would take time and the meeting itself had not yet begun. I put it to my colleagues that the public needed reassurance, that some form of message had to be given and this would be best done by someone in authority and in uniform, and that I thought it had to be me. To different degrees, all of my colleagues disagreed: it was too early, we didn't know enough, things weren't clear. Dick Fedorcio was dead set against the idea. For probably the only time in my life, I overruled unanimous advice to the contrary, from senior and trusted colleagues, in relation not to a policy decision but something immediate and irrevocable. Dick phoned the main TV channels and agreed a pooled statement to a single camera at ITV's Millbank Studios in central London.

Just after 11am, accompanied by Joy Bentley, the press officer who would be with me through almost all of the events of the next four years, I stood there and delivered a very simple series of messages: the incidents were very serious and there would be loss of life but above all that people should stay where they were for the time being and that a long-rehearsed and well-planned operation by all the emergency services was now swinging into action. As I finished I had an unbidden thought that if such an operation wasn't swinging into effect as I spoke, then someone else would be talking to them tomorrow because I wouldn't have a job.

Sometime after I returned to the Yard I was told that COBR was actually discussing what public announcements were to be made and by whom while I appeared on the screens in the room. Fortunately, after initial consternation, there was broad agreement that the messages and the messenger had been right, particularly as every few minutes the scale of what had happened became more apparent.

In the early afternoon I left the Yard to visit the police and others working at two of the scenes, Tavistock Square and Russell Square. It would be another couple of days before I went down into the tunnel beneath Russell Square station because it is a cardinal rule that police chiefs are there to encourage, not to interfere with a crime scene, however vast. But already it was obvious that something terrible had happened. Exhausted emergency service personnel stood about, covered in dirt but anxious to talk and equally anxious to know from me the scale of what had happened elsewhere. Tavistock Square was even worse. Because debris, including human remains, had been blown at least that distance, I stayed about 30 yards from the bus. It took me a number of return visits to notice the irony that one of the principal statues in Tavistock Square is that of Mahatma Gandhi, the great advocate of non-violence.

In the early evening I went out again and visited Edgware Road and Aldgate, the Jaguar passing almost alone through empty streets. Wherever I went, though, I drew strength from the way that so many people had responded with so little thought for themselves. I felt the same deep admiration for the staff of the County Hotel and the British

Medical Association, near to the bus, who set up temporary triages, as for the parish volunteers of St Mary and St Mark's Church, Paddington, who opened their doors so that emergency staff could have a rest, or the staff of Marks & Spencer at Edgware Road, who not only provided the first triage site at that location but also emptied their shelves of bottled drinks for emergency workers and minor casualties alike.

Over the coming weeks many more stories would emerge but I learned of only a fraction of them in these early visits. But it was outside Russell Square Underground Station on that afternoon that I first became aware of something that I would use again and again to show how extraordinarily the Met had reacted to the events of 7/7. The system has now changed, but in 2005 new officers joined as police recruits and went to the Met's training college at Hendon in north-west London for eighteen weeks of residential training. Thereafter a group would be allocated to a Street Duties trainer at the police station where they were to work. The group would then work together for a further ten weeks before they could patrol on their own. A group from Camden, led by Sergeant Neil Drinkwater, were near Russell Square tube station on 7 July. They were in week five of the course, which meant they each had been a police officer for less than six months and they were still in full-time training.

As members of the public began to stream out of the station's entrance it became obvious to Neil Drinkwater that there had been a serious incident on the tube. He radioed that position to the Camden control and then decided to investigate. He told the Street Duties officers that they did not have to come with him but they all volunteered to do so. They went down the steep steps into one of London's deepest tube tunnels, then walked along the tunnel in the dust and the darkness, not knowing whether the roof might collapse, never absolutely certain that the electricity was switched off. As they climbed into the bombed carriage they entered a scene of medieval carnage. I have always regarded that action as deeply emblematic of an organisation whose values are in the right place. All of these officers were also highly commended.

After returning from Russell and Tavistock Squares I held a series of meetings to try to assess the emerging situation and our response. Then I received a telephone call saying that a visitor was arriving. Tony Blair had flown down from Gleneagles and was coming to the Yard. I had met the Prime Minister before on many occasions but in nothing like these sombre circumstances. Together with Charles Clarke, Tony Blair arrived at Scotland Yard at about 4.30pm. They sat in my office for ten minutes while Paul Stephenson and I briefed them about developments in the last couple of hours. Then I took them down to the second floor of the Yard, where I knew that a briefing was going on for those senior officers who would be taking on the late-afternoon responsibility for both returning London to normality and guarding it against further attack. The control room at Scotland Yard is a place of restricted access and, as the three of us walked along the corridors, officers pressed codes into doors which swung open. The briefing officer was Superintendent Roger Gomme, a public order expert. The small room was crowded by the time we entered.

Roger was mid-speech. It was probably the toughest afternoon of a tough career. No one knew what would happen next. For him, what happened next was that the Commissioner entered the briefing room. That was 95 per cent unusual – on a highly unusual day. In all the activity, the call from my staff that I was coming down to him hadn't got through. If Roger was surprised to see me, he was even more surprised when the Prime Minister and the Home Secretary walked in as well. We have chatted many times since then about that moment. Roger did very well. He welcomed us all before carrying on with the briefing. The Prime Minister listened and, at an appropriate pause, he told those present what a great job they were doing, what a challenge we faced and how proud he was of them. The three of us left. A slightly gobsmacked Roger continued.

We went downstairs to the front of Scotland Yard. I said goodbye to the Prime Minister and his team left. Charles Clarke and I remained for a moment standing on the small tarmac area inside the Yard's armed perimeter. His protection team, anxious to move on, moved forwards. The Home Secretary had his hand on the door of his car as he turned to me and said, 'Ian, find the fuckers' and got in. I smiled a bit grimly but said nothing.

There was no reason at this stage to assume that the acts had been the work of suicide bombers, although we had prepared for such acts. After 9/11 the UK's police forces, led by the Met, had developed strategies to counter suicide attacks, based on the acquisition of intelligence about either an individual who was suspected to be a suicide bomber or a particular event that was to be targeted by a suicide bomber. The strategies and tactics were collected together under the codename Operation Kratos and they shared one particular feature. In normal circumstances an armed police officer can only fire their weapon if they have reasonable cause to believe that someone, including themselves, is in imminent danger of death or serious injury. Under Kratos a codeword could be given to a firearms officer to shoot dead – the technical term is to fire a critical shot at – someone against whom they had no information on which to base reasonable cause. In these circumstances they would be acting as the agent of the senior officer who had the intelligence. There would be no warning, no shouts of 'Armed police.'

However, there had never been a suicide attack in Europe and the Madrid train bombings of fifteen months before, which killed 191 people and led to the fall of the Spanish government, had not been carried out by suicide bombers. (In the search for those perpetrators a Spanish police officer was killed by the terrorists during a raid on their flat, just as a man known as Kamel Bourgass had murdered Detective Constable Stephen Oake in a raid in Manchester the year before: facts which weighed heavily on our minds in everything that we did on 7 July and throughout that summer.) But 9/11 had been a suicide attack.

I was directly involved in the immediate British response to 9/11. On that September lunchtime in 2001 I was having lunch with Justin Russell, the Prime Minister's special political adviser on policing. The Prime Minister was at the TUC conference, which was apparently going to be difficult. At that time texting was not yet in common use by adults and Blackberries were unknown, but we both had pagers. Five minutes or so after we had started the main course, within ten seconds of each other our pagers went off. Both of them roughly said the same thing: 'Incident in New York: return to the office immediately.'

As it was for an earlier generation, when everyone remembered where they were when they learned that John F Kennedy had been killed (which I can just about remember, although I was only ten), and more recently the death of Diana, Princess of Wales, the attack on the Twin Towers is a moment that psychologists describe as 'flash-bulb memory'. The restaurant is one of those for me. I am not sure that psychology has a term for what followed next; perhaps 'searchlight memory' would be appropriate, as I spent the next few hours grappling with the implications of the one single event which, in my lifetime, has changed the world.

Back at Scotland Yard I saw the pictures of first one and then a second plane flying into the World Trade Center. Only three years earlier I had stood on top of one of the Twin Towers with my wife and children. (It is one of the few mercies of that terrible day that the planes hit the towers before the viewing platform was open to the public.) For two weeks earlier in 2001 I had attended the National Executive Institute Course of the FBI in Washington DC and in Canada. One of my fellow students on that programme was Fred Morrone, Superintendent of Police and Director of Public Safety, the Port Authority of New York and New Jersey Police Department. During the hours that followed the 9/11 attack, he returned to his control room in the Twin Towers and, when they collapsed, he was killed.

I knew that the then Met Commissioner, John Stevens, was by chance on a plane midway to the United States. Once he left the ground I was the Acting Commissioner, so it was no surprise to me that two things happened on my return to Scotland Yard. The first was a telephone call from the Permanent Secretary at the Home Office, John Gieve, asking us to mobilise every asset we had to help the Americans 'find who had done this'. The second was a call to represent the police service at COBR. Below ground in Westminster lies a series of government control rooms, each one deeper and further away from Whitehall than the last. The headline above the first extract of Andy Hayman's book *The Terror Hunters*, as it was serialised in *The Times* in 2009, was 'The lost politicians and cronies who make chaos out of a crisis'. I don't agree. I believe that COBR, when properly run, is an extremely effective mechanism of government.

The briefing room is long, low and at that time dominated by large television screens at either end, on which CNN and SKY were playing silently. At moments of serious crisis it always feels crowded, even though there are officials in another room who are available to supply more information on any topic required. I had been in COBR before but I had never – and have never since – been in such a dramatic meeting, even after 7/7. The Prime Minister, having returned from the TUC conference without giving his speech, was in the chair. Present were the heads of MI5 and MI6, the Foreign Secretary, the Defence Secretary, the Home Secretary, military officers and others. The conversation was urgent and yet disjointed, all of us struggling to comprehend what had happened and what was happening: the attack on the Pentagon and the loss of another plane in mid-America were reported during the meeting. Everyone was trying to predict the implications for the UK. We all knew instinctively, none more so than the Prime Minister, that the world was changing. I should say we all understood that this was a terrorist attack but, of course, we had no idea of what might happen next. There was a moment in the discussion which did not involve me, about health and concerns over increased hospital admissions of people suffering from psychosis, frankly a second order consideration. I looked up at the screens and saw the first tower come down. I and one or two others gasped. A silence fell. We all knew that this was war, in our time, on our watch.

My other overwhelming memory is of a sudden announcement that a number of planes were approaching the UK from the Atlantic, each with an emergency distress signal operating. We would soon learn that this is what happens when a plane is turned through 180 degrees from its original course, but initially it led to a deadly silence. The military – with the Prime Minister and all of us looking on open-mouthed – began a stuttering discussion about scrambling fighter planes to meet the incoming airliners. It only took about two minutes to understand what was actually happening yet what was being considered was beyond belief.

It is an interesting coincidence that, in talking afterwards about 9/11, Bernard Kerik, who replaced Bill Bratton as New York Police Commissioner, used to say that he had known how to get hold of almost every emergency service but nobody around him knew a telephone number for the US Air Force. However, while he was no doubt shouting that to his colleagues, one of my thoughts, rather shamefully, was to wonder whether being under a very well-known central government building with a dozen planes apparently intent on exploding in the heart of London might be about as unwise a place to be sitting as possible.

Al-Qaida was far from unknown. Just a month before 9/11, in August 2001, my family and I were driving across Italy on holiday. Josh, who was subsequently to be with me on 7/7, was then thirteen, in the back of the car and bored. He said to me, 'OK, Dad, you're a policeman: who is the worst criminal in the world?' And so I told him – and a rather astonished rest of the family – about Osama bin Laden, about the attack on the World Trade Center in 1993 and the bombings of the US embassies in East Africa in 1998 and the destroyer the USS *Cole* off Aden two years later. So, while those planes on 9/11 literally came out of a clear-blue sky, the deadly organisation which lay behind that terrible day was by no means unknown.

With the Good Friday agreement of 1998 in Northern Ireland I had thought that the threat of terrorism would be lifted from the UK for the rest of my police career. For their part, in the run-up to and after that agreement, the intelligence services, particularly MI5, had began to cast about for a new role, particularly with the diminution of the other threat from Eastern Europe. They had started to work on organised crime as an economic threat to the nation. For some reason, however, their cover of Islamic terrorist groups was much looser than it could have been, much to the outrage of a number of allies, including France, which dubbed London as Londonistan, subsequently the title of a book by Melanie Phillips. There has always been a worthy British tradition of sheltering radicals, from Marx onwards, but you do not have to share all of her views now to see this as an error. This all changed immediately. Even so, the very audacity of the 9/11 attack was to have one particular and unfortunate consequence: its sheer scale fixed the eyes of the world – and by association the eyes of law enforcement and intelligence – largely on to attack from elsewhere, as opposed to attack from within, inspired from elsewhere.

And then came bombings across the world: in Bali, Riyadh, Casablanca, Mombasa, Istanbul and Madrid, all of which seemed to have been carried out by or connected to Al-Qaida, and all of us, certainly in Britain, Europe and the United States, saw this as an external threat on a scale not faced since the Cold War. But there was another story. Both of the so-called 'shoebombers', Richard Reid (himself a convert to Islam) and Saajid Badat, who were involved in an attempt to blow up transatlantic airliners in 2001, were born and raised in Britain. The same goes for the two young men who went to Israel in 2003 to carry out a suicide attack in Tel Aviv, as it does too for Ahmed Sheikh, the murderer of Daniel Pearl in Karachi in 2002. Dhiren Barot, arrested in 2004 for planning to detonate a 'dirty bomb' in either London or New York, had come to Britain as a small child. It was Britons who were to pose the threat which would emerge both below the streets of London and on a bus. And we did not see them coming, to the extent even that, shortly before 7/7, the national threat level, used to estimate the likelihood of an attack, was officially lowered.

July 2005 had begun pretty normally for me. Despite many invitations, I had a fairly austere approach to corporate hospitality, during my time as Commissioner, for instance, going as an official guest to just one football international and one rugby international. However, my wife is a divorce lawyer and would have regarded it as grounds for a petition of unreasonable behaviour if I had declined the annual invitation to the Commissioner and his wife to watch the Men's Final at Wimbledon from the Royal Box. So Sunday 3 July 2005 saw us watching Roger Federer beat Andy Roddick with hardly a sweat.

The Monday could not have been much more different, with the launch in a Brixton cinema of a new campaign to combat gun crime in the black community under the banner of the Met's Trident campaign. Trident is a hugely successful partnership between the Met and the black community. In the late 1980s London had first begun to experience drug-related murders within its African-Caribbean, particularly Jamaican, community. The Met acted as it usually did and set up a squad to investigate what were then called 'Yardie' killings. Yardie is a Jamaican slang word which broadly denotes a gang member. I remember talking to one of the officers involved at the time, who said that they were meeting silence and making little progress.

As part of its response to the Macpherson Report into the murder of Stephen Lawrence, in 1999 the Met created Trident, a full-time dedicated unit working with the community, supported by its own independent advisory group, some of whom were from the black church movement. John Grieve was the prominent senior detective who had headed up the Met's response to Macpherson and had helped to introduce the idea of independent advisers. I remember his comment to a sceptical colleague who had pointed out that you couldn't solve murders at a vicarage tea party: 'You can in this community: it will be the churchgoing mothers who will lead us to the killers.' These murders were extremely difficult to solve. For instance, those of seven-year-old Toni-Ann Byfield and the man she believed to be her father, in September 2003 in Harlesden, were declared virtually uninvestigable by the reviewing officer (all unsolved murders are automatically subject to peer review at various stages) but were solved by a mixture of investigative audacity, perseverance and community cooperation. The result was the conviction in 2006 of Joel Smith, who received forty years' imprisonment.

At this particular launch I met two of the characters behind Trident. Cindy Butts is a young black community activist who had made such an impact on the MPA during its first four years that she was voted in as one of its Deputy Chairs in its second and third terms, while Lee Jasper was then the Mayor's adviser on community relations and policing. Lee has many admirers and many detractors. I am broadly an admirer and on Trident, as on many other things, this former black radical, whom I first met in the controversial Mangrove Club when I was a young police officer in Notting Hill, was a star. The campaign in London's

Evening Standard by Andrew Gilligan, the journalist whose broadcast launched the Hutton Inquiry on to the BBC, to oust Lee from his post was part of that paper's unrelenting push to unseat Ken Livingstone in the run-up to the 2008 mayoral election. After Lee was suspended a Scotland Yard investigation subsequently found he had no case to answer, in that no evidence emerged which required the police to treat him as a suspect for criminality and his conduct was never referred to the Crown Prosecution Service (CPS). That was for later: for now, he and Cindy were part of the public face of Trident, proof to the black community that the Yard was serious about solving their crimes, not doing investigation to them but with them. Trident's average clear-up rate for murder during my time as Commissioner was nearly 75 per cent, an unthinkable achievement twenty years before.

The main events on the Tuesday were a routine monthly meeting of the Management Board and a discussion with Paul Stephenson on how the efficiency drive which I had announced on my first day as Commissioner, known as the Service Review, was going to be presented the next day to the Management Board. This was going to be pretty tricky because some of the review's conclusions were likely to be unpalatable to a number of my colleagues. There followed something quite unusual, a dinner between the members of Management Board and Bob Kiley, a former CIA agent and then the Mayor's Transport Commissioner, and his colleagues from Transport for London (TfL). We had a lot to talk about, principally because the creation of TfL in 2000 had raised the distinct possibility of its contracting out policing and security to another organisation, either the British Transport Police or even a private security firm. In the event it had contracted with the Met, however, and there was much to discuss. After the business issues had been gone through, one of the topics we discussed was the next day's announcement of which city was to host the Olympics. No one expected London to have a hope.

The Management Board met again the next day for almost the whole day to examine the Service Review. The discussion went surprisingly well but the main event we all remember was, of course, the Olympic announcement just after 12.30pm. We were away from the Yard and the room did not have a television but Dick Fedorcio had brought a radio. We listened and heard the pause before the heavily accented word 'London'. We all cheered and thought what wonderful news it was for London and for Britain.

It did not take long for a more sober mood to settle on our room as we individually and collectively contemplated the challenge for the Met in the run-up to and the staging of the Games in 2012. We were also concerned with the events going on at the G8 meeting at Gleneagles, where the Met was giving substantial assistance to Fife Constabulary. At the end of the meeting I went back to the Yard and agreed to do a pre-recorded interview that evening about the winning of the Olympics with the BBC's *Today* programme, for transmission the next morning. It was to be one of those pieces of bad luck over which one cannot have any control. I was asked about the obvious threat of terrorism to the London Olympic Games and, while emphasising that there could never be complacency nor absolute security, I replied, quoting a then recent report from the Inspectorate of Constabulary, that the Met was regarded as the 'envy of the world when it came to counterterrorism'. This remark was broadcast the next morning and to all but the most discerning listener would have seemed live. Less than an hour later the first three bombs went off on the London Underground, at about 8.50am.

More or less simultaneously Mohammed Saddique Khan, thirty, detonated his bomb on a westbound Circle Line train, just outside Edgware Road Station, killing six people, while Shezad Tanweer, twenty-two, detonated his on an eastbound Circle Line train, just outside Aldgate Station, killing another seven, and Jermaine Lindsay, nineteen, set his bomb off on a Piccadilly Line train far below street level between Russell Square and King's Cross stations, killing twenty-six of his fellow passengers. About an hour later Hasib Mir Hussein, eighteen, blew up the bus in Tavistock Square, killing himself and thirteen other passengers. The other bombers had gone south, east and west from King's Cross, where they had arrived by train from Luton, some 30 miles north of London. The Northern Line going north from Euston (100 yards' walk from King's Cross) was temporarily closed and it may be that Hussein was on a bus because he could not get on to a northbound train.

Much is known now that was not known on that day. There were only four bombs, not six. We know now that these were suicide attacks. We had no idea yet what kind of explosive had been involved and few of us had heard of the hydrogen-peroxide-based formula which was the bombers' weapon of choice. We did not know then that this plot had been long in the hatching, perhaps since Khan went to Pakistan in July 2001. (It seems certain that the planning had already begun when Khan and Tanweer went to Pakistan in November in 2004.) The connections which would later be established between them and other men, not part of the 7/7 plot, but subsequently convicted in other terrorist trials, were not yet clear to the Met.

We didn't know any of these things but those who lost their family members or friends and those who lost limbs and livelihoods want to know if anybody knew. We know now that there were some traces, particularly around Mohammed Saddique Khan. Ignoring hindsight, the key question is whether the combined actions of MI5, the Met and West Yorkshire Police were negligent in regarding Khan and his associates as too peripheral to the men they were already following, who were involved in a number of known and active plots, to bother with. A report by the Parliamentary Intelligence and Security Committee was published in May 2009, when the all of the trials concerning 7/7 had been finally concluded. It was entitled 'Could 7/7 Have Been Prevented?' and paragraph 212 was pretty straightforward:

> Having taken everything into account, and having looked at all the evidence in considerable detail, we cannot criticise the judgements made by MI5 and the police, based on the information they had and their priorities at the time ... We believe that the decisions made in 2004 and 2005 were understandable and reasonable.

This conclusion does not assuage the grief felt by those who believe that, if something had been done differently, the bombers would not have succeeded. But that is to be sure that something would have been elicited by further surveillance. Furthermore, understandably but unfortunately it is to hold police and secret service agents to an impossible standard and to misunderstand the nature both of surveillance and intelligence and of the choices over resourcing that have to be made. Surveillance teams are very expensive and there are never enough of them. Those in charge have to achieve a balance between the competing demands of crime and terrorism and between differently prioritised targets. In the years after 7/7, when surveillance capacity had been massively reinforced, the list of potential terrorist target groups almost always far outstripped the capacities of teams available to deploy against them, and truly agonising choices had to be made. Even then, surveillance is a blunt instrument where days can be spent with no useful product and where, even if intelligence is gained, it is difficult to decipher, like a prospector panning for gold, except that these nuggets do not shine out. Select for further work or discard for now? Information, rumour or disinformation? Act or don't act?

One of the oldest adages about counter-terrorist policing is the statement of an anonymous Irish Republican spokesman after the IRA had blown up the hotel where the annual conference of the British Conservative Party was being held in 1984, failing to kill the Prime Minister, Margaret Thatcher, although other people died. 'You have to be lucky all the time,' he said. 'We only have to be lucky once.' The scale of what the 7/7 bombers had done, coupled with our knowledge of previous plots involving poisons like ricin or the attempt to create a 'dirty bomb', made that statement an agonising challenge. The dilemma of when to take action against an apparently emerging threat was to haunt police, security agencies and government in the years ahead. It would lie at the heart of the 'ninety-day' debate over prolonged detention and would be seen again in relation to almost all the suspected and actual plots, from that concerning airliners in 2007 to the arrest and release of a number of Pakistani students in the north-west of England at Easter 2009: act potentially precipitately or wait and risk disaster. And it made the presentation of such choices extremely difficult to make clear to the public.

Nothing made this clearer to me than an interview I did with Jim Naughtie on *Today* after a police raid on a house in Forest Gate in east London in 2006. He asked me two questions, one after the other. The first was whether Eliza Manningham-Buller, head of MI5, who had recently announced her resignation, was doing so because MI5 had had a trace of one of the 7/7 bombers before they struck – this was Mohammed Saddique Khan – but had not followed it through. The second was why I had not resigned over the Forest Gate raid when the Met followed through what was believed to be more than a trace but had not found the terrorist device which it believed to be in the house. I answered the questions separately: it was only afterwards that I realised that these two questions represent entirely incompatible positions. Resign if you don't act (or someone in your organisation doesn't) but you or they are wrong. Resign if you do act (or someone in your organisation does) but you or they are wrong.

I only wish I had been quick enough to recognise the contradiction while still on air. The French have an expression for this: 'l'esprit d'escalier', or 'staircase wit', what you realise you should have said in the room, when it mattered. (In fact the Independent Police Complaints Commission report on Forest Gate subsequently made clear that, given the nature of the intelligence, the Met had no choice but to act when we did.)

But all this was still in the future and what lay ahead of the Met on and after 7 July were many separate but concurrent tasks: to investigate the greatest single act of murder in modern English criminal history (English because the death toll was less than the 270 killed in 1988 above and in Lockerbie in Scotland); to identify the dead and injured; to coordinate the efforts of emergency, health and transport services and local authorities to restore the city to some form of functionality; and to protect it from further attack. Equally we had to communicate as much information as possible to a frightened and potentially restive population and a media desperate for facts, of which we really had very few. This, of course, meant that very little authoritative information could be given and, as subsequently in the case of John Charles de Menezes, the media would have to rely on witnesses and survivors, sometimes with unfortunate results.

In his recent book *Voodoo Histories: The Role of the Conspiracy Theory in Shaping Modern History* the commentator David Aaronovitch notes the unwitting case of the *Guardian* journalist Mark Honigsbaum on 7/7. Two of the early witnesses to whom Honigsbaum spoke at the scene at Edgware Road said that the bombs had blown up under the train, an account which he duly filed. Despite the fact that he subsequently corrected the copy, having spoken to survivors who had been closer to the blast and were certain that the explosions had occurred inside a carriage, Honigsbaum recognises that his 'comments, disseminated over the internet ... were already taking on a life of their own'. Aaronovitch argues that this early account was the beginning of a number of the conspiracy theories which would eventually swirl around 7/7 that it was, as was suggested about 9/11, a government plot to justify war in Iraq.

But on 7 July we knew very little for certain. We did not know the number of dead or injured or who was responsible or why. However, two of the features of Al-Qaida-inspired terrorism are that they very rarely claim or admit responsibility and they seek always to inflict mass casualties. This meant that it was in their direction that our thoughts immediately turned.

It was the task of the Management Board to ensure that all this was being done and that the appropriate staffing and command lines were in place. To this end we put into effect the operational plan that we had developed and practised, which was well meant and good on paper but was subsequently found to need refinement. I created two Gold Commanders, as they are known, the officers in ultimate charge of an operation; these were Andy Hayman for the investigation and Alan Brown for the logistics to support everything else. But no plan survives contact with the enemy: this left potential room for both duplication and omission. After the summer a review of all the events suggested a better course, which was an entirely different briefing and meeting process, together with the establishment of a single lead Gold responsible to me, with all other Management Board colleagues working in support. This pattern would then apply whatever the situation, although the selection of the Gold would depend on the nature of the challenge, with different Assistant Commissioners appointed in the response to terrorism, for instance, or some form of multiple serial killing similar to that of the Washington DC snipers or a pandemic.

In the meantime everyone got on with the roles assigned to them and did their best. I knew the investigation and the resourcing would be under full steam. In fact both turned out to be the biggest undertakings of their type in the Met's history. Operation Theseus, the investigation into the bombings, had, by 2009, when the trials connected to 7/7 came to an end, examined 37,000 exhibits, attempted to trace nearly 25,000 people and analysed the use of tens of thousands of telephones. Meanwhile, for the first time in the memory of any of us, the Met called for 'mutual aid' from forces outside London to help with security and the investigation, this being the term used for forces supplying manpower when an individual force cannot undertake a task on its own. Mutual aid was what the Met supplied to others, not something it asked for.

Beyond this, my main concerns were the fear of what these bombings, let alone a repeat attack, would do to the possibly fragile relationships between communities in the likely event that the bombers did turn out to be Muslims, together with a deep worry about the problems relatives and friends were facing in tracing relatives. I had been in charge of the identification of the dead at the 1987 King's Cross fire, an experience which made my concern about this more acute. Part of the standard modern response to a disaster in which lives are thought to have been lost is the setting up by the police of what is known as a Casualty Bureau. This is a unit designed to log details and descriptions of casualties and match them against those being enquired about, or reported as suspected to be missing, by relatives and friends using a telephone number which is given out on all media channels. The Met has a large casualty bureau at the training school at Hendon. While not in use it serves as classrooms and offices but it can be – or should be able to be – brought on line very fast. It had only recently been stood down from work on the Tsunami of Boxing Day 2004, in the aftermath of which the Met had led the efforts to identify the British citizens missing in that catastrophe. It should take a maximum of four hours to staff up (which allows time for the first outlines of a major incident to become clear), but as everything was being got ready on 7/7 it was then found that there was a serious telephone fault. Desperate efforts were made by BT to correct this but locating the fault and testing the system took hours. When it was finally repaired and the number was given out in the late afternoon, the fifty or so operators were simply overwhelmed. It is now known that nearly 44,000 calls were attempted in the first hour: the vast majority of callers simply got an engaged tone and so redialled, adding to the queue.

There was a combination of previously unforeseen factors behind this number of calls. After the news of the bombings emerged, London's transport systems stopped and many people were neither at home nor at work, so seemed to be missing. Mobile telephony became unreliable under the pressure, but the Met had decided not to do something we could do, which was to disable the networks to leave the frequencies free for emergency services – although unfortunately and temporarily, the City of London did take that decision. Unlike with air travel, there are no passenger manifests and no one knows what tube or bus someone else would have caught. The age of individuals going to work in London is such that many were being enquired after by lots of friends as well as family. And, of course, inevitably the media coverage was enormous.

Despite best efforts, including the Met's sharing its casualty function with linked bureaux in other forces, the experience for many families was quite terrible. People went from hospital to hospital enquiring fruitlessly, while others living outside London drove to the capital to do so. For the rescuers, one of the many distressing features was the sound of mobile telephones ringing amid the dead. It took days to sort this out. I know because a few days afterwards contact was made with my wife on behalf of a friend of a friend of a friend in the remote hope that I might be able to cut through this delay, and by that means one family got to know a little earlier that their twenty-eight-year-old daughter would never come home. This was not much better than my experience at King's Cross in 1987, which was the first time a casualty bureau had been set up in modern times, where the same number that was given out to the public was initially given to my staff in the temporary mortuary, so we could not get through to them either. The plight of friends and relatives remains one of the extra horrors of that day, a conundrum which is not yet fully fixed or perhaps fully fixable, although line capacity of at least 1,500 trained casualty bureau staff can theoretically now be established.

There were also some tricky issues to negotiate with the government. At one meeting of COBR I was asked how soon it could be announced that the affected tube lines would restart. 'Days,' was my crisp answer. 'These are crime scenes.' One question that was already being raised was whether the long-planned commemorative event (scheduled halfway between VE Day and VJ Day) on the following Sunday to mark sixty years after the end of the Second World War should be cancelled. At first, apparently, this seemed to be my call but I was relieved when it was announced that the Prime Minister had made the decision that it should not yet be cancelled, mainly on the grounds that, whatever had happened, these people were not the Luftwaffe and many of those attending would have lived through the Blitz.

By nightfall on 7 July a truly profound silence had fallen on the city. As I left the Yard after making my last visits to those officers who would be working through the night at the scenes, I was proud but deeply perturbed. I was absolutely positive that the Met had done its best and that its best had been very good indeed. I already knew that some officers – along with many other people – had voluntarily put themselves at huge risk. But what would happen now? Who were the bombers? Would they strike again or, if they were dead, were there others out there? I knew that the number of casualties was huge and dozens of people were dead, that many people were still missing and relatives and friends were desperate for news. I went home and sat silently with my son, watching the news. All this twenty-four hours after the euphoria of winning the

Olympics. What conceivably could happen next and what were we not doing that we ought to be were my last thoughts before sleep.

I returned to the Yard early the next morning. The most striking feature was the absence of reports of crime and disorder. It was as if London was holding its breath. The evening before had been remarkable in the way that so many people, with very little public transport, had just walked home for hours and yet, that following morning, many were already on their defiant way back. The next few days were full of developments: the discovery of the car at Luton, full of explosives, of the bomb factory in Leeds and of the steady rise in the confirmed death toll. The Met had to ruin the plans of one couple to have their wedding reception on the playing field/parade ground of the Honourable Artillery Company on the Saturday, when we commandeered it on the Friday to build the largest temporary mortuary ever put up in a couple of days. The plight of the families of victims prompted an idea borrowed from the New York experience of 9/11: the creation of a twenty-four-hour family assistance centre, staffed by volunteers ranging from bereavement counsellors to local authority liaison officers, which was established in Victoria. The Mayor, Ken Livingstone, spoke on television from Singapore and perfectly caught the public mood of defiance in London:

> This was not a terrorist attack against the mighty and the powerful. It was not aimed at Presidents or Prime Ministers. It was aimed at ordinary, working-class Londoners, black and white, Muslim and Christian, Hindu and Jew, young and old. It was an indiscriminate attempt at slaughter, irrespective of any considerations for age, for class, for religion, or whatever.
>
> That isn't an ideology, it isn't even a perverted faith – it is just an indiscriminate attempt at mass murder and we know what the objective is. They seek to divide Londoners. They seek to turn Londoners against each other.

When he got back to London I joined Ken in his first press conference after the bombings. He promised solemnly that the injured and the relatives of the dead would have the front-row seats of honour at the opening ceremony of the London Olympics in 2012 (a promise which I hope Boris Johnson will keep). In a sense this was the real beginning of my working relationship with Ken. As we went through the next few weeks, whether travelling together on the tube one day with photographers to show the public we believed it to be safe, attending the various memorial services or sometimes just talking quietly together in one or other of our offices, I began to appreciate more deeply his vision for London, he my vision for policing and both of us the connectivity between them. Ken came to the Yard one evening in mid-July and met with a large group of first responders from the emergency services. He spoke so passionately about what they had done. It reminded me of how he had handled a debate organised by the Met Police Federation for mayoral candidates before the inaugural 2000 election. Given my memory of him at the GLC, I had been stunned when the police audience had cheered him to the echo because he knew who they were and the other candidates did not. I was fascinated by the way they swarmed round him in the Yard, and he stayed for hours.

The memorial services that followed were remarkable and entirely without rancour against any one community: Ken had been right about the indiscriminate nature of the slaughter. I remember the mounds of flowers at King's Cross; Jonathan Sacks, the Chief Rabbi, announcing at an interdenominational outdoor service that 'there may be hundreds of languages spoken in London but there is one universal language, the language of tears'; the Hindu chants on the evening air of the Embankment; much later, the solemn rituals of national grief in St Paul's Cathedral.

Within a short period, however, investigators were beginning to suspect a suicide attack and within days the investigation was providing clear leads to suggest that this was the work of individuals claiming adherence to Islam. If clues were not enough, videos were posted on the internet, so-called 'martyrdom' speeches. The one recorded before the attack by Mohammed Saddique Khan was unambiguous and, oddly, all the more chilling for being spoken in a broad Yorkshire accent. Part of what he said was: 'Your democratically elected governments continuously perpetuate atrocities against my people all over the world ... Until we feel security, you will be our targets ... We will not stop this fight. We are at war and I am a soldier. Now you will taste the reality of this situation.'

It was, of course, the authentic British reply to the inadvisability of announcing a war on terror. Although I attacked this concept in public many times afterwards, first in a public speech in Berlin in 2006, I was not perceptive enough to denounce it at this stage. However, in the days immediately after 7/7 I became more and more certain that it was vital, as the senior police officer in the country, to be seen to be making clear that the police were not blaming an entire community for these attacks or condoning those who did, as some voices in the tabloid press were capable of doing. In this, of course, they were given marvellous opportunities by the idiocies of men like Abu Hamza, the hook-handed preacher of violence, apparently provided by central casting. At that stage I was much helped in my decision to take this on myself by Tarique Ghaffur, the country's senior Asian officer. I had inherited Tarique as an Assistant Commissioner and he reminded us often of the nature of difference and of how vulnerable the Muslim and other minority communities would be feeling. It is a great sadness to me that, years later, our relationship ended in acrimony.

Although I had already attended a meeting between the Prime Minister and leaders of the Muslim community, my first personal positive step in this direction was, in the week after 7 July, to keep a diary commitment to address a meeting of the Three Faiths Forum, founded by the inspirational Sir Sigmund Steinberg, who also founded the Anne Frank Trust. The forum brings together representatives of Christians, Jews and Muslims and they were pleased to have the Commissioner put across the message of understanding between faiths. From them I picked up the vital message that people of faith would rather hear from someone of faith than from an agnostic.

On Friday 15 July, just eight days after the bombings, I went to address the Forest Gate Mosque, a mosque connected to Pakistan, a country where we already feared a connection, during Friday prayers. I introduced myself to the elders as a committed Christian but one who recognised the validity of the other Abrahamic faiths. I asked for their support for police actions and promised our support and protection to them. The television news crew filming the event was clearly surprised at the approach. But I knew that a long road lay ahead, in which Muslim people, whether they were wearing rucksacks or not, would feel watched and distrusted, as would many other minorities, as many people cannot distinguish easily between Sikh, Hindu and Muslim in the street. For good measure I also visited Sikh gurdwaras and Hindu temples to give the same message.

I continued with a series of visits to front-line staff, particularly the investigating teams at the Yard and those involved in victim identification and evidence recovery. Four days after the bombings, dressed in a green overall, blue overshoes and a facemask, I went down to the tracks below Russell Square Station with some of the officers involved in this distressing but painstaking work. To stand in the carriage where the bomb had exploded was a sobering experience. A huge hole had been ripped in the floor and the wall of the train. Officers pointed out that the effect of the blast was to smash the steel and glass against the walls of the tunnel about a foot away, only to hurl it back inside the carriage in fragments. No one nearby could have survived. As we walked to and from the train along the tunnel from the platform, I reflected again on the bravery of the first officers on the scene that morning. Now the tunnel was lit with arc lights, now we knew that its roof and walls had been carefully examined for their structural soundness, now we were certain that the current had been switched off; then they had known none of those things. Even now it was unnerving to hear tube trains moving in linked tunnels nearby; that morning it must have been terrifying. It is also worth reflecting on the job which the men and women I was with were actually undertaking. By this stage victim identification and evidence recovery meant a fingertip examination of the underside of the carriage for fragments of human tissue and bomb fragments, working in very high temperatures – up to 40°C – because there were no trains moving and the trains provide the ventilation. Vermin were a terrible problem: rats underground, pigeons in Tavistock Square. These men and women were doing a magnificent job, one which they could never have imagined when they joined the service. I had seen some of this before at King's Cross but it did not get any better with the years.

After I came up I walked round Russell and Tavistock Squares and spoke to the Salvation Army team who were providing tea and cold drinks for the emergency services, as ever without asking for any thanks, as well as to some of the officers guarding the scenes. Police dog handlers are often of long service and have pretty much seen it all. I remember speaking to a couple of them, who were quite emotional about the way that so many members of the public kept coming up to them and just saying thank you and well done. On my very first morning a few months before, I had been asked during a radio interview what I had hoped my legacy as Commissioner would be. I had answered that I hoped that, during my term of office, Londoners would realise what extraordinary things the men and women of the Met did for them and take them a bit more to their hearts. For that short while in July 2005, that is exactly what had happened.

On the same day a particular Londoner wrote to me from Buckingham Palace:

> Following the successful conclusion of the G8 summit and the weekend's major public events in central London, I would like to express my thanks to you not only for the security arrangements for those events but also for the outstanding work that is being done by the men and women of the Metropolitan Police in the aftermath of the London bombings. I have nothing but pride and admiration for the way in which all your officers are performing their duties often under the most extreme pressure. I would be grateful if you would pass on my warmest appreciation to each and every one of them.
>
> ELIZABETH R.

One of the innovations I had introduced was a broadcast to the force using our intranet. It was a great pleasure to let the Met know of the Queen's letter but also to let them know of the volume of messages from round the world that were now being received. Along with colleagues in Australia and New Zealand and various cities in America, Bob Mueller, the FBI's director, rang me to express the admiration felt in the USA for Londoners as a whole and for our bobbies and their calmness. Of course, he would have felt himself to be in the same war. In the days that followed I gave separate briefings to the British and foreign press corps, opened meetings aimed at community reassurance, attended Chief Constables Council (which is very unusual for a Commissioner) to thank my Chief Constable colleagues for all their support, briefed MPA members and the Mayor on the progress of the investigation and kept in touch with No 10 and the Home Secretary. I was able to do this because Andy Hayman or Peter Clarke, his deputy and the National Coordinator of Terrorist Investigations, were briefing me daily or twice daily on the progress of the investigation. I had a number of conversations with and attended meetings with Eliza Manningham-Buller and her deputy at MI5, Jonathan Evans, as well as with colleagues from MI6, Government Communications Headquarters (GCHQ) and the Home and Cabinet Offices.

Quite early on, concern began to centre on three individuals from the Leeds area. Met officers were deployed full-time in Leeds with the agreement of West Yorkshire Police. At this stage the arrangement whereby the Met had primacy for counter-terrorism was an unwritten gentlemen's agreement formed in the days of Irish Republican terrorism and, in the future, events like Forest Gate were to produce a number of awkward arguments inside the Association of Chief Police Officers (ACPO) over accountability and liability in a more litigious age. However, right now, the Chief Constable of West Yorkshire, the late Colin Cramphorn, a former Royal Ulster Constabulary man, had unreservedly welcomed the Met in. The news from both West Yorkshire and Luton, where the bombers' car had been found, was grim. The car had contained more explosive devices, which had been wrapped with nails to cause maximum injury, while the preliminary examination of a house in the Beeston area of Leeds had found clear evidence of bomb-making. The forensic scientists there were particularly concerned with a bathtub containing a large amount of a jelly-like substance which they were unsure how to stabilise. Until it had been, the property could neither be declared safe for surrounding residents to return to their homes nor be properly searched. No one knew what clues might be inside. All of us felt that the hands of Al-Qaida were all over what was going on and the sense of foreboding was strong.

We had to wait for less time than we expected for foreboding to become reality again. Exactly two weeks after 7/7 an attempt was made to explode more bombs in London. And after that came 22 July and the death of Jean Charles de Menezes and separate plots to blow up airliners, film the beheading of a Muslim British soldier and cause carnage in nightclubs.

After the summer of 2005, as terrorism and crime became central to the way Britain and its citizens understood their place in the world and their individual relationship with the state, media interest and political position-taking would transform my role as Commissioner, which would itself become a subject of deeply divisive political controversy. The chapters that follow give my account of all these events and more, but I believe that they are best seen not on their own but in the broader context of the history of British policing and particularly that of London. I have policed controversy but so did a number of my predecessors. The fact that, in early October 2008, for the first time in weeks, my resignation took what we then termed the emerging credit crunch off the first page of every national newspaper, including the *Financial Times*, would have been of little surprise to those who went through an earlier and somewhat parallel period, when the controversy was over whether a police force should or should not be established at all.

2

Peel

One of the most popular series of historical novels recently written in Britain are those of Patrick O'Brian about the post-Nelsonian navy. They explore the relationship between an English sea captain, Jack Aubrey, and the surgeon, botanist and secret agent who sails with him, Stephen Maturin. Aubrey's motivations are plain: honour, patriotism, ambition and courage. Maturin's principal reason for his involvement in the war is much less immediately understandable to the modern mind. Despite being a liberal Irishman, with an ambivalent view of many matters English, he has a profound hatred of Napoleon as a tyrant. In this O'Brian, as he does in so much of his writing, captures the detail of the age.

As is well attested in the excellent recent biography of William Wilberforce by William Hague, the war with France delayed the abolition of slavery because so many of those who initially supported the French Revolution were supporters of emancipation and either lost political influence or dropped both causes. In parallel, there is no doubt that the Napoleonic Wars or, perhaps more accurately, the way France developed from the Revolution until the final defeat of Napoleon also delayed the creation of a modern police force in Britain and moulded its initial shape.

The idea of a police force was not new. Glasgow's was, in fact, the first city force in Britain, there was a Thames Police to look after the river's shipping and the British had established police forces in a number of colonies, including the Royal Irish Constabulary. However, London was different and its police force was to be different. For nearly

forty years before the first Metropolitan Police Act of 1829, parliamen-
tarians of all stripes had often debated policing. The previous system of
night watchmen was clearly inadequate and the reliance on the quasi-
privatised Bow Street Runners and occasional military support were
unsatisfactory. It was not at all clear what was wanted.

What was clear, however, was what was not wanted, which was
some form of 'continental' police service. Legislators looked across
the Channel in horror at the police as agents of the state and, above
all, as the employers of paid spies and informers. The bogey figure was
Joseph Fouché, who, having been a particularly bloodthirsty supporter
and indeed instigator of the Terror and a friend of Robespierre, was
appointed Chief of Police by the Directory after Robespierre's fall and
execution. This appointment continued under Napoleon both in his
pomp and after Elba and then finally under Louis XVIII. If anyone
during that tumultuous period knew where the bodies were buried, it
was Fouché. The comment 'Whenever three people talk together in
Paris, one of them works for me' is often wrongly attributed to him:
it was said by De Sartine, a lieutenant-general of police of the Ancien
Régime from 1759 to 1789. But Fouché would have wholeheartedly
applauded its sentiments. Interestingly, the French foreign intelligence
service, the General Directorate for External Security (DGSE), still
traces its origins to Fouché: its strapline is 'Where necessity makes law'.

This was totally unacceptable to the instincts of libertarian England.
However, even if they did not emulate France, the Tory government of
the time could have chosen the military model already in use in Ireland,
with barracks, sabres and guns. But they chose something very different, something that had never been tried before. This was an organisation low in numbers and low in powers. It was an organisation whose
primary objects were neither the detection of crime nor the suppression
of public disorder but were based on the opposite approach: the prevention of crime and the maintenance of public tranquillity. Its initial
uniform of a tall black hat and swallow-tailed coat was far from military. It was unarmed. Of its first twin Commissioners, although one
was a retired Peninsular War veteran, Charles Rowan, the other was a

lawyer, Richard Mayne. The Commissioners and their force were supposed to be independent of ministers.

Peel wanted the police to be very close to the public and even remarked that 'the Police are the public and the public are the Police'. The model he created in London spread across Britain, first in towns and cities and later across more rural areas. It also spread rapidly across the common-law world, with numerous city forces across the Empire and in the United States being founded in emulation of the Met. In terms of its preventative role, its modest powers and its separation from the state, what Peel created was a gift not just to Britain but also to the world.

I have read a lot of histories of British policing and in doing so have been struck by two peculiarities. The first is that very few were written in the past thirty years and the second is the significance that the authors attach to the uniqueness of the English style of policing. Here is a Captain Lee, whose *A History of Police in England* was published in 1901: 'amongst all our institutions, it would be hard to find one so eminently characteristic of our race, both in its origin and in its development, or one so little modified by foreign influences, as the combination of arrangements for maintaining the peace, which we call "police".' Thomas Critchley, who published the second edition of his *History of the Police in England and Wales* in 1972, contrasts in his preface the events of 1968 in Paris and Chicago with those in London and refers to 'a tolerant, mature society well matched by a tolerant police force' and quotes from an unnamed American at Oxford University who describes the 'flexible and temperate efficiency' of the British police and states that she 'never knew what safety felt like until I came here'.

There is an old joke which populates Heaven and Hell according to stereotypes of different European nations. In Heaven, the place is run by the Swiss, the cooks are French, the engineers are German, the lovers are Italian and the police are British. In Hell the Swiss are the lovers, the British are the cooks, the Italians are the administrators and so on.

There is something very significant about these choices, something about the image portrayed by a nation. The fundamental question is whether Britain and, in particular, England and Wales can still put forward a strong claim to be the heavenly constabulary and whether, nearly forty years after Critchley wrote those words, Britain any longer possesses the kind of police service which he described and whether the political and social context in which it works supports such tolerance.

It is a question with both historical and practical significance. Ian Loader and Aogán Mulcahy have contributed what might be described as a history of recent British policing, although they refer to it as a work of cultural sociology. But whatever it is, its title and argument are very pertinent to this question. This 2003 book is called *Policing and the Condition of England*, echoing the title of the famous nineteenth-century polemic by Thomas Carlyle *The Condition of England*. In it, a bit close to that heavenly constabulary, the authors argue that the period since the Second World War has been one in which policing has changed from being a sacred institution, central to the idea of English-ness, to a merely secular or profane one, a fascinating thesis.

While this may explain much of the hankering for a past golden age, a change so profound has some very practical consequences. For the British system gives the police a much greater role in law enforcement and criminal justice than elsewhere. In his 1986 book *The Governance of Police* the well-known criminologist Laurence Lustgarten argues that 'in the edifice of English criminal justice, the police are the keystone. From comparative analysis [of other legal systems] there emerges a striking conclusion. Police in England ... enjoy a unique dominance within the institutional structure of law enforcement.' Of course, this may or may not be appropriate. Perhaps it needs to be changed but change should not occur unthinkingly and arbitrarily.

All countries find a method of controlling the police function. The aim is invariably to prevent any one agency or minister from having control over the entire function. Hence, France has two major police forces, the Police Nationale, which answers to the Ministry of Justice, and the Gendarmerie, a part of the Defence Ministry. Italy has a number of separate police forces, each reporting to a different ministry. On the other hand, German police forces, both federal and local, perhaps understandably, have extremely limited powers, needing to seek authorisation for detention of an accused person from a prosecutor after very few hours. While the names of some of its Police Departments are world famous, from New York to Los Angeles and from Chicago to Miami, the United States has over 16,000 separate police forces. Beyond these local forces stand a range of more powerful agents, including the elected District and Federal Attorneys and the Federal Bureau of Investigation (which is only one of about fifty Federal agencies with some law-enforcement capabilities).

Equally the role of police and prosecutors differs from country to country. In those countries which broadly follow the inquisitorial system of the Napoleonic code, the job of the police is to prepare an investigative record either for or under the direction of an investigating magistrate, and in France these detectives are called the Police Judiciaire. Under this system the accused is not normally allowed to plead guilty: the case must be proved by the state. In those countries (largely the Commonwealth and the United States) whose systems have evolved from English common law, the police have a much more dominant role in the preparation of evidence. Even here systems differ, with American prosecutors, for instance, having their own investigators, who often take over the more difficult cases from the local police.

Responsibilities for the investigation of terrorism vary widely. In New Zealand, for instance, until fairly recently the head of the national police also led the equivalent of MI5. The United States has a confusing distinction between the roles of the FBI, the CIA and the newly created Department for Homeland Security. And France has a long history of bitterly divided intelligence agencies, with traditions linked to the different Second World War legacies of the Vichy regime and of De Gaulle and the Resistance.

All these matters intertwine but perhaps none is as important as accountability. In France the most senior police officer is the Préfet de Police of Paris and is appointed by the Council of Ministers. The postholder is unlikely ever to have served as an operational police officer, with the current incumbent being a graduate of that traditional launching pad for politicians and senior civil servants in France, the École Nationale d'Administration. In the United States police chiefs are appointed by local mayors and hold office at the mayor's pleasure. They are usually now police officers but their careers can seem a little truncated. Bernard Kerik, for instance, a recent Commissioner of the NYPD, had only six years' police experience, including being Mayor Giuliani's protection officer, when, after a period in the New York prison hierarchy, he was appointed Commissioner by Mayor Giuliani. Kerik was in post on 9/11 but subsequently faced a series of financial and other investigations.

In Britain the system is entirely different on all these points. Police in England and Wales have almost complete responsibility for the preparation of criminal cases, up to the point of decision whether a suspect should be charged, although in very serious cases the wise detective seeks advice from the prosecutors in the Crown Prosecution Service on the conduct of the investigation. Responsibility for the investigation of terrorism belongs to the police, although the working relationship with the security agencies, particularly MI5, is very close, with officers from MI5, MI6 and the government's listening agency, GCHQ, sharing intelligence with officers of the Metropolitan Police in a combined unit called the Joint Terrorist Analysis Centre, an arrangement almost unthinkable in many other countries. Importantly, during the bombing campaign of 2005, MI5 officers were based full-time at Scotland Yard. This means that police in Britain are responsible for the investigation of the complete range of criminality, from the most local to the most serious, from drunkenness to terrorism, a situation uncommon elsewhere.

Most important of all, the system of accountability is almost wholly different from the model encountered in either America or continental Europe. The police chief is not directly accountable to central or local government and his or her responsibilities are separated entirely from those of the judiciary. In an arrangement finally formalised after the 1962 Royal Commission (the most recent) to consider the role of the police in Britain, the so-called 'Tripartite Arrangement' gives overlapping but differently emphasised powers and responsibilities to the Home Secretary, the Chief Officer and the local Police Authority (largely but not exclusively made up of elected members of local authorities). In this the Chief Officer is an equally important partner: he or she does not enter or leave office at the whim of another single person and, although he or she remains accountable for the actions of the force, he or she has independence as to how operations and investigations are conducted.

These three elements of public accountability but operational independence and of responsibility for almost all elements of criminal investigation for all types of crime set the British system apart from those of almost all other countries. It is worth considering how this happened, how the police became so central to both criminal justice and the relationship between local and central government, for it did not come about by accident.

English police histories all begin with the Anglo-Saxon hue and cry but the story of modern policing begins in the 1750s. It seems that the experience of civil war a century before (immediately after which Cromwell introduced a system of militarised police, largely to combat frivolity rather than criminality) left the eighteenth-century mind deeply concerned with political and personal liberty, even in the face of uncomfortable facts. In 1743 the poet William Shenstone commented that London was 'really dangerous at this time: pickpockets, formerly content with mere filching, make no scruple to knock people down with bludgeons in Fleet Street and the Strand', while Horace Walpole wrote in 1752 that 'one is forced to travel, even at noon, as if one were going to battle'. Old systems failed. Almost everyone sensible bought or lied their way out of the duty of being a parish constable or 'Charlie', while the magistracy had become widely corrupt, often described as 'trading justices', unpaid by the state but requiring a fee for the administration of any kind of justice.

This was not a problem for London alone, as the Industrial Revolution swept away old certainties and ties, but it was London which saw the worst of examples. To give but one example, the famous criminal

Jonathan Wild openly established himself as a society figure while organising burglaries the proceeds of which he returned to the owners for a fee. (Perhaps there is some echo here of the way the Kray brothers were lionised.) The proposed solutions varied widely: there was much support for more and more savage punishment; there were alternative proposals to reform the moral character of the poor; there were those who argued that time should be given for the reform of criminal law and prisons to take effect. What almost nobody seemed to support was the creation of a police force to tackle the criminals. While the two Fielding brothers, the novelist Henry and his blind brother John, together with their successor Patrick Colquhoun, began to rescue the reputation of magistrates by becoming successful and honest Chief Magistrates at Bow Street Court in central London, as well as creating a police for the River Thames and the mounted bounty hunters known as the Bow Street Runners, Parliament endlessly refused to consider widespread reform.

Henry Fielding was the principal witness before a Parliamentary Committee established to consider the policing of London in 1770 but which had little result. Despite the severity of the Gordon Riots in 1780, during which London was abandoned to the mob for nearly a week (and Bow Street Magistrates' Court was sacked), a 1785 Bill proposed by the government of William Pitt the Younger to provide a Metropolitan Police force under Home Office influence was howled down by the vested interests of the City of London and the magistracy. Pitt withdrew the Bill and then the whole concept of police fell under the shadow of the French Revolution and the guillotine, followed by the creation of a police establishment designed covertly and overtly to serve the interests only of the Emperor: for its time, the very emblem of terror and state control, perfected by Fouché.

Nothing changed: the horrors of the Radcliffe Road murders of 1811, when two whole families in Wapping, east London, were brutally slain, or the Peterloo Massacre of 1819 in which eleven people were killed by mounted Hussars attempting to control a demonstration near Manchester created waves of panic and discontent, but Parliamentary Committees of 1816, 1818 and 1822 rejected the concept of a public police as incompatible with the freedoms of Englishmen. Two passages of the 1822 report are frequently quoted: 'a system of police would ... make every servant a spy upon his master and all classes of society spies on each other' and:

> It is difficult to reconcile an effective system of police with that perfect freedom of action and exemption from interference, which are the great privileges and blessings of society in this country; and Your Committee think that the forfeiture or curtailment of such advantages would be too great a sacrifice for improvements in police, or facilities in detection of crime, however desirable in themselves if abstractly considered.

In the next decade, however, different currents began to run. Benthamite experiments in prison reform were making prevention of crime and the reformation of character fashionable. To a conservative cast of mind, France was restored to its ancient liberties. The success of London's river police in reducing crime was obvious. The way forward would lie in the squaring off of the most powerful vested interest in opposition and in the earlier experiences in Ireland of Robert Peel. The surprise was to be the model of policing that emerged and particularly the model of accountability which Peel facilitated rather than created.

Before becoming Home Secretary, Peel had been Chief Secretary for Ireland between 1812 and 1818. He had noted that the Dublin Parliament had seen the measures put forward in Pitt's defeated 1785 Bill and enacted them in Ireland in 1786. While the early beginnings of the Royal Irish Constabulary were military in form and nothing like the way in which the Metropolitan Police would subsequently be modelled, accountability for the police function had been taken away from the magistracy and placed under men directly appointed by the Crown for the purpose. As soon as he became Home Secretary, Peel set up the 1822 committee whose conclusions have just been mentioned but, finding himself defeated here, he turned to reform of the criminal law, although there is ample evidence that he continued to be interested in the creation of a professional police.

After a short period out of office he returned as Home Secretary in a new government under the Duke of Wellington in January 1828 and immediately set up a further Committee of Enquiry into the State of the Police in London. His first move was to exclude the City of London from the scope of the inquiry, which left the other seventy or so wards and parishes of London without what had previously been the main and most effective voice of opposition. His second was to be economical with his description of the changes he intended to make. Introducing the work of the committee, he remarked that he intended 'to proceed slowly with the experiment, with a cautious feeling of the way'. In fact his Bill swept away the old system in its entirety, watchmen, parish constables and, above all, the role of justices in the control of public order (it was their duty to 'read the Riot Act') and created a new agency in the state, to be run by two Commissioners answerable to the Home Secretary and hence to Parliament. This could have been a state police but for two factors. First, Peel was adamant that this should be a preventative police and it is noticeable that in the Instructions provided to the fledgling service it was Peel who added the word 'principal' to the very first sentence: 'It is to be understood at the outset that the principal object to be obtained is the prevention of crime.' One hundred and forty-five years later, on my first evening as a police officer in training, I was set the task, in common with all recruits, of learning by heart what were by then termed 'the primary objects' of the police, scarcely changed from the words agreed between Peel and his two Commissioners, Rowan and Mayne. They read:

> The primary object of an efficient police is the prevention of crime: the next that of detection and punishment of offenders if crime is committed. To these ends all the efforts of police must be directed. The protection of life and property, the preservation of public tranquillity, and the absence of crime, will alone prove whether those efforts have been successful and whether the objects for which the police were appointed have been attained.

The second factor was astonishing. Other than this kind of general direction and his brilliance in the selection of these two men, whose characters and experiences were both compatible and complementary, Peel did little else, leaving almost all details of how this new institution was to be organised.

It was at 6pm on a Tuesday evening, 29 September 1829, that the new police marched out from their bases across London and began a completely new tradition of policing, which spread rapidly across Britain and the English-speaking, common-law world. Yet what was created was not Peel's invention but principally that of Colonel Charles Rowan, who determined on this police, dressed in civilian attire, low in powers and numbers and including no detectives or spies. That is clear from the evidence Rowan provided to a Parliamentary Select Committee in 1834: asked as to his freedom of manoeuvre, he replied: 'Everything that has been done since the commencement has originated with the Commissioners; the whole of the organisation has been made by them alone; the Secretary of State has approved of their regulations.'

But there were some things which were not yet clear, notably who was in charge. The Chief Magistrate at Bow Street thought he still was and he and his fellow magistrates were particularly hostile to the new police and their Commissioners, a position which made the enforcement of the law acutely difficult. Peel appeared to make no effort to smooth over this disagreement before Wellington's government fell in November 1830 and the Commissioners were faced with an even trickier situation than any of their successors: a new Home Secretary who did not believe in a police force at all. However, Melbourne and the Whigs were also in a dilemma. They had spent decades condemning Tory governments for suppressing public disorder with troops and now at last London had another, much less bloody mechanism; yet they disliked the police. Melbourne's response and that of his successors, Duncannon and Russell, was to embark on a policy, as Reith puts it, 'of sidetracking demand for abolition of the police by making show of warmly sharing popular feeling against them'. Never was this more acute than during the riot at Cold Bath Fields in Clerkenwell in May

1833, when Melbourne ordered the Commissioners to disperse a public meeting and arrest the ringleaders. An officer was killed and yet another Parliamentary Committee was set up to examine its circumstances. The Commissioners provided written evidence of the verbal instructions they had received and Melbourne denied issuing them. The Committee did not believe him. However, from that time on, the right was firmly established for the Commissioners to be certain that, in Rowan's words to an interfering Chief Magistrate in 1837 who wished to give orders about arrangements for the funeral of William IV, 'our men were to be solely under our orders and directions'. This was not a judicial function or one for ministers.

After the 1830s the Commissioners established their primacy and the Metropolitan model spread around the country. There were certainly difficult moments. The much-debated establishment of the detective branch was rapidly followed by a corruption scandal over bookmaking involving four of the five most senior officers in command. The 1877 'Trial of the Detectives', as it was called, shocked Victorian London but led to the professionalisation of the detective function by Howard Vincent, who went to, of all places, France to study detective methods, suggested the formation of a Criminal Investigation Department and acquired the position as its first Director, with the rank of Assistant Commissioner. All detectives came under his command thereby and a seed was sown which would flower in bitterness during the years shortly before I joined the service. Meanwhile, however, the name of Scotland Yard gradually became synonymous with success in detecting crimes both around the world and all over Britain. There was a reason in Britain, however, for the Met being so dominant: if a difficult murder occurred in the patch of one of the many small police forces across the country (there were well over 150 at one time), then, if the Chief Constable 'called in the Yard' in the first twenty-four hours, the Yard paid: if not, with or without the Yard, the costs were borne locally.

In 1886 a public meeting in Trafalgar Square turned into a riot which spread across the West End and led directly to the enforced resignation of the Commissioner, Sir Edmund Henderson, although whether he was made a scapegoat for damage to the government of the day or resigned because his Pall Mall club was one of those whose windows were smashed is not entirely clear. The next Commissioner, the apparently irascible soldier Sir Charles Warren, lasted less than two years before he in turn resigned, over a disagreement with the Home Office following public consternation about the murders by Jack the Ripper. One interesting point about these murders is that the Crime Museum at Scotland Yard possesses a book owned by Detective Chief Inspector Donald Swanson, the senior investigator in the case, which makes clear that he believed he had solved the murders. There had been a witness to the third murder, that of Elizabeth Stride. DCI Swanson was the senior investigator to whom those more usually described as hunting the Ripper, like Inspector Frederick Abberline, reported. Swanson believed that the murderer was Aaron Kosminski, a Pole who had been arrested following an attack on his sister two years after the last Ripper murder. Kosminski was taken, of all bizarre places, to the Hove police convalescent home and confronted with the witness to the Stride murder, who positively identified him. He was declared mentally unfit to stand trial and died in 1919 at Leavesden Asylum in Hertfordshire. This is all known to Ripperologists but not accepted as proof positive.

The next challenge for the Met was terrorism. Taking its name from a band of second- and third-century Irish warriors called the Fianna, the Fenian Brotherhood had been founded in America in the 1850s and quickly became a powerful movement for Irish independence from British rule. After an attempted uprising in 1867, three Fenians were hanged in Manchester and in December a bomb planted by Fenians exploded at Clerkenwell Prison, killing a number of people. In 1883 there was a relentless series of dynamite explosions in London, including at the office of *The Times*, in Whitehall and on the Underground, leading to the formation of a new unit, the Special Irish Branch. As Irish republican activity waned, the word 'Irish' was dropped from the unit's name. It had a lot to do as London became home to more and more immigrants from Eastern Europe, including some who were members of politically militant groups, commonly referred to as 'anarchists'. All this reached a climax in 1911 in the Siege of Sidney Street, during which a small number of militants were killed. This incident was another watershed in the political control of the Met, with much criticism being levelled at the Home Secretary, Winston Churchill, for interfering in the command of the scene. The Irish returned in another series of bombings in 1939 and 1940 and the government reacted by passing the first legislation to include an extended period of police detention, in this case five days. They would return again to dominate my early days as a young officer.

Over more than a century the doctrine of the 'operational independence' of Britain's police slowly took root. The London local authorities launched spasmodic requests to control the force, always rebuffed by both the Commissioners and the Home Office, the second disdainfully referring to the inappropriateness of local politicians to supervise the Met's 'imperial' duties. Part of the aftermath of the police strikes of 1918 and 1919 was a national standardisation of conditions and pay. However, the pre-eminence and independence of Chief Constables and Commissioners steadily grew over operational affairs. The Royal Commission which led to the 1964 Police Act and the Tripartite Arrangement supported this position but it reached its apogee in the 1968 case of R *v* the Metropolitan Police Commissioner *ex parte* Blackburn. Blackburn was a campaigner on moral issues and former Labour MP who fretted that the Metropolitan Police was not taking sufficient action against illegal gaming, which was probably true, and he sought to make it do so. Although the lower courts supported his position, the Court of Appeal did not and Lord Denning, in a typically trenchant judgement, declared that a Chief Officer of police 'is not the servant of anyone, save of the law itself. No Minister of the Crown can tell him that he must, or must not, keep observation on this place or that: or that he must, or must not, prosecute this man or that one. Nor can any police authority tell him so. The responsibility for law enforcement lies on him. He is answerable to the law and to the law alone.'

Although this judgement has been trenchantly criticised (Lustgarten, for instance, asserting that 'seldom have so many errors of law and logic been compressed into one paragraph'), this judgement has become the cornerstone of British policing, enabling senior police officers to take decisions deeply unpopular with both local and national politicians. Examples on both sides of politics abound, from the Chief Constable of Northumbria who insisted on the purchase of baton rounds for the control of rioting in the teeth of opposition from his Labour-dominated Police Authority, who were themselves over-ruled by a Conservative government's Home Office, to my own decision at the site of the Newbury Bypass to refuse to use new legislation against protesters for unlawful trespass because it was operationally inappropriate at that particular time. (We did use it later.) Operational independence also lay behind the Met's decision to investigate 'cash for honours', an investigation unthinkable in many other jurisdictions (although not all, as the honourable example of the United States over both Watergate and the Monica Lewinski affair shows clearly). For nearly forty years this position has been supported by politicians of all sides as a matter of principle. This is what makes Boris Johnson's decisions, taken immediately after my departure from office, to issue a press statement after the arrest of Damian Green MP, and then to speak on the telephone to him later on so astonishing, actions described in the words of the official report into complaints made about these events as 'extraordinary and unwise'.

It must be said that the doctrine is sometimes in the eye of the beholder and there can be little doubt that, to some beholders, the 1984–5 miners' strike was the moment that the political consensus around policing began to unfurl with consequences that are yet unfin-ished and to which we will return in later chapters.

However, with that caveat, operational independence is one of Peel's greatest legacies, but one of the others was to have some unfor-tunate results, despite the nobility of its motivation. At the time of the foundation of the Metropolitan Police, the normal system of appoint-ment to public office of all kinds was through patronage, whether in the Church, government or the armed forces. Twenty-five years before the Northcote-Trevelyan reforms of the Civil Service and even longer before the abolition of the purchase of commissions in the Navy and the Army, however, Peel determined that policing 'should not be an occupation for gentlemen'. He wrote to the Commissioners in December 1829:

> All nominations for the police, as well as original nomination as promotions from inferior stations, should depend exclusively upon the character, qualifications and services of the persons selected. I am convinced that on the strict adherence to this principle must entirely depend the efficiency and character of the new establishment.

This was a real change from what the British were doing and would continue to do across the Empire, with police forces from India to Canada to Hong Kong having an officer cadre and direct entry at commissioned ranks. In Britain Peel's injunction has been maintained ever since with only a few exceptions. Commissioners were appointed from the great and the good until well after the Second World War, as were Chief Constables of rural but not usually urban forces. The 1930s saw a brief experiment to introduce an officer class to the Met, called the Trenchard Scheme, named after the Commissioner of the time, which aimed to attract well-bred men and to accelerate them up the ranks. It was abandoned during the Second World War and never resurrected.

The effect of all this was to provide the police with energetic, ambitious and intelligent men and women from the striving working class, a genuine meritocracy which still exists to this day, as Robert Reiner's 1990 book *The Chief Constables* reveals. But the class structure, while far less rigid than in the 1830s, remains a feature of British life and the unintended consequence of Peel's dictum was to separate the police from the establishment and make the real nature of police work a mystery to middle-class commentators, who just do not have family members in the police force (but do read a lot of detective fiction!).

The consequences of this are many but two are of particular interest. The first is that catastrophes like the shooting dead of Jean Charles de Menezes are examined and pronounced upon by people who have no understanding of police operational methodology, whereas they are likely to know much more about military doctrine or medical ethics, a matter to which I will return towards the end of the book. It also meant that, during the profound social changes of the second half of the last century, the police force fell behind the curve of that change and was left to adjust on its own, a feature which shaped the service I joined in 1974. Much else, of course, happened to policing in Britain between what Peel created and the Met of the 1970s but Peel's legacy remains a truly profound influence on London's policing.

3

Recruit

One of the curiosities of being a police officer is how many people tell you that they had thought of joining the police but then provide no particularly cogent reason for not having done so (unless they were too short – no longer valid – or were colour-blind). Obviously people consider many options before launching into a particular career but almost invariably during these conversations people peter out in a slew of comments about not being sure about the qualifications needed or other family pressures but then lead to the direct question, 'But you, Ian, you, with a degree from Oxford – what made you join the police?' When I gave the Dimbleby Lecture in 2005 the producer actually explained that he asked me to undertake it because he wanted to know 'why someone like you would become a policeman'. That's the polite way: more direct was the comment made at a wedding early in my career to my then girlfriend, now my wife, to the effect that this woman had 'never met a policeman socially before'. Felicity has long known what the answer should have been – 'Oh, how many times have you been arrested?' – but, of course, didn't think of that at the time.

More than thirty years later, *The Times* continued in the same vein. Commenting favourably on my performance during my first few months in office, including the London bombings, the paper drew attention, however, to the language I had used in a Police Authority meeting. It appeared to be surprising that the Met Commissioner, in the course of many comments during a three-hour meeting, should use words like 'invidious, encapsulate, ex-cathedra, antithesis, pervading and counsel of perfection'. It is difficult to imagine anything similar being written about the Chief of the Defence Staff for doing the same.

There can be no doubt that class is still an issue in relation to policing. This is not meant as an autobiography but in some ways my motivation for joining the police still needs some explanation. I was born in 1953 in Chester. I had a conventionally happy but somewhat lonely childhood, in that my parents were not young when I was born (my father was forty-seven and my mother thirty-six) and my elder brother was six years older than me and mostly away at school. My father, Jim, had been the youngest of seven sons of a doctor. Most of his brothers became doctors but my grandfather had become ill before my father left school and, although my father had wanted to be a doctor, there was no money available to help him qualify.

He spent his career with Lever Brothers, running the dock at Port Sunlight near Liverpool for the last twenty years of his working life. He was a disappointed but gentle man, of whom I was immensely fond. My mother, Sheila, was more complicated, outgoing but frustrated. She had been the younger daughter of a wealthy Sheffield steel merchant who had gone catastrophically bust and then died in the 1930s, leaving his family destitute in middle-class terms. Her childhood sweetheart had died at Dunkirk. Ours was a tense house sometimes: in my mother's view we lived in the wrong street and there was too little money for her social aspirations, although, thanks to a legacy from one of his brothers, my father ensured that both my brother and I went to public schools, even if relatively minor ones. My brother, Sandy, left his early and became an articled clerk to a local solicitor without going to university. I had no expectation of doing so either until I had one of those life-changing moments which only a great teacher can deliver. I was in my O-level year at my school in Shropshire, Wrekin College, when my housemaster, Desmond Minty, asked me which university I wanted to go to. I replied that I didn't want to go to university. 'Oh no,' he said, 'you misunderstand my question: I am asking you whether you want to go to Oxford or to Cambridge because that is where you are going.' And so I did and I went to Christ Church, Oxford, because that was where Desmond had gone himself.

But, like everybody else, I took a number of things from my family and school which shaped my future life choices. First and foremost was a sense of service to others. Both my parents had been youngest children and the house was full of books by authors like G A Henty and Rosemary Sutcliffe, tales of exploration and derring-do: it was almost a late-Victorian or Edwardian upbringing, with very little connection to the 1960s unfolding outside. This draw towards public service inspired not only me: my brother later left private law practice and joined local government, becoming a senior figure among local authority Chief Executives and being awarded a CBE. From some combination of influences I also emerged with a very strong sense of fairness and dislike of injustice. As a tiny example, my father's dock had a train on the edge of the wharves, gleaming with brass and polished green paint. I used to go with him to his office on Saturday mornings in the school holidays and I was allowed to drive the train, a great treat for a nine-year-old. Then one day my father told me that one of his staff had asked if his son could do the same and my father had decided that he just could not let anyone else do that. But he also said that this would not stop me. I apparently refused to do it again if others couldn't. And from my mother – and although I did not always get on with her terribly well, I bless her for this – I got a streak of rebelliousness. This emerged first in my decision not to study biology O level but to replace it with almost anything else. With any other subject and most other children, this would have been entirely unremarkable. However, my father had long before decided that I would be the doctor that he had not been allowed to be and I had spent my childhood telling all everyone that, when I grew up, I was going to be a doctor. It took me a year to tell him that I had deliberately chosen subjects which would rule out a medical career.

And so when I am asked why I became a police officer in a way that means that the questioner actually wants to know, I give a one-word answer: 'rebelliousness'.

Christ Church, of which I am now immensely fond and proud but about which I knew practically nothing before I got there, was an odd sort of place in the early 1970s. I read English Language and Literature. I had wonderful tutors and I pursued the normal undergraduate pastimes of too much drama, both on stage and in my endless and usually unsuccessful attempts to persuade young women to go to bed with me. There was too much drinking and too much wasting of time. I had curly hair down to my shoulders, an enormous beard and an old car. However, the college was still all-male and struggling to shake off a continuing and unfortunate aristocratic reputation, especially among students at other colleges. There was a minor but irritating streak of upper-class nastiness, of which the now famous Bullingdon Club was only one example. There was little academic pressure and a strong connection to a London set at the weekends. For those of us not in that set there was sometimes a sense of being out of place, something which was reinforced in me when I spent two weeks in the John Radcliffe Hospital in Oxford after my appendix burst. Even though they lived in the city, none of the nurses or patients had ever been inside an Oxford college nor would have ever dreamed of doing so.

I had gone up to Oxford wanting to be an actor. At that time applicants for Oxbridge had to do a seventh term at school, after their A levels, to take an entry examination. I had decided then to apply for a scholarship scheme run by the English Speaking Union to provide places at American and British schools for students from the other country, some of which were available for the two terms after the Oxbridge entrance process was over. This was perhaps the luckiest break I have ever had. There were thirty-two scholarships in the United States and of those thirty were on the east coast and thirty-one were in boarding schools. I was allocated to Harvard High School, the day school in Hollywood. I went there from January to June 1971 and then travelled alone around the States for a further couple of months by long-haul bus: a life-changing and enjoyable experience.

Perhaps not surprisingly for a school in Hollywood, there was a fine drama department (a lot better than the rugby playing, in which I also took part) and an English accent was much in demand at this and the affiliated girls' school. I was convinced that the dramatic life was for me. I was soon unconvinced. My audition for the famous Oxford University Dramatic Society (OUDS) was unsuccessful, much to my callow surprise. I took to directing and put together Christ Church's offering for the first-year college drama competition. We got to the final with a little-known play by Johnny Speight (creator of Alf Garnett) called *If There Weren't Any Blacks, You'd Have to Invent Them*, an attack on prejudice of all kinds. The cast was entirely made up of my friends from college, with the exception of a cameo performance by Tina Brown, later to be editor of *Tatler*, *Vanity Fair* and the *New Yorker*. We put on our production as the first of two finalists. About two minutes into the other play it became clear to me that I had no long-term future in drama. It was a production of part of Peter Weiss's 1964 play *Marat/Sade*, directed by one Mel Smith, with costumes and, as far as I could tell, a cast largely drawn from the National Youth Theatre of the time. The judges were kind but emphatic. We lost.

This did not matter too much as there were still eight terms left. But these passed quickly and the question of what I was to do for a living began to gain importance. I had no idea. Drama was gone and I didn't want to go into law because my brother had done that or into commerce because my father had done that. I toyed with hospital administration but realised this would seem like second best to the medicine which I had rejected. I even contemplated medicine again but it would have taken another seven years to qualify and I could not bear that. I filled in a questionnaire for the university careers service and went to see them. They astonished me by suggesting the national graduate entry scheme for fast-track selection and promotion in the police. A number of things came together. First, such a prospect fulfilled both the public service preference and the interest in people that I had emphasised in the questionnaire. Also it would allow me to be the outsider I slightly enjoyed being. However, most important of all, it positively rang the bells of rebellion. We were the tag end of the sixties generation and I was far from conservative, widely expected to enter the liberal arts in some way and nothing I could have done could have much more profoundly shocked my friends, it was something no one in my family had ever done and would upset the narrow provincial background from which I assessed myself to have come. It was completely quixotic. And there was one other thing, something that seemed important to me: I couldn't give an acceptable reason to myself why I shouldn't try it.

I am sure now that it was the right choice for me but I am equally sure it was a hard thing for my parents to swallow and I am not proud of the arrogant way I remember dealing with their concerns. My parents were Conservative by party and by inclination, members of the golf club and of the Church of England, as were all their acquaintances. They felt that they had made many sacrifices to get me to Oxford, they had never heard of anybody becoming a police officer and, as my mother said, 'What would we tell our friends?' I don't remember using the word 'bourgeois' to dismiss their views but I might as well have done: the more they argued, the more determined I became, although to be fair, their reaction and that of many others made me think harder and harder about what I was doing. My brother had meanwhile moved far to the political left. (On the way back from there he later stood as the Labour Party candidate for Chester in the 1979 General Election, which made my decision seem moderately bearable to my parents in comparison.) I don't think he liked the idea of the police at the time either but was all for upsetting the membership of the golf club.

Many years later I became good friends with Ben Simpson, who is the son of Joseph Simpson, Commissioner of the Met from 1958 to 1968. Simpson was the first Commissioner to emerge from the Trenchard Scheme. Ben has an early scrapbook of his father's which makes clear the disbelief he faced from friends and family on entering the police, including a significant delay to his marriage.

Nevertheless, I proceeded with my idea. I went to see the Chief Constable of Cheshire, whom my father inevitably knew from the golf club, who decently encouraged me but made it clear that the only place for an ambitious and well-qualified young man to join was the Met. I went through the national selection process, which was and still is based on the model used by the Civil Service for fast-track selection. My only apparent bloomer was turning up to the interviews without a tie, a mistake I learned years later that I shared with John Gieve, the former Home Office Permanent Secretary, during his evaluation for the equivalent Civil Service selection. We were both successful: for my part, I got one of the twelve or so places awarded that year.

On 21 October 1974 I went to the Metropolitan Police Training School at Hendon in north-west London, known inevitably as the Peel Centre. Long after my father's death my mother told me that she had seen him cry only once: the day I left to join the police, apparently concerned about the kind of horrific sights he was sure I would encounter. Hendon had just opened and was a modern facility, boasting good accommodation. What I really enjoyed about the sixteen weeks I spent there was the pleasure of meeting people from so many different backgrounds and of quite disparate ages. Among the thirty or so recruits who joined that day, there were other graduates, like Tom Lloyd, who had just come down from New College, Oxford, and went on to be Chief Constable of Cambridgeshire, but the class also contained ex-soldiers and bricklayers, a former mining engineer who was to become a lifelong friend, Neil Robins, a sprinkling of school-leavers and ex-service personnel, a postman, a bus conductor and a couple of disillusioned teachers. One man left on the second day. This was the year that Equal Opportunities legislation became applicable to the public services, including the police, and there were nine women in the two parallel classes of fifteen recruits. Everyone was white but then so had everyone been at Christ Church and the presence of women was a positive advance on the whole of my previous educational experience since primary school.

The teaching was a mixture of rote learning of law, practical exercises in making arrests and giving evidence. There was an emphasis on physical fitness and self-defence, particularly on how to deal with someone threatening to use a knife, which turned out to be useful later on when I was trapped in a police cell with a man brandishing a meat cleaver, and a bizarre exposure to a room full of CS gas, which appeared to be something the Met expected to use pretty soon (but never has). It was great fun. It was also, as I would later say in earnest warning to many classes of recruits and their parents, completely and distressingly absorbing. This is why to those who work in it the Met is simply known as 'The

Job'. When I joined I had quite a steady girlfriend, who waved me off
from a London hotel on the morning I drove to Hendon. She ditched
me within a couple of months because, although we had spent most
weekends together in the meantime, I wouldn't and couldn't talk about
anything except policing.

Like anybody who has been through such a period of training, none
of us could wait for the real job to start. So after sixteen weeks incarcer-
ated in the suburbs, Police Constable 245C Blair started work at West
End Central in Savile Row, in the very heart of London's West End, a
police station whose patch covered all of Mayfair to the west and Soho
to the east. It was probably a more interesting end to a liberal education
than most people have.

My two years at West End Central were wonderful. I really enjoyed
meeting most of the people I worked with. I learned an enormous
amount from them, including how it is apparently safe at night to go
through red lights at eighty miles an hour on an empty Regent Street:
'You look in the shop windows on either side,' said the Area car driver.
I went into brothels, gaming dens and the great mansions of Mayfair,
saw more pub fights than I can remember, was taught how and when
and when not to make an arrest, the latter being the very epitome of
'discretion is the better part of valour': 'Never try and arrest them when
the bastards outnumber you,' explained my sergeant. My first arrest was
a down-and-out and very smelly drunk, my next a shoplifter and then,
after that, a pub fight in which both I and my prisoner fell through a
pub window, but I was soon given the reward for making lots of arrests:
the chance to work in that Area car and later on the plain clothes crime
squad.

There were moments of real humour, as when a visiting Australian
rugby team had to be dissuaded from rearranging the seats of a striptease
club in the road outside, which they were doing rather slowly because
they were bolted to the floor. I recall intervening in a fight outside an
Orthodox church involving apparently innumerable people in cleri-
cal vestments, waving a number of items of church property in a thoroughly unclerical manner, and then discovering that the Ecclesiastical

Courts Jurisdiction Act under which I thought I was making arrests only applied to the Church of England.

To my knowledge, my mother had never seen a prostitute but she was capable of recognising a lady of the night when she saw one. She was not impressed when an obvious working girl addressed me as 'Ian' when I was showing my mother the area where I worked. It was endlessly varied, meeting characters in the underbelly of a great city whom very few people encounter. It was exciting, sometimes moderately dangerous: astonishingly, after a few early weeks a lone officer was almost unsupervised, able to pick and choose what to investigate, always listening to the radio to be first to a 'good shout'.

The Met I joined had, as I look back on it, a number of abiding characteristics, many of which flowed directly from the early years after its foundation but some of which were of more recent origin. There were very few Londoners in its ranks, something I would later try to change. Its relationship with its public was patronising at best and oppressive at worst. It was confronting three major challenges simultaneously: corruption, a fear of public disorder, which was a mask for not knowing how to deal with the new immigrant population, and genuine, life-threatening terrorism on the streets of London. At the same time it enjoyed strong, united support from almost all politicians and the judiciary and most sections of the press and, partly as a result, support from most law-abiding people. And, although the Met was almost staggeringly old-fashioned, it provided a young and keen officer with the most wonderful job.

The uniforms were shocking: nylon shirts, trousers that came up beyond the waist and soaked up rain beneath, while the shapeless macs above let it in as well. No wonder it was drummed into me that a good copper didn't get wet: Claridge's staff kitchen was a favourite haunt. No officer of inspector rank or above was allowed to work in his shirt sleeves, even in his own office: if a summer's day was too hot for full serge, they had to wear the thin blue nylon jackets accurately dubbed 'ice-cream jackets'.

Supervision of officers' activities was virtually non-existent: some worked hard, some not at all. Senior supervision consisted of, first, the

Chief Inspector, then the Superintendent, then the Chief Superintendent, coming down to the front office of the police station and checking the various registers, all of which were invariably correct in terms of being properly written but bore no resemblance to anything of importance. No one ever spoke to one of these ranks unless spoken to. None of them was ever seen in the hurly-burly of the charge rooms.

What was equally odd was the chaotic legislative framework in which the police had been working for so long. In 1982 I visited the United States to look at its investigative techniques about rape. When I observed an interview with a suspect I was astonished to find it being tape-recorded, something not yet seen in Britain. (The suspect was equally shocked when I announced, for the purpose of the recording, that I was from Scotland Yard: he protested volubly that he 'ain't done nothing that bad'.) A defence lawyer was also present: all reforms that were still years away here, although their shape was becoming visible. Before 1986, under the early-twentieth-century arrangements known as the Judges' Rules, there were no lawyers available to suspects, no taping of evidence and, of course, no video recording of what happened in cells or the charge room. Prisoners held for serious offences were routinely locked up for days before being asked anything. One of the greatest absurdities of all was that if two officers saw something or interviewed a prisoner together, their accounts were required by the courts to be identical word for word, despite the utter illogicality of this.

While most officers were honest, for some officers the complete absence of any supervision of their investigation led to short cuts which must have been clear to lawyers, magistrates and judges, but nothing was done. In Raymond Chandler's *The Long Goodbye* the hero, the private detective Philip Marlowe, is treated very badly and points out to the police detective in charge that what he is doing is against the rules. The response is 'Listen, buddy, there ain't a police force in the world that works within the law book.' This was true in Britain as well and these short cuts, brilliantly defined as 'noble cause corruption' by the American academic Edwin Delattre in his 1994 book *Character and Cops*, were the breeding ground for the real corruption that followed.

As always, there are advantages in any situation and the great strengths that the police enjoyed from this insularity were those of teamwork and a willingness to tackle any problem. Even on the wettest of days or the darkest of nights, a call over the radio that an 'officer requires urgent assistance' would empty the canteen and divert other officers to the scene from almost any task. The sense that your mates would come through hell and high water was palpable and was also necessary because, while officers today face far more risk of an attack with a knife or gun, my early period was very physical. Pub fights were everyday occurrences, rolling on the ground with a prisoner not uncommon, so the sound of a siren getting nearer was very comforting. We believed that the Met's Dad was bigger than anyone else's Dad and that included the Provisional IRA.

My early years of service coincided with the height of the early IRA campaign in London, together with occasional interventions by Palestinian terrorist groups. Calls to suspect packages were routine and you just had to get used routinely to opening them. This was the time of the bombings at the Park Lane Hilton in 1975, the Balcombe Street siege in 1975, the attack on the Europa Hotel in Mayfair in 1978, the death of a Met bomb-disposal expert, Ken Howarth, blown up in 1981, the bombings in Hyde Park and Regents Park in 1982. It was in the aftermath of bombs in 1974 in pubs in Guildford, Woolwich and Birmingham frequented by military personnel, which killed twenty-eight people and injured hundreds. I went to some of these scenes, the Hilton, Hyde Park and Balcombe Street, and was acutely aware of them all.

There was a sense that the Met could do anything and memories are of farce and of fear. To take one example of farce, after a series of attacks on Israeli interests a bright decision was made that the El Al offices on a corner of Regent Street should receive a police guard on the door. One winter evening, just as light was failing, probably in 1975, it was me. I was unarmed, which in my view rather took away the point of being there. A dark car drew into the opposite kerb of the sidestreet on which the offices were situated. The back door opened and a long tube with holes in it was pushed out. It was pointing at me and I took the decision that it was a machine gun and ran round the corner. I stopped and looked back and watched an elderly lady walk away on her crutch.

To take an example of fear, five years later, my sergeant and I, both armed, got a call to a man with a pistol in a pub on the borders of Chiswick and Hammersmith. Another man met us outside and told us where the man was sitting, with his back to the wall of the lounge bar. He apparently had a gun in a plastic bag. We called for assistance but went into the pub, which was pretty full. The man who had been described was sitting where we had expected. Two cops walking into a bar quieten things down a bit but not as fast as what happened next. I told the man to stand up. He did so but his hands were behind his back. I told him to raise his hands above his head very slowly. His arms came from behind his back and he raised them out sideways. In his right hand was a revolver.

Now what really quietens a pub is when that happens and the two cops jump backwards, pulling their own guns out. The man just stood there with the gun pointing upwards at the ceiling. Had he brought his arms forward rather than out sideways, I have no doubt that I would have shot him. We were maybe five feet apart. The silence was absolute. The barman had thrown himself on the floor behind the bar; the customers were cowering in their seats. The gun turned out to be a replica. In 1980, he had not even committed a criminal offence, but we confiscated it by getting him to sign it away.

I reflect on that event often, partly because the man was standing in front of the partition wall between the lounge bar and the snug and, had we fired and missed, we would probably have killed somebody behind it, but also because, in the years that lay ahead, such an incident would become a major part of my life. Yet the incident was also part of the thing I loved most about the police: the sense that we could do anything, that there was nothing beyond the reach of our can-do approach.

But, however enjoyable at the operational level, that can-do was 'can do by ourselves' and that was not all for the good for the police service as a whole. As policing developed in Britain, despite the Fenians and the corruption cases, the anarchists and the General Strike, a rather benign and, particularly in rural areas, somewhat bucolic model of policing emerged. The bobby became an icon of Britishness and the fictional *Dixon of Dock Green* beamed this ideal into millions of homes. During the 1950s and 1960s a political, judicial and media consensus arose that policing was best left to the professionals, with the Met, in particular, largely being left to run itself, as Martin Kettle noted in the *Guardian* in 2008:

> Until very recently, London's police were a law unto themselves, controlled only, if at all, by a Home Office that rarely picked even a small fight with the force. Historically, the Met was an alien force to Londoners, often staffed and sometimes even led by people with no community roots in the capital ... Until the 1980s, the Met to all intents and purposes ran itself.

However, probably because of this and its separation from the establishment, the Met increasingly lagged behind a Britain that began to shake off its post-war exhaustion, which is probably why it seemed so old-fashioned when I joined. The police did not know whether to be hard cop or soft cop in relation to pornography, drugs and drink-driving. These last two were bringing the police into conflict with a wider public and especially with the 'chattering classes'. Whatever Critchley had thought, the police were profoundly shocked by the violence at Grosvenor Square in the Summer of Love, 1968. They were out of sync, as the musicians of the time would have put it, not members of what Andrew Marr so brilliantly described as 'the democracy of narcissism' in his description of the sixties in his recent book *A History of Modern Britain*. The words 'peelers' and 'bobbies' went out of fashion, replaced by 'the cops' and then 'the fuzz', 'the filth' and 'the pigs'.

The consensus was going to crack and the police were going to be on their own. Dixon was fictional. The 1977 book *The Fall of Scotland Yard* by Barry Cox and others tells the story of one of the first obvious signs of decay. It begins with the words: "'Like catching the Archbishop of Canterbury in bed with a prostitute," observed a leading criminal lawyer on breakfasting with *The Times* on Saturday, 29th November 1969.' The front page of *The Times* bore the headline 'London Policemen in bribe allegations. Tapes reveal planted evidence.'

The story was truly sensational. *The Times* had obtained tape recordings of Met detectives soliciting bribes and planting evidence. The phrase that echoed for years to come was one of the CID officers saying to Michael Smith, the name used throughout the piece as a pseudonym for the small-time professional criminal who had alerted *The Times* to the story, that he would look after him if he got into trouble with the police anywhere in London 'because I'm in a little firm within a firm', clearly an indication of a network of corrupt officers. He continued, 'Anywhere in London, I can get on the phone to someone I know I can trust, that talks the same as me. That's the thing and it can work – well, it's worked for years hasn't it?'

The *Times* story was not the first revelation in recent decades that all was not well. That had come six years earlier with the inquiry into the activities of Detective Sergeant Harry 'Tanky' Challenor. Challenor was an ex-SAS soldier with a Military Medal for service behind enemy lines. In 1962 he was sent to West End Central and effectively given carte blanche to clear up Soho, a task to which he applied himself with gusto. A series of criminals found themselves at the Old Bailey on serious charges, much to the satisfaction of Challenor's bosses. But then, in July 1963, his methods of planting evidence and fabricating confessions came to grief when he made an arrest at a demonstration outside Claridge's against the presence in Britain of Queen Frederika of Greece. The detainee was a man called Donald Rooum, a member of the National Council for Civil Liberties. He was carrying a banner but Challenor had him charged with possession of an offensive weapon, in the form of a half brick, an imprisonable offence. Rooum was sophisticated enough to have his own coat, in the pocket of which the half brick had allegedly been found, examined forensically. There was no brick dust. Challenor and two young officers working as aides to CID were charged with perverting the course of justice. Challenor was found unfit to plead and sent to a psychiatric institution. The two aides were sent to prison.

The Home Office and the Met reacted by setting up an inquiry under a distinguished barrister, the very title of which indicates their approach: 'An enquiry into the circumstances in which it was possible for Detective Sergeant Harold Gordon Challenor of the Metropolitan Police to continue on duty at a time when he appears to have been affected by the onset of mental illness.' Tanky was represented as a lone aberration. When those few criminals who were prepared to testify to the inquiry protested that they were all like that, their evidence was discounted on the basis that, in a contemporary phrase, 'they would say that, wouldn't they?' The waters closed. More than ten years later I was a young officer on a coach taking us to a demonstration. The sergeant read out the names of the officers supposed to be present. The name Challenor evoked hoots of laughter.

The waters closed but the *Times* story disturbed them again irreversibly. The Yard was forced to bring in an outside inquiry team, for the very first time in its history, led by an Inspector of Constabulary, Frank Wilkinson, who would be frustrated at many turns and who would conclude, Cox and his co-authors reported, that there were only three sorts of detective in the Metropolitan Police: 'Those who were themselves corrupt, those who knew that others were corrupt but did nothing about it and those who were too stupid to notice what was going on around them.' The Home Office was so worried about what had been uncovered that in 1972 it appointed perhaps the greatest of all modern Commissioners, Robert Mark, with the clear brief to root out corruption. Mark was an outsider, although a friend of Williamson, and he had been prepared for what was to come by a brief period as Deputy Commissioner. And he did his utmost to clear out corruption ruthlessly.

Mark is credited with the remark 'The basic test of a decent police force is that it catches more criminals than it employs. And the Met is failing that test.' He famously replaced the head of CID, Peter Brodie, with another Assistant Commissioner, Colin Woods, whose previous career had been entirely in uniform. When told that this was like putting a Chinese chef in charge of a French kitchen, Mark apparently replied that 'at least the kitchen will be clean'. He introduced compulsory interchange between uniform and detective officers. He destroyed Howard Vincent's concept of a single CID with a separate hierarchy, independent of the rest of the Met, placing detectives working in police stations under uniform command, although not those on central squads. Then he went after the villains of the piece. Under Mark's tenure a whole raft of allegedly corrupt officers were removed. He set up Department A10 under a uniform commander, to investigate suspect officers, taking away from the CID the responsibility of investigating its own colleagues. Taking a step which in our more litigious times would be inconceivable, the unit used a 'Confidential Memorandum 4'. This told suspect officers that they had lost the Commissioner's confidence and gave them a stark choice of immediate resignation or of suspension and possibly arrest, and by this means they forced a now unknown but estimated hundreds of detectives to leave the force.

Investigations from inside and outside London continued. Lancashire Police broke open the corruption of the Met's Drug Squad, resulting in trials and convictions in 1973, and a Met Deputy Assistant Commissioner, Gilbert Kelland, himself smashed the Vice Unit, sending to prison more than ten other detectives and two Met Commanders, the most senior ranks ever convicted in the Met's history, in a series of trials that went on across 1976 and 1977. In this, he had the assistance of a group of outstanding officers, including John Smith, later to be Deputy Commissioner, and John Hoddinott, later to be Chief Constable of Hampshire; both went on to be Presidents of the Association of Chief Police Officers.

Meanwhile, an innocent, I was entering the CID. Fairly unusually, I had been appointed to the crime squad at West End Central with about eighteen months' service, in early 1976. The crime squad was and is a group of would-be detectives, detached from their normal uniformed colleagues and working in plain clothes as the foot soldiers of the CID, either carrying out basic surveillance or limited enquiries. I immediately loved it. I had whole cases to deal with, from start to finish, and had responsibility for building the evidence to the point where the case went to court. I went to Bow Street and Marlborough Street Magistrates' Courts. I enjoyed the acerbity but humanity of the Stipendiary Magistrates like St John Harmsworth. I remember him dealing with a former Polish Air Force captain, now an alcoholic semi-vagrant, charged with being drunk and disorderly.

> **Harmsworth**: Captain K, have you anything to say?
>
> **Captain K**: No, sir.
>
> **Harmsworth**: Captain K, you and I have appeared together in this court for fifteen years. Never before have you had nothing to say. Let us celebrate that: have a conditional discharge. See you tomorrow.

I admired the Detective Sergeants, with their fur-collared overcoats, joshing with the barristers. But I also felt the chill. West End Central was probably little different from anywhere else and most officers there were doing their best. Nevertheless, the office was divided into cliques and there was suspicion among us as to just who was primarily working for the Commissioner and who mainly for themselves.

Robert Mark undoubtedly made a huge effort to clean up the Met but he made two mistakes. The first was to paint himself into a corner over what needed to be done to prevent corruption. He firmly resisted the determination of the Home Secretary, Roy Jenkins, to introduce an independent element into the way complaints against the police were investigated, unshakeable in his belief that the police were in the best position to do that alone. When the Home Office produced legislation to create the Police Complaints Board, an even more toothless tiger than its successors the Police Complaints Authority and the Independent Police Complaints Commission, of which more later, he refused to serve any longer (and painfully made an advert for tyres, albeit for charity, which for a while hurt his reputation badly). The second mistake was to not tell his successor, another outsider to the Met, David McNee from Strathclyde, what he must have known, that corruption was not a one-off event in a particular place and time but endemic in big-city policing. As a result, the watch slept and all the lessons had to be relearned right up to the end of the century.

In the 1980s a further corruption investigation, Operation Countryman, came and went. Countryman was led by a senior officer from Dorset Police and had possibly the worst ever name for a police operation, given the view from the Met that provincial detectives were 'swedies' rather than 'The Sweeney' (Sweeney Todd being cockney rhyming slang for the Flying Squad). There were almost no convictions despite enormous hype; and one of the officers who faced trial later received the Queen's Police Medal for Distinguished Service.

Twelve or so years later I found myself appointed head of internal investigations for the Met. Three weeks after that the largest corruption inquiry since Countryman emerged. The consequence was that Mark's legacy was fulfilled, as I describe in the next chapter.

Robert Mark once said, 'The police are the anvil on which society beats out the problems and abrasions of social inequality, racial prejudice, weak laws and ineffective legislation', and there was no doubt that race was emerging as an issue on which that anvil would receive some ringing blows. The first intimation had been the Notting Hill Riots of late August and early September 1958, fourteen years before Mark took office. At this time there were some 100,000 people of Caribbean descent living in London, with 7,000 or so in the Notting Hill area alone. This period also saw the remnants of Mosley's fascist groupings whipping up the issue of immigration and the emergence of a new form of white working-class identity in the shape of 'Teddy Boys'. The riots began with a gang of white youths attacking a mixed-race couple on Saturday 30 August and went on for over a week. Although the primary violence was committed by white youths, the African Caribbean community also organised their own gangs in defence. The police not only arrested the white attackers but also the black defenders, and the black community was very critical of their actions. Writing over forty years later, in 2002, the Home Affairs editor of the *Guardian*, Alan Travers, said that the riots 'ensured a legacy of black mistrust of the Metropolitan Police that has never really been eradicated'. Notting Hill became a focus for some of the conflict that arose out of that mistrust, particularly during the last evening of its now famous and largely peaceful August Bank Holiday Carnival, which itself had been founded the year after the riots to celebrate minority culture. When I served as a Detective Sergeant at Notting Hill Police Station in 1979, the sense of being almost a garrison was very strong. All Saints Road, not more than half a mile from the police station and part of what was called 'the frontline' by the black community, was virtually a no-go area and 'the Mangrove Club' in that street was raided regularly and robustly. In 1980 I served as a uniform Inspector underneath the raised roadway of the Westway and faced stone-throwing black youths at the end of yet another Carnival that ebbed away into mob violence, and very frightening it was too.

As I began my police career one of the most popular television shows ever made by the BBC was making millions laugh. In one episode first transmitted in 1975 Basil Fawlty, the proprietor of the disaster-prone seaside hotel named after him, complains about his wife to a permanent resident of the hotel, an elderly man known only as the Major. The conversation goes like this:

The Major: Strange creatures, women. I knew one once ... striking-looking girl ... tall, you know ... father was a banker.
Basil: Really?
The Major: Don't remember the name of the bank.
Basil: Never mind.
The Major: I must have been rather keen on her because I took her to see ... India!
Basil: India?
The Major: At the Oval ... fine match, marvellous finish ... now, Surrey had to get thirty-three in about half an hour ... she went off to powder her ... powder her hands or something ... women ... er ... never came back.
Basil: What a shame.
The Major: And the strange thing was ... throughout the morning she kept referring to the Indians as niggers. 'No no no,' I said, 'the

niggers are the West Indians. These people are wogs.' 'No, no,' she said. 'All cricketers are niggers.'

Basil: They do get awfully confused, don't they? They're not thinkers. I see it with Sybil every day.

The Major: I do wish I could remember her name. She's still got my wallet.

Basil: As I was saying, no capacity for logical thought.

The Major: Who?

Basil: Women.

The Major: Oh yes, yes ... I thought you meant Indians.

I quote this as a reminder of how casually racist Britain was in 1975. Racist jokes were commonplace and, in most quarters, considered totally acceptable: who now would tell a joke about Rastus and Lisa? But many did, including me and many of my friends. The first black person I ever entertained in any house in which I lived was in 1977. My parents never did, not because they were particularly prejudiced: they just didn't know any. A country that had spilled its blood to help destroy Nazi Germany still had no concept of or regard for the experiences and values of those over whom it had ruled for centuries in taking up the 'white man's burden'. They had forgotten the sacrifices made by the non-white Commonwealth in both world wars. Any reader now of John Buchan or Rider Haggard has to get past the assumption of white superiority within their pages. Every white adult in Britain in 1975 had had their formative years shaped before the Civil Rights legislation of the United States and the much weaker Race Relations Acts in Britain had outlawed discrimination.

This needs to be remembered as the history of the relationship between the police and minority communities unfolds and we try to understand why that relationship became such a lightning conductor for relationships between races as a whole. I do not think that police officers then were inherently more racist than other people, and I am absolutely certain that they aren't now, whereas I am often shocked by the casual attitudes current in other spheres. I believe that what made the police relationship with minorities so troublesome was the power to use force which the police possess. As one witness said to the Lawrence Inquiry years later, the African-Caribbean community feels 'over-policed and underprotected'. Discrimination by police was more visible and had such dramatic effects on people's lives. A decent police force is a necessary underpinning of a decent society and for many black people in Britain it wasn't decent, for too long.

So the years that followed 1975 and *Fawlty Towers* were full of incidents which became *causes célèbres* between the police and the black community: above all, the disproportionate number of deaths of black men in custody, usually associated with violent struggles on arrest, and the explosive riots of the 1980s, first in Brixton in 1981 and then in Tottenham in 1985. The disorders in Brixton were on a scale not witnessed since the Gordon Riots 200 years earlier. More than 300 people were injured, including many police officers, and many buildings and vehicles destroyed in three days of rioting. Crucially, the events were the first of their kind in Britain to be extensively captured by television cameras. In some ways the black community took heart from the government response. The public inquiry into the events, chaired by Lord Scarman, blamed high-handed police tactics in the days that preceded the riots, particularly the overuse of 'stop and search' and the hated 'sus' law, a nineteenth-century statute which allowed the arrest of someone suspected of being about to commit one or more of an indeterminate range of offences, which the black community believed was being used discriminately against them. Scarman's report forced the police to set up regular direct meetings with committees of community leaders (which still occur today) and led to the abolition of 'sus'. The more radical end of black opinion, however, was disappointed. Scarman also blamed unemployment and deteriorating social conditions for the increasing alienation of black youth, but crucially he did not accept the charge that the Met was a racist institution. That would be for another day and another tragedy, the racist murder of Stephen Lawrence.

The riot on the Broadwater Farm Estate in October 1985 had its immediate origins in the death from heart failure of an African-Caribbean woman, Cynthia Jarrett, during a visit to her home by police after her son had been arrested. Hours later parts of the estate were in flames and Police Constable Keith Blakelock was dead and his colleague PC Richard Coombes was so seriously injured that he never made a full return to duty. It was the first deliberate murder of a police officer in a riot for generations and Blakelock's was an horrific death at the hands of an enraged mob. The impact was the almost complete alienation of the community from the police, made worse by the intemperate remarks of Bernie Grant, leader of Haringey Council and the first black council leader in Britain, who failed to condemn the murder. It was then made worse by a botched police investigation, as a result of which convictions were quashed and some of the investigating officers put on trial. Like other Commissioners, I have met Keith Blakelock's widow, Elizabeth, and their family and I told her that the Met will never give up its efforts to bring his killers to justice, but with each passing year, I fear, that must become less likely.

Perhaps the best that can be said about these events is that they placed the relationship between the black community and the police at the centre of policing in London, with many community leaders and many senior police officers recognising that something had to be done to prevent a total breakdown in trust between a force that was now policing an increasingly multi-racial city. But it would be a long, bitter road. And it was very tough for those who were on the inside, the early black and minority police officers of London, whose experiences were sometimes a mirror image of the black community whom they served.

I served briefly with Norwell Roberts, the first black officer in recent times, who joined the Met in 1967, coincidentally on the same day as Paul Condon. I was on the crime squad and he was a detective at another central London police station and we did one or two operations together. I very much doubt he remembers me from that time, but I have always remembered him because I had never seen a black officer before. The man I got to know better was David Michael, who was a Detective Constable at Notting Hill when I was serving there. He always joined in the office banter, much of it directed at him. He kept a large, old-fashioned sweets jar on his desk, of which the sole occupant was a large and grisly plastic spider. It was, he said, 'for feeding honkies to' (a West Indian term of the time for whites). We all thought that was frightfully funny. What a good chap he was, one of the boys. I met David again when I became Deputy Commissioner in 2000. By then he was a Detective Inspector with a fine record but also with a long history of disputes and indeed an Employment Tribunal settlement against the Met. I could see the toll that his experiences in the Met had taken: the ready smile never returned until his retirement party. It is still there now and David remains a great ambassador for the service.

When I was in Surrey as Chief Constable years later, during the discussions that swirled around the Lawrence case, a young black officer told me a poignant and revealing story about himself. He was a cricket fan and at work he supported England: only at home did he feel safe to support the West Indies. It was just one small indication of the personal sacrifices so many minority officers had to endure to make the police service a welcoming and fulfilling place for those who were to come afterwards. As with all communities, not every minority officer would behave well and some would cynically use race as an excuse, but the early pioneers like David Michael, Leroy Logan, Paul Wilson, George Rhoden and Roy Hope, who attended the Special Course at Bramshill Police Staff College with me and rose to become, as a Chief Superintendent, the highest-ranking black officer of his time, were genuine pioneers and, like all pioneers, endured much on the journey.

A similar story can also be told about the women who fought for equality throughout most of the same years. Their story was different in that the breakthrough to higher rank came much earlier but many of the early high-flyers gave up marriage or, if married, gave up the prospect of having children to battle through. I believe that the struggle is now over as much as it ever will be in the police or any other profession. As Commissioner I used to try to drop into police stations without warning. One day I called in at the Plaistow station and joined a group of women having lunch in the canteen, who turned out to be the local Sapphire team, the rape investigators. They ranged in age from about twenty-four to about forty and I asked them about their experiences as women employees. The older ones talked about how good the job now was at supporting women with small children in terms of flexible working and the younger ones were confident that this would now be the case if they wanted to start a family. All of those, including me, with more than five or six years' experience acknowledged that this had not always been the case. When I left office nearly 30 per cent of new recruits were women, many very senior posts were held by women, both in uniform and in the CID, and you could almost see the culture changing as you watched.

4

Cop

After my time on the crime squad at West End Central I was appointed to the CID and transferred to Wembley, where I served for six months as a Detective Constable. It was not without incident. The CID at Wembley was the fiefdom of Detective Chief Superintendent Jack Slipper, a famous detective whose reputation was oddly enhanced by the way that Ronnie Biggs had eluded his grasp in Brazil. He was not sure about any detective with less than three years' service. It was here that I used – in part – the self-defence techniques that I had learned at Hendon. I was called down to the charge room because a prisoner was asking to see me. He was a man whom I had charged with 'going equipped to steal' a week before and he had arrived at the front counter of the police station, insisting on seeing me. He had then made such a huge commotion at the front counter that he had been arrested. When I came into the charge room, he suddenly pulled a meat cleaver out of one of his cowboy boots and forced me back into a cell. The instructor's voice from Hendon came back to me. I shouted at someone behind him, he looked around for a moment, and I hit him very hard indeed. He was later convicted at the Old Bailey of attempted Grievous Bodily Harm. When I received a Commissioner's commendation for bravery it was quite a surprise as I had not thought I had had much choice.

It was a much more amateur time: while raids are now risk-assessed and police use hydraulic jacks on premises which have to be forced, these were the days of just turning up with a sledgehammer. It would have helped if we had always got the right address. I recall one suspect we were seeking coming out to give himself up because he had been woken up by the sounds of us smashing down his neighbours' door and then emerged roaring with laughter at whichever benighted crime squad officer had written down the wrong house number on the warrant.

Thereafter I was promoted and went to Chelsea as a uniform sergeant for a few months. This early promotion was a feature of the Graduate Entry scheme. I am not sure that it is true that the first promotion is the hardest transition but it was a challenge to be a sergeant with only three years' service, when most of those whom I was supposed to be supervising were much older and much more experienced. Those brief months at Chelsea also included some new experiences. I was involved in policing the violent disorder at Grunwicks, the first industrial dispute the Met had faced for many years. I was to face many more, but the first experience of a spitting, jeering, threatening crowd throwing missiles is unnerving. It was at Chelsea that I understood very clearly for the first time that those with money and supposed breeding did not expect their children to be arrested, as I did with a couple of what are now called 'hoorays' still at a familiar public school, who decided that walking along the roofs of a line of cars was good fun. The parents expected that if they paid the owners, that would be fine. I disagreed.

At Chelsea, I also had the most frightening moment of my whole police career, meat cleaver not excepted. The fire brigade went on strike and the army were called in with their 'green goddess' replacement fire engines. There was a fire in a hotel and it was for police and management to ensure the hotel was empty. I went too many floors up and suddenly I thought I was trapped. I wasn't but I rushed down stairs at the speed of a falling lift and shook outside. There was no one in the building.

It was then off to Bramshill. The Graduate Entry Scheme inevitably meant, unless you fell off the scheme by failing the sergeants' exam, attendance on the Special Course at Bramshill, the Police Staff College in Hampshire, an echo of the Army's Sandhurst and centred around one of the most beautiful Jacobean houses in Britain. The course had been designed in the early 1960s as a year-long university-style programme to provide a cadre of selected officers for future promotion to high rank. After the postwar abandonment of the Trenchard Scheme, an inquiry a few years earlier had discovered that graduate entry to the police service had effectively dried up. Together with the introduction of scholarships to universities for serving officers, the Graduate Entry Scheme and the Special Course were the alternative to the recreation of officer entry, like that in the armed services. This was partly done to honour Peel's original vision, but more to placate the Police Federation, to whom the concept of officer entry was anathema.

The Special Course was not extraordinary in content; nor was there a gulf between the respective ability and intelligence of the twenty-nine sergeants from all over the country with whom I was to spend a year. What was different was their previous educational experience. The course of 1978 – the sixteenth – straddled a period of change, as the number of graduates increased, so that it contained graduates like myself but also bright people who had practically no educational qualifications. As a result the teaching staff faced a huge challenge to retain both the confidence of those for whom the environment was challenging and the attention of those who were used to it. Once again I loved it because this was the very mixed company that I craved. As I could do most of the course work and examinations fairly easily, I had time to listen to the different experiences of the officers of many ranks from forces around the country who were on the various courses run at Bramshill. I learned a great deal and once more made lifelong friends including many who would later become Chief Officers. It also meant that I had more time than my colleagues to spend on the main piece of work required, which would now be termed a thesis, and that was a good thing because I ended up doing two, or at least one and a half.

Here I shudder to look back at my naivety. There is a regulation which prevents police officers from taking an active part in politics, a wise rule that stems from an earlier time when police officers of all ranks, together with women, prisoners, lords and lunatics, were not allowed to vote. So I decided to survey anonymously all the officers at Bramshill, of whom there were more than 300, on whether this was an appropriate restriction.

My questionnaire also asked respondents about their voting history and intentions, as it was clear that a general election was not far off.

The head of the college was, in my view, rather unfortunately entitled the Commandant. I was summoned to his office and politely but firmly told to choose another subject. I had done a lot of work, however, and can now reveal that this previously unpublished piece of research showed, less than twelve months before the landslide election of Mrs Thatcher in May 1979, that a considerable number of these officers, particularly from the North of England and from Wales, were and intended to remain Labour supporters, something that I think would have surprised many commentators at the time. But it didn't surprise me, as it had become increasingly clear to me that only a few years of police experience would be enough to convince most people of the stark inequalities of life in Britain at the time. Nor had the Labour Party yet lurched to the left and become seen as anti-police, following the impact of its electoral disaster and the miners' strike of a few years later.

So another subject: nothing controversial this time. I chose best practice in rape investigation and produced a competent review of the literature, which probably won me the baton of honour I received at the end of the course. But one thing was obvious: almost all the research was American and some forces there had revised their approach in the light of the concept, apparently unknown in Britain, of Rape Trauma Syndrome, which described a specific pattern of emotional and behavioural response to this violation.

At the end of my time at Bramshill I returned at the beginning of 1979 to spend another year in the CID, now as a Detective Sergeant, at Notting Hill. I think I probably enjoyed this more than any other posting for many years to come. I was lucky as this was an energetic station with excellent Detective Inspectors, including John Grieve. It was here that I began to put my learning about rape into action. One case was that of a young American girl who was raped on her first night in London, her first night outside America. The arrest was straightforward but, after many twists on the way, the trial began at the Old Bailey. The trial judge was Michael Argyle, QC, a rather eccentric judge of the old school. He effectively adopted the prosecution case and was very dismissive of the defendant and his barrister. After the jury had retired, the defendant stood in the dock, discussing with the prison officers the likely length of his sentence. The jury came back after a very short retirement and acquitted him, clearly believing him not to have had a fair trial. Argyle swept his law books off the desk and dismissed the jury. The victim was now completely traumatised and knew no one in London, so, against every rule I could imagine, I took her home with me. I had been married only a few months and when my wife got home from work she was understandably surprised. It was this case that set me off on a drive to reform the Met's approach to rape. Although the investigation took place while I was at Notting Hill, the trial had occurred after I had received the last promotion available under the Graduate Entry scheme, as a uniformed Inspector, in charge of a team of roughly twenty-five officers at Shepherd's Bush.

A year later, at the beginning of 1981, it was back to the CID at Cannon Row, in the shadow of the old Scotland Yard on the Victoria Embankment. Again there were some who were sceptical about a Detective Inspector with six years' service. My Detective Chief Inspector, the late Ted Fosbury, was an old hand, who had taken the statement under caution from Harry Roberts, the murderer of three police officers in Shepherd's Bush in 1966. He was a little concerned to find that he had become a CID officer before I had been born but in the end we became good friends. He used to regale me with his experiences as a young cop when, after a tough war, he returned to a West End where everybody was on the make, spivs, shopkeepers, police and public. A little later on I had my first experience of being the number two to a Detective Superintendent in charge of murder inquiries. There were no permanent homicide squads then and they were formed from the CID wherever the murder occurred. My two back-to-back murders were of a dowager duchess and of a prostitute at the lowest end of the market. Neither was solved in my time, although years later a man was convicted of the first, after confessing in prison. This case had two particular features. One was that the confession showed that no amount of detective legwork would have solved it. It was a mugging. A mugger had just got off a bus at Victoria Coach Station, carried out an opportunistic attack on an old lady and got back on a bus before the police had even been called. She subsequently died of the injuries sustained when she was knocked over. All the house inquiries were in vain, except one, when life imitated art. I went to see the daughter of the dowager duchess, in a pretty palatial home in deepest Gloucestershire. I was delighted when my sergeant and I were shown into the drawing room with the words, 'My lady, the gentlemen from the Yard are here.'

In June 1981, while still at Cannon Row, I became the investigator of an extraordinary incident when a seventeen-year-old youth, Marcus Sergeant, fired a blank pistol at the Queen, in what appeared to be an assassination attempt, during the Trooping of the Colour. In those days trials which were to take place at a Crown Court were subject to a formal preliminary committal process at a Magistrates' Court. And the police were normally given four or five weeks to take statements and prepare the necessary paperwork. Sergeant had been charged with treason. A week after the events an Assistant Commissioner came unannounced into my office, a much more senior figure than anyone I had ever met or thought about meeting. He told me, not as a suggestion but as an unassailable fact, that he had just come from a meeting with the Private Secretary to the Queen, whom he had assured that the committal would take place by the end of the coming week. With that and without seeking any response, he walked out. It happened, just. Sergeant was sentenced to five years' imprisonment.

While I was at Cannon Row, I dealt with a case of blackmail. The suspect was charged on Christmas Eve and I had to find someone to type the charge sheet. There is no offence of blackmail – it is just a short-hand expression: the actual offence is 'demanding money with menaces.' I went to Bow Street Magistrates' Court and asked that the charge sheet be brought along afterwards. Some combination of my handwriting and an early sherry on Christmas Eve meant that the prisoner was arraigned for 'alternating nicely with menaces.' I have always thought that a pretty accurate description of policing.

In 1982 Roger Graef's famous 'fly on the wall' TV series about Thames Valley Police included the now notorious sequence of a rape investigation, which showed detectives treating a rape victim very badly. While I was at Cannon Row I came across an advert for a bursary to spend time abroad studying a policing topic. I applied to examine working practices in rape investigation in the United States. To my genuine surprise, because other applicants were much more senior in rank, I won the bursary and later in 1982 travelled to New York, Newark, San Francisco and Los Angeles. It was, with the exception of New York, which seemed little different from London, a revelation. The officers I met were specialists in the investigation of sexual assault, had received specific training, including the issue of Rape Trauma, and were connected to a number of charities dedicated to such victims.

Two women died by accident in Trafalgar Square during the celebrations on New Year's Eve 1982. Again I was the number two on the investigation into how this accident had occurred but this time I caught the eye of the senior officer who had been in charge of the police operation on the night, Hugh Annersley, later to be Chief Constable of the Royal Ulster Constabulary (RUC). Kenneth Newman had just been appointed Commissioner and decided to introduce the concept of strategic planning to the Met, based on a police version of the fashionable idea of the time, Management by Objectives. Strategic planning units were set up at the Yard and in each of the four geographic Police Areas into which the Met was divided, one of which Annersley commanded. Within a few days of ending the Trafalgar Square inquiry I was based at Paddington working for him.

Here I had time to continue the research I had been doing on rape. On my return from my bursary trip to the United States I had produced a report that I have no doubt would have gathered dust, except for one more difference I had discovered between that country and Britain. US police departments kept open records of the number of cases which were 'unfounded', cases which police in Britain would refer to as 'no crimes', that is cases in which the investigating officers did not believe that a rape had occurred or in which the victim had withdrawn the allegation. I was very interested in this figure because I knew that research showed that one of the most devastating complications of Rape Trauma is for the victim to feel she has not been believed and the film about Thames Valley Police had ended with the traumatised victim withdrawing the allegation.

That unfounded rate varied widely between a number of US police departments which I either visited or surveyed after I got back. My 1985 book *Investigating Rape: A New Approach for Police*, published with the aid of the Police Foundation, is sometimes kindly credited with a change in the way the Met and British police forces approach rape. But the book does not and could not have contained the whole story. In it I noted that Kansas City Police Department was the far outlier of the American forces surveyed, with a rate of some 14 per cent cases unfounded in 1977, while the other forces had far fewer. Kansas had also supplied figures for 1982, which added in another category of 'allegation withdrawn by victim', which raised the combined figure of cases that were not proceeded with to 18 per cent. Police departments in America also had high proportions of their cases categorised as 'inactive' or 'unsolved', so that no department I found solved more than half the rape cases, with most achieving much less. The 1982 clear-up rate for reported rapes in England and Wales was 68 per cent.

I then wrote in the book that 'except for the physical search of crime records', in Britain there was no way of discovering what proportion of reported rapes were classified as 'no crime'. But that is precisely what I did at Paddington and it was this that changed the Met's approach to rape. Police stations were wearily used to requests from these new planning departments for statistics. So I just added another one. Each station was asked to provide a return of all allegations of rape made over a set period, making clear what had happened to the investigation. There was a variety of possible outcomes but the obvious divide was between those cases where the crime had been fully investigated and solved or not and those where the crime had not been investigated because it had been classified as 'no crime', either with or without the additional rubric of 'victim withdrew allegation'.

When the figures came in from the police stations, they were pretty stark. Less than 20 per cent of the cases had been fully investigated. That meant that the Met's clear-up rate was of only a fifth of all cases, which meant it was five times too high. In 1982 the Metropolitan Police recorded 285 rapes, of which 161 were solved, an official clear-up rate of 56 per cent. It was actually detecting only some 12 per cent of all the allegations being made by distressed women in London. I was quite a junior officer and I had a bomb in my hands. I decided to seek some top cover.

I went to see a redoubtable woman called Thelma Wagstaff, who was to be the first woman detective to become a Commander in open competition with men and who, at this point, was a Detective Chief Superintendent at the Yard. At first she was quite suspicious of my motivation but when she saw the figures she was appalled: she signed the order spreading the research across the whole of London. The pattern was the same. The vast majority of allegations of rape were being written off as not having occurred, either with or without the agreement, such as it might be, of the victim. Thelma took the figures to the Assistant Commissioner Crime, and afterwards described him as being incandescent, though whether that was because of what was happening or the fact that it had been discovered, she declined to say, with a smile. The Assistant Commissioner sent staff out to redo the figures. They came back with the same results and the whole approach to rape investigation changed.

Thelma and I were given the task of setting up sexual offence investigation training courses across the Met, focused on the needs of the victim but using these figures as the clinching argument to the Detective Inspectors, who came to the course accompanied, for the first time, by women constables, who were to be given the task of direct contact with victims. A film was made to encourage women to report the crime and training was given to a wonderful group of women volunteers from Victim Support. A national course for rape investigators was set up at Bramshill.

Even now, more than twenty years on, rape investigation is far from perfect. Rape is a very hard crime to investigate, let alone to take to a successful conclusion at court. The vast majority of the officers who were taking the decisions to write these cases off were doing it to save the victim from becoming dragged into a system where the case would end either with there being insufficient evidence to charge the suspect or, if a charge was brought, in acquittal. Jury attitudes to women who had been drinking, who had mental impairment of any kind or who were raped by an acquaintance were even more judgemental than now. A 'good' rape, as it was described, was one that did not have any of these features and would be more likely to succeed. However, this unofficial filtering of cases entirely ignored the needs of the victim and largely stamping it out has improved the lives of thousands of women.

This improvement has continued, with the creation of specialised units to deal with sexual assault and much closer liaison with the NHS in London. I am also proud of the fact that, even though many hundreds of officers were shown these figures over those years, they were never leaked. The number of rapes in London in 2008 was 2,124, with a clear-up rate of 33 per cent. The total figure, while still likely to be lower than reality because of under-reporting of this crime, is a much more likely total than the 1982 figure in a city of 8 million inhabitants; the clear-up rate is much nearer the norm I had found for American cities. Angry as the Assistant Commissioner was, he would preside over a change for the better but one that, as always, was driven from within.

Hugh Annersley was replaced by Edgar Maybanks and I was then to accompany him as he took charge of the siege of the Libyan People's Bureau, after the murder of WPC Yvonne Fletcher. This was my first contact with an operation involving government, the secret services and the military. It was an extraordinary feeling to see the Met, as it always does, turn away in a matter of minutes from many activities to concentrate so much thought and so many resources on a single urgent task. It was an experience that I would recall on 7/7. I had never before worked such hours and it was bitter to suspect that, as the diplomats left the Libyan People's Bureau, the murderers were among them. However, I know that the case still remains open, although there have been recent revelations indicating that the case can only be tried in Libya.

Later that year I was taken into the central planning unit at the Yard and had my first sight of the leviathan that is the Met, as Newman struggled to modernise it. This was not going to be easy: most of the plans were ridiculously oversized and very easy to ignore. As one weary Detective Inspector said to me, 'The trouble with these plans and targets is they assume my CID office is full of swans. Some of them are not swans. Some of them are arseholes, even when they are sober, which is not very often.' Perhaps the funniest moment was when I was dispatched to request the Special Branch plan. There clearly wasn't one but I was told it would be delivered in half an hour. Right on the dot, an envelope arrived. On the piece of paper inside was typed: 'The plans of Special Branch are secret.'

In May 1985 I left the Yard to become the Detective Chief Inspector at Kentish Town, a busy, run-down part of north London. I really enjoyed my nearly three years in post there. What job other than the Met could take you from such contrasts as murder inquiries to strategic planning and back to murder inquiries (but now in charge). I do not read much detective fiction but I do like the work of P D James and her detective Adam Dalgleish. There is a passage in her book *A Taste for Death* which I read about this time and which really resonated. Dalgleish is called to the scene of a murder and sees the body for the first time: he has a silent conversation with the corpse to the effect that he does not know who he is but promises to find out who killed him. That is precisely what I felt and I had never seen it in print before. As Bill Griffiths, who ran the Met's homicide units many years later was fond of saying, 'There is no greater privilege in policing than to investigate the murder of another human being.' It is an indication of how far the Met has professionalised itself since the 1980s to reflect that, at that time, I was allowed – I did volunteer – to run a murder enquiry out of my CID office, which involved a forged letter to obtain the key to the victim's flat where a professional hit man was waiting. The Met now has a specialised homicide command, with 850 detectives.

Years later, when I was Deputy Commissioner, I met Phyllis James. As delicately as I could I pointed out to her that her later books were increasingly unlike the reality of how murders are now investigated and offered to arrange for her to visit a murder incident room. She gently replied that she wasn't sure her readers either knew that or would care very much. Fiction is fiction.

But it was not murders or rapes or armed robberies or drugs busts or any of the other staples of detective life that I remember most from Kentish Town but the King's Cross fire. That November evening in 1987 I was walking up the steps of my house in Wandsworth, expecting to spend time with my wife and one-year-old daughter, when the pager in my pocket went off. As I put the key in the door the telephone in the hallway started ringing. Then the police car arrived. I was now to take charge of the identification of the dead.

The fire had begun under a long escalator and then, as the officer in charge of the fire crew was examining the blaze, it suddenly changed into a fireball which killed him and engulfed passengers in the ticket hall above. At scenes of disaster the normal axiom, for speed and to preserve evidence, is to rescue the injured and leave the dead where they are, but so dark and appalling was the scene that the Fire Brigade could not be sure who was alive and who was dead so they took the decision to move all the bodies up to the surface. By the time I arrived a number of bodies were lying in black plastic sheeting on the floor of a local church hall, with more arriving every few minutes.

We had to treat this as a scene of crime and with a small group of detectives, I went down into that hallway after the bodies had been removed. As in the rescue effort after 7/7, the trains which provided the ventilation to the Underground had all stopped. The smell of burning was almost overpowering, underlain by a sweet smell of burned flesh about which none of us said a word. I worked through the night and could still smell it the next day on my clothes.

During the night the bodies were shifted to the main local authority mortuary behind Euston Station. I had attended post-mortems for many years but as the night and then the next day wore on, this became like a grotesque dance of death as body after body was unwrapped, many twisted and unrecognisable, although not all.

The process of identification was severely hampered by the fact that, because they had been moved, the bodies had become separated from their property; there was, of course, no DNA. I found out later that, after the previous major rail crash in London, at Hither Green almost exactly twenty years before, the Met had stopped a funeral cortège because the coffin contained the wrong body. We nearly had to do the same, having to explain to a grieving family that the body which had been identified as their family member was not that person. As a result we then had another family that had to be told that, although they had been informed that their missing family member was not among the dead, he or she was.

One of the other problems which those of us involved in the post-mortems were to discover later was that, because there was no passenger manifest, as each sack was opened, each of us was wondering whether we would know the person inside. In those days there was no post-incident debriefing and the pub was usually the therapy. Not long afterwards one officer had a partial breakdown. I felt very sick a couple of weeks later, when I walked around a corner and smelled a barbecue without seeing it first.

Thirty of the thirty-one bodies were identified reasonably quickly but we were left with one unknown. I was offered the services of a forensic artist, Richard Neave, who was prepared to reconstruct a face from the skull. He took the head with him in a box accompanied by a note from me advising police officers not to open it if they stopped him but to telephone me. Unfortunately, the reconstruction led nowhere and it would take a further sixteen years to identify the body, known as Body 115 and buried unnamed, as that of Alexander Fallon, a Scot who had fallen on hard times.

In 1988 I left Kentish Town on promotion to Detective Superintendent to lead a review of the way CID offices in London were organised, before going to Kensington in uniform to learn how to run a Met division. The head office of Penguin Books was just off Kensington High Street. During my time there in February 1989 Ayatollah Khomeini issued his Fatwa against Salman Rushdie for writing *The Satanic Verses*, published by Penguin. I was responsible for requesting armed police to guard the building. Kenan Malik's 2009 book, *From Fatwa to Jihad*, made me recall those days, which was part of Britain's and my journey from the burning of books in Bradford to the bombs of London.

Then, in 1991, I was selected to become the staff officer to Her Majesty's Chief Inspector of Constabulary, John Woodcock, the principal policing adviser to the Home Secretary. Promotion to Chief Superintendent soon followed. This post provided an even more lofty helicopter view of the service than working for the Commissioner. During my time the Home Secretaries were the Conservatives Ken Clarke and Michael Howard. This was the time of the ill-fated Sheehy Inquiry into the police service, which is remarkable for having had almost all its recommendations either rejected at first or, if introduced, subsequently rescinded.

Working at the Home Office gave me a direct view of the interface of the government with the police service, which probably made it easier for me to clear the main hurdle for those who aspire to senior rank in the police, which is to pass the extended interview process controlling access to the Strategic (then Senior) Command Course at Bramshill. Without attending this course, it is not possible to become a Chief Officer. In 1993 I went to the college to undertake the course, after two years with John Woodcock.

I have already noted the benign political consensus over policing after the Second World War and the sense in which the Home Office was less interventionist and certainly not as concerned to seek significant change as it had been in earlier decades, although there had been some significant amalgamations in a rather haphazard way in different parts of the country. Perhaps the best example is the contrast between two events at the beginning of the 1980s. There was much public concern over a higher than normal number of neonatal deaths at Birmingham Children's Hospital. In an acrimonious debate in the House of Commons, the Secretary of State was forced to defend her position. A little while later West Midlands Police accidentally shot a toddler dead during an armed raid. There was no political disagreement over the position adopted publicly by the Home Secretary: that this was an operational matter for the local Chief Constable.

There were some changes. A series of miscarriages of justice had stained the reputation of the police, beginning with the overturning of convictions in 1980 for the 1972 murder of Maxwell Confait. This led to a Royal Commission on Criminal Procedure and hence to the ending of the old casualness of police interrogation, the creation of the Crown Prosecution Service and the introduction of tape recording and legal representation during interviews with suspects. The Confait case was followed by those of the Birmingham Six and the Guildford Four, whose convictions for Irish Republican bombings in those cities were also overturned. But these were matters supported by all political parties.

It was – unwittingly – probably the Conservative government of Mrs Thatcher that broke the cross party consensus. There is no question that, by the time the miners' strike of 1984–5 was over, there was a widespread perception that the police had become very close to the government. This was also the period of Labour's wilderness years, with the Militant Tendency at full blast: the defeat of the miners made many Labour supporters and politicians much more hostile to the police, with one delegate to a national party conference describing the service as 'the salmonella in the sandwich'. The Conservatives had always had an almost axiomatic tendency to support the police and throughout the next decade saw law and order as their prerogative. Then something happened which went in completely the opposite direction.

Nineteen ninety-three was to prove a seminal year for policing. First a little-known Shadow Home Secretary announced that Labour was to be the party of law and order in Britain. A former barrister, Tony Blair, had asked the Labour leader, John Smith, for the Home Office brief, convinced that the working class was the most affected by crime. With his quick realisation of the depth of public outrage at the death of a Liverpool child, James Bulger, at the hands of two other children in early 1993, Blair then stole the initiative on crime from the Conservatives with his phrase 'tough on crime, tough on the causes of crime'.

There had been many terrible murders in British history, from the Wapping murders that preceded the Met's foundation, via Jack the Ripper, to the twentieth-century horrors of Rillington Place and Chevy Chase, the Black Panther, the Moors Murderers to the Yorkshire Ripper in the 1980s. However, the Bulger murder coincided with a new mood in Britain. Other murders had excited a grisly fascination and, in nearby areas, understandable panic: but the death of this little boy, his abduction captured on CCTV beamed into millions of homes and carried out by children only just of the age of criminal responsibility, seemed to be taken as a harbinger of moral decline. This moment also coincided with an apparent shift in the expression of emotion, first perhaps caught in the public expression of raw grief in response to the Hillsborough disaster in 1989, so different from the British tradition of the stiff upper lip and reaching its apogee in the country's reaction to the death, eight years later, of Diana, Princess of Wales. Jamie Bulger's death came halfway between these two events.

Crime suddenly emerged as a key issue of public concern and, at the same time, an area not so much of division but of intense competition between the main political parties. As Labour under Tony Blair moved apparently inexorably to power, it seemed to be aware of the success of the Republican Party in the United States, particularly the view attributed to Newt Gingrich that whatever you did in power, you could scarcely be too right-wing in seeking to gain it. Without the classic American issues of abortion and gun control, crime filled that position perfectly. Blair exploited the position by opening up a competition for toughness with the Conservative Home Secretary, Michael Howard, and mercilessly capturing law and order from the Tories before and after the 1997 election. In time, the effect of this would be dramatic. A 2007 survey by MORI found that crime is 'a bigger cause for concern for Britons than the citizens of any equivalent Western European nation and even the United States'.

All that was for the future and would be a major part of the context I would inherit as Deputy Commissioner and then Commissioner. In the summer of 1993, however, I finished the Senior Command Course and returned to the Met for the first time for almost two and a half years. I had been appointed to head a unit called CIB2, as a Detective Chief Superintendent. This was the successor unit to Mark's anti-corruption drive: CIB stood for Complaints Investigation Bureau and 2 was the investigative team. My new job was to investigate the misdoings of police officers. Despite what Mark had created, I was very concerned by what I found: the watch slept. There were five or six separate squads to cover different parts of the Met but there was no coordinated intelligence between them. I could smell corruption underlying the workload of each of the squads and there seemed no sense of urgency. There was a nasty inquiry going on into alleged drug dealing among officers in Hackney but no one seemed to be considering whether that might be happening elsewhere. Three weeks after I arrived the biggest corruption inquiry since Countryman dropped on to my lap out of a clear blue sky. It was to preoccupy me for the next three years but it was also to be the catalyst for a significant part of the changed Met that I was to inherit.

In an unconscious echo of the *Times* investigation of twenty-five years before, a small-time but persistent criminal called Kevin Cressey had gone to the BBC's investigative programme *Panorama*. He claimed that Met detectives on the Regional Crime Squad were requiring him to pay £40,000 for evidence against him to be dropped. The programme makers filmed him handing over the money. The BBC then contacted America's Drug Enforcement Administration to confirm some details. The DEA contacted the FBI liaison officer in London, known as the Legal Attaché, to ask what was going on. He contacted the officer in charge of the South East Regional Crime Squad, who called me in.

We, of course, did not know all this. We did not even know the names of the officers allegedly involved. All we had was a copy of a fax from the BBC to the Americans but it was clear that the *Panorama* programme was imminent and that the programme makers had film evidence of apparent corruption. It was obvious that, unless we did something, the first the Met would know about the facts would be a few hours before transmission of *Panorama*, too late to do anything but watch the Met's reputation shredded in public. I went to see the

Assistant Commissioner with overall responsibility for discipline and complaints, Peter Winship, and laid out a plan to him.

The plan was to obtain a Special Procedure Production Order, effectively a warrant to require the BBC to hand over its journalistic material, which could only be granted by a senior judge at the Old Bailey and was issued very rarely. We had two advantages: this was Wednesday and *Panorama* would not broadcast until Monday, and the BBC did not know we knew anything. However, it was also possible that, even if we got the warrant, the BBC could appeal against its requirements for long enough to permit the programme to go ahead. We needed to make a bargain. We got the warrant on Thursday and Peter rang the BBC and got through to the Duty Officer. An hour later, holding the warrant, he and I met with the controller of BBC1, Tony Hall (who was moving house that day and had reluctantly come in), and an apparently even more senior individual in the BBC bureaucracy, Richard Ayre, the Director of Editorial Policy. It was a very tense encounter. We were effectively threatening to send police into the hallowed halls of the BBC; they were threatening to take out an injunction to stop us. But I had a devil's bargain in mind. If they would hand over their evidence in a useable form, I proposed, we would not arrest those involved until an hour or two before the programme went out. They confirmed that this was to take place on the following Monday. We agreed my proposal and they undertook to provide the evidence by noon on the Friday. But that was not enough. I needed to see what they were going to broadcast. Amazingly, they gave me a copy of the unfinished programme.

Peter Winship was immensely supportive but he had a problem. The next morning the relatively new Commissioner, Paul Condon, was holding a meeting in Bromley in south-east London with his ten or so top officers, including Peter, a group then known as the Policy Committee. My post was sometimes described as 'the prince of darkness' and it was always possible for me to have direct access to the Commissioner, although I had never asked to do so before. Peter was sure that the Commissioner had to know of the problem that was about to hit him, so I went first thing on the Friday morning to brief the top team of the Met about the programme. They watched in silence. Paul Condon was clearly very irritated by what he saw and a bit irritated at having his meeting interrupted. He thanked me and then turned not to Peter Winship as he should have done but to Bill Taylor, the much more powerful Assistant Commissioner Specialist Operations, but still known, as almost all his predecessors since Howard Vincent had been, as the ACC, the Assistant Commissioner Crime. 'Sort this out, Bill,' Paul said. Bill held responsibility for the Met's relationship with the Regional Crime Squad. He came outside with me and Peter and I explained the plan. Bill disagreed. He was clearly angered by what he had seen on film. Bill told me that, when the BBC sent over its evidence at lunchtime, I was to arrest the detectives involved. When I said I could not do that, he made clear that that was what he expected to happen.

I had been driven down by a sergeant, who was present to hear this conversation. I got back into the car and for about three-quarters of an hour we drove back in silence to the office where the incident room was now being set up. As we reached the car park outside the building on the banks of the Thames, the sergeant said, kindly and firmly, 'Guv'nor, don't do anything stupid.' But I felt I had no choice. I rang my contact at the BBC and told them not to send the evidence over as we were not yet in a position to receive it. I then went back to see Peter Winship as soon as he was back at the Yard. I told him what I had done and explained that, if the decision was to be that the officers were to be arrested when the evidence was provided, a new arrangement would have to be negotiated with the BBC and a new senior investigating officer appointed because I had given my word and I could no longer continue the investigation. As I said this I knew I was putting my whole career at risk: it was very unlikely that the BBC would cooperate, the investigation would be seriously damaged and I would be disobeying what seemed to me to be the direct order of an Assistant Commissioner. Peter sat there in silence for a moment but he did not try to change my mind. He just said, 'I'll ask Bill to come here and discuss it again in more depth.'

It was a hell of a moment. Bill Taylor came up. I knew I had one more chance. I did not tell him that I was on the brink of resigning from the case, let alone that I had effectively sent back the evidence. I again explained, at greater length as I probably should have done the first time, the deal I had made with the BBC, emphasising that I assumed that the material it was going to provide would take days to examine and that, even if we got it that day, I would not be in a position to make arrests much before Monday night and that I was sure that in any case we would need the assistance of the BBC to interpret it. Bill Taylor grinned. He was actually a man of long experience and great subtlety. 'You are a chancer, Ian,' he said, 'OK: just make sure you get them.' Then he left. And so Operation Gallery, as it was known, because my office looked over the Thames at the Tate Gallery, swung into action. I rang the BBC, who brought over the material, and a number of arrests were made shortly before the *Panorama* programme was shown. As can happen to all Commissioners, Paul Condon was launching an important initiative the next morning and found his press conference being dominated instead by the allegations of widespread corruption. Kevin Cressey had fled to northern Cyprus, where we placed him under surveillance. He thought he was a witness and was surprised when I arrested him at Gatwick on his return.

Three points are worth recalling about this case. First, the depth of the web of corruption: my investigative team was as tight as a drum but still someone else tipped off Detective Constable John Donald, the principal officer investigated by the BBC probe, and we lost him for a crucial twenty-four hours from the Monday lunchtime. Second, Kevin Cressey got it wrong: he was not a witness. It is OK going to the BBC to film you bribing a police officer but it is still a criminal offence and, much to his surprise, he received seven years' imprisonment (less than the eleven years received by Donald). Third, and most important, this case proved to be a watershed in the Met's approach to corruption. It was now possible to convince the Commissioner and others that this case indicated that corruption was not cyclical in the sense of occasionally arising at intervals, which had been always been the view in London, as in New York and Sydney for that matter, but a constant threat. While I was investigating this case, others began a wide-ranging reappraisal of the threat, and in time this not only reinvigorated my sleepy hollow of CIB2 but also led to the creation of the dedicated anti-corruption unit that I was to inherit as Deputy Commissioner seven years later.

In the autumn of 1993 I applied to be appointed as an Assistant Chief Constable in Thames Valley Police, created during Roy Jenkins's amalgamations, which covers the counties of Berkshire, Buckingham-shire and Oxfordshire. I had applied earlier in the summer for a vacancy but had not been successful. Suddenly, to everyone's surprise, a very long-serving Assistant Chief Constable there suddenly applied for and got a job elsewhere and so another vacancy occurred. I decided to give myself the almost unique opportunity to be rejected twice by the same group of Police Authority members (who choose officers of and above the rank of Assistant Chief Constable: Commander in the Met). It turned out that the selection process was going to be unusual.

The Thames Valley Police Authority had decided to agree to a BBC request to make this particular appointment part of a TV series on how people get selected for jobs, called *Situation Vacant*. I was telephoned to be told that I had been shortlisted for appointment and then given this news. I was told that I did not have to agree personally to appear in the series. It took me only a couple of milliseconds to work out that, if this was what the Authority wanted to do, they would want candidates to cooperate. I was successful at interview. Years later the Chairman of the Authority admitted that he had personally discounted those candidates who declined to be filmed, on the grounds that he wanted someone 'who could stand in front of Reading when it was burning and tell the televi-sion that everything was under control, even if it wasn't', an interesting premonition of the events of 7 July 2005. One small source of amuse-ment in the years that followed was that a majority of the members of the first selection panel, which I had failed, told me privately that they had voted for me on that occasion. Someone wasn't being truthful.

Taking the overall supervision of the Cressey case with me, my family and I moved to Oxfordshire. This was a tough decision. My wife was a very successful lawyer running her own firm but, to ensure that the family stayed living together, she merged her practice with a central London firm and became a consultant. The years in Thames Valley were full of incident: my first job was to be in charge of police operations, which would later include the policing of the Newbury Bypass, Swampy and all. I then took over the personnel portfolio, which involved me in two of the police service's early large, gender-based employment tribunals. After a brief time as what was then known as the Designated Deputy to the Chief Constable (an overelaborate construction emerging from the Sheehy Inquiry, later abandoned), I was appointed Chief Constable of Surrey in late 1998, the first chief that force had had in many years who had not served there before.

Again things were tumultuous. One late afternoon a woman member of staff came into my office and asked if she could have a private word. When she left I was certainly feeling the loneliness of command. I went upstairs and sought out the longest-serving Superintendent in the force. He was surprised to see me walk into his office. 'To whom do you owe most loyalty – to Surrey Police or to the Deputy Chief Constable?' I asked. The Deputy was a very long-standing and powerful member of the force. The reply was instant: 'The force, sir.' I then told the Superintendent to take an initial brief statement from the woman who had come in to see me. He came down later and told me that we had real trouble. We had. I called in Her Majesty's Inspector, by now Peter Winship, who had left the Met, as well as the Clerk to the Authority, Paul Coen, and its Chairman, Alan Pearce. The Deputy, Ian Beckett, whom I had known for many years, was suspended and subsequently stood trial at Southwark Crown Court for indecent assault. He was acquitted and left the service.

After I had been at Surrey for some fifteen months I was asked by the Permanent Secretary at the Home Office, David Omand, to have lunch with him at the Reform Club. After a while he looked at me and asked if I was 'wedded to Surrey'. I was and must have looked puzzled. He said, 'We will shortly be looking for a new Commissioner for the Met and I want you to think about applying.' I left with a mixture of elation, surprise and trepidation. Commissioner? At this stage in my service and with what was happening in the Met?

While I had been in Thames Valley and Surrey, the Met was going through one of its most difficult periods and the cause once again was race. Paul Condon is a very decent man and was a good but unlucky Commissioner. London has a very low murder rate in comparison with most great cities. One of my speaking tricks, in fact, whether at a seminar or a dinner party, is to ask people how many murders they think there are a year among London's 8 million-plus inhabitants. Most people think it will be about 1,000. It is usually somewhere around the 150 mark (a third of the rate in New York) and was 144 during my last twelve months in office. Nevertheless, it was a murder that defined Paul Condon's commissionership, a murder which occurred in 1993, only a few months after he took office, as the death of Jean Charles de Menezes occurred a few months after I took over and defined my commissionership in the eyes of many observers. At about 10.30pm on the night of 23 April 1993 an eighteen-year-old black man, Stephen Lawrence, was waiting at a bus stop with a friend in Eltham in south-east London, when they were confronted and chased by a group of white men, at least five in number, perhaps as many as nine. He was stabbed in the chest and had no chance of survival. So began one of the most painful chapters in the long history of Scotland Yard.

The story of the Lawrence case has been told too often to need repeating here in any detail. But it was of huge significance in changing the policing of London and indeed Britain. I do not believe that the officers involved in the initial Lawrence investigation were themselves racist: it was the longer-term response of the Yard that famously laid it open to the charge of 'institutional racism', a term which was to change so much. This is, again, because of history. The impact of the events at Broadwater Farm had seared the Met. There was a clear need for the force to reach out to the black community and the Met tried but based its approach on the seventies and eighties doctrine of 'equal opportunities'. Officers became determined not to be seen to be prejudiced in their behaviour and to treat everyone the same, regardless of colour or creed, although individual decisions did not take away a collective tendency to stop and search African-Caribbean young men disproportionately.

I was not in the Met during these events but I have reflected long on what apparently happened. Those who carried out the initial Lawrence investigation showed themselves to be less competent than they could have been. In this, however, they reflected the shortcomings that would have characterised many investigations of what would have been seen as a routine murder inquiry by understaffed and overburdened homicide teams in the working-class areas of outer London at the time. The officers appear to have assumed it was a common or garden fight. They failed to understand the racial tensions which simmered in the streets of Eltham, a part of London which houses the headquarters of the tiny British National Party. They failed also to understand the high expectations of the Lawrence family for appropriate public services. Beyond them, the Met as a whole was about to learn something vital through the determination and networks which characterised Doreen and Neville Lawrence, Stephen's parents: that the need to treat people equally was not itself enough. Treatment had to be equal in terms of competence and respect but police also had to understand and, where possible, adjust their service in line with the experience and expectations of different communities. Learning that would take six years.

It is now alleged that most of Eltham knew who had killed Stephen Lawrence. That knowledge does not seem to have been within the possession of the inquiry team. Although the right suspects were eventually arrested, the Crown Prosecution Service dropped the charges for lack of evidence. The Lawrences were not satisfied. With the utmost determination they followed every avenue to find out who had killed their son and why the police had failed to prosecute anyone. They enlisted the help of politicians, journalists and, above all, the black community, both in Britain and overseas, with Nelson Mandela as just the greatest of luminaries. The *Daily Mail*, perhaps the most unlikely of newspapers, named the suspects and branded them murderers. With the help of a young Asian solicitor, Imran Khan, and the civil rights barrister Michael Mansfield, the family mounted the almost unheard of initiative of a private prosecution for murder, which failed. The Lawrences made an official complaint against the Met. They bearded the incoming Labour administration and its likely new Home Secretary, Jack Straw, with demands for a public inquiry. And the response of the Met was to defend, to insist that the original inquiry had been properly conducted. It had formally reviewed what had been done and the results of that inquiry had gone to the Commissioner, who had accepted its conclusions, including the idea that the Lawrences and their supporters were troublemakers. Whatever his instincts might have been, Paul Condon at first succumbed to the classic temptation of Met Commissioners: to support his officers rather than open up the whole of the case again to independent scrutiny. This allegation would subsequently be made against me.

Condon was deeply disappointed when, a few days after taking office in 1997, Jack Straw announced that a public inquiry would take place. For Mansfield, in particular, this was an opportunity of a lifetime to bring the Met's sins to light, while a new investigation undertaken by Kent Police exposed the threadbare nature of the original investigation. Set against the normally restrained British legal process, the public inquiry, which opened in March 1998, was a circus. Along with other officers, the Commissioner was made to face an unrestrained set of cause lawyers, in front of a hostile public gallery and a panel, under the chairmanship of William Macpherson, who were properly determined to ensure that the voices of the voiceless were heard. The final report was delivered in February 1999 and was extremely critical of the Met.

Of course, I knew that the report was likely to be very difficult and I meant well when I chose to make a speech to the Social Market Foundation, a couple of weeks before Macpherson was due to report, about diversity and the proper response of the police service to the Lawrence case. I said that part of the response:

> must be the elevation of inclusiveness to be the hallmark of British policing. By inclusiveness, I mean something very specific: an active

reaching out to a diverse community. In common with many organisations, the police service is replacing equal opportunities with diversity statements. By inclusiveness, I mean going past that to making the welcoming of diverse traditions central to the police service.

This was front-page news in the next day's *Guardian*. Under the headline 'Police Chief: "this can't go on"', Alan Travers, the Home Affairs editor, described me as 'a key modernizer inside the police force' and said that the speech 'did no harm to his prospects of succeeding Paul Condon'. I had not meant that to be the inference. My speech was a bad piece of timing for Condon, who was unable to respond to a forthcoming report but was quietly building the future. He had determined to acknowledge openly the need for fundamental change. He had asked John Grieve, by then in charge of counter-terrorism and a hugely respected figure, to lead the Met's response, which he did in two ways. First, by creating a new Race and Violent Crime task force, he operationalised anti-racism, making the arrest of racists a task of which skilled detectives were to become proud. Second, he invited a group of the long-term and sternest critics of the Met to become its advisors on matters of race. The Independent Advisory Group (IAG) was made up of amazing people, like Beverley Thompson, John Azah and Ben Owuso, who came from many communities suspicious of the Met. John Grieve and his successors in post would make IAGs an integral part of the Met's working culture, not only in relation to race (as in the case of Trident) but also later in terms of gender, faith, sexuality and disability.

Paul Condon showed real mettle. He dug in, ignored the calls made for his resignation and used his political capital to establish a bargain with Jack Straw by which he stayed on for another twelve months or so to take the pain for his successor. It was a brave choice because the strain undoubtedly affected his health for the worse. But it could only be part of the necessary medicine.

The famous definition of 'institutional racism' at the heart of the Macpherson Report was a significant part of both the solution and the problem. The concept had been around for many years and some activists regarded the failure to brand the Met with such a label had been a shortcoming of the earlier Scarman Report into the Brixton disorders. It was expressed in the Stephen Lawrence Report as follows:

> The collective failure of an organization to provide an appropriate and professional service to people because of their colour, culture or ethnic origin. It can be seen or detected in processes, attitudes and behaviour, which amount to discrimination through unwitting prejudice, ignorance, thoughtlessness and racist stereotyping which disadvantage minority people.

The words 'unwitting prejudice, ignorance, thoughtlessness and racist stereotyping' were helpful in providing much of the way forward for reformers like John Grieve to break the stranglehold of thought which characterised the Met's approach to race. Unfortunately, the whole definition was nuanced and complex and many officers took it as an accusation of personal racism and were incensed. Their anger encompassed the Commissioner who had accepted it. Some of the mass briefings of staff were listened to in sullen silence. Many officers were hurt, confused and angry. And not only did Condon have to deal with Lawrence but, at the same time, he also faced an outflow of money from the Met to the regions and inside the Met a crisis of pay for young officers (another result of the Sheehy Inquiry). Recruitment to the Met was stalling and the number of officers leaving was rising. Paul could deliver much but he could not deliver a full meeting of minds with a Home Secretary who wanted someone else in charge.

My lunch with David Omand was a few weeks after my speech to the Social Market Foundation and I have no doubt now that it influenced him to call me. The Commissioner's post was advertised shortly afterwards. After much thought I decided to apply. I could not see what harm it could do me. Alan Pearce, the Chairman of the Surrey Police Authority, was very supportive.

The selection of the new Commissioner had always been an odd process but it was becoming exponentially more complex each time. In 1971 Robert Mark was summoned to the House of Commons by Reginald Maudling, the Home Secretary, who greeted him with the words 'Are you going to do this ruddy job for us?' Having impressed the Home Office Permanent Secretary with the way he had managed the amalgamations which led to the creation of Strathclyde police, David McNee, Robert Mark's successor, got a phone call asking him to come down from Glasgow. He was to brief Willie Whitelaw about the new computer system that was to underpin his new command. He arrived and instead found himself in a long and affable discussion with the Home Secretary, the Chief Inspector of Constabulary and the Permanent Secretary. He was then informed that he might be offered the position of Commissioner and duly was. McNee's successor, Kenneth Newman was asked by the Chief Inspector of Constabulary whether he would prefer to replace him or to be the Commissioner. After answering that he would wish to be the Commissioner, he was subsequently called to see the Home Secretary, still Willie Whitelaw, and, after a short conversation, offered the job. Peter Imbert, next, was brought back to the Met as Deputy Commissioner in 1985. Newman retired in 1987 and Imbert was offered the post of Commissioner by Douglas Hurd, without anything recognisable as an interview. After that, Paul Condon, then Chief Constable of Kent, was interviewed by the Home Secretary, Ken Clarke, together with three others including John Smith, the long-serving and much-loved Deputy Commissioner. Smith was seen as the clear favourite but Clarke picked Condon.

By the time Paul Condon retired, the legislation to create the Metropolitan Police Authority was in sight and the process became much more formal. The Chair of the MPA's predecessor body, the Metropolitan Police Committee, was involved in a first interview chaired by the Permanent Secretary at the Home Office, David Omand, and also present were a Civil Service Commissioner and an Inspector of Constabulary. Three names then went forward for interview by the Home Secretary, Jack Straw: these were John Stevens, then Deputy Commissioner, Charles Pollard, a long-term Chief Constable of Thames Valley and my former boss there, and me, with not much more than eighteen months as Chief Constable of Surrey.

I was much younger and had far less experience than the other two and, during the next bit of the process, I relearned one thing about interviews and learned another for the first time. I had received feedback that my performance on the first board had been 'outstanding'. Looking back, I am not surprised: I had not thought that I had an earthly chance. I was completely relaxed and probably therefore seemed assured and confident. By the time I got to the second interview, I had realised that I might be about to become the Commissioner with less service than anyone in recent history and I tried too hard, prepared too much and was very nervous: I gave a pretty poor interview: lesson relearned. The lesson learned for the first time came from the process: Jack broke nearly every rule of formal interviewing, making statements rather than asking questions and, if there were questions, they were 'closed' rather than the 'open' type which allow the candidate to argue the case for and against. So the new lesson was that senior politicians are not experienced interviewers, something I was to see again and again on the Police Authority which was to follow. Nonetheless, Jack was much more than an interviewer: he knew exactly who he wanted to be Commissioner, John Stevens, and he was correct. For reasons which I will elaborate further in this chapter, John was absolutely the right man for a particularly difficult time in Met history.

A few months later John's old job as Deputy Commissioner was advertised and again David Omand asked me to apply. This time, seeking a job outside Surrey was a lot less straightforward. Alan Pearce again supported me but warned that, if I failed, my relationship with the Police Authority as a whole and my reputation in the force would be badly damaged. Having a Chief Constable applying for the job of Met Commissioner was seen as a fillip to the reputation of any force: applying after only eighteen months as Chief Constable for another job was not in the same league. I had to think very hard. It was a difficult time for Surrey: the suspension of the Deputy had sent shockwaves through the force and it was facing a major increase in responsibility as a result of a recent Home Office decision to change the boundary between Surrey and the Met, small beer for the latter but a huge project for Surrey. I remember standing by the fax machine in my office with half an hour to go before the deadline for applications closed. I pressed the button. Jack Straw selected me.

John Stevens became Commissioner on 1 February 2000. I joined him two weeks later. Appropriately, it was Valentine's Day, just right for a massacre, and that is what we were facing.

The task that lay ahead for John Stevens should not be underestimated. The Met was in deep trouble and it would take most of the five years of his term of office to rebuild its numbers, morale and reputation. I will never forget that first afternoon. I thought it would be good to visit a Met police station on my first day as Deputy and it seemed rather appropriate that it should be West End Central, where I had started thirty years before. It was a rather different welcome from the first occasion, with the Chief Superintendent standing saluting on the steps. I was given a brief and rather confusing tour of the building – confusing because, during the intervening years, the Met had carried out a major renovation of this imposing building in Savile Row. While the outside had been left untouched, so I recognised it instantly, inside it had been completely gutted and rearranged, so I was immediately disorientated as we started to walk around. Then I did what I had so often done as Chief Constable of Surrey and met alone, except for my staff officer, Superintendent Sue Akers, with a group of staff who worked at the station. To put it bluntly, they despised senior management, politicians and the press, were largely contemptuous of the public and thought their pay was derisory, particularly those with shorter service. They were sullen and unsmiling. They seemed thoroughly demoralised and when, to lighten the mood, I asked why, if it was this bad, they weren't leaving, two of them said they were. I decided it was not really necessary to ask them what they thought of Macpherson's recommendations and as I left I reflected that this was a group who had been selected to meet the new Deputy Commissioner. What on earth were the rest like?

The next few months and indeed years were very challenging. John

quickly succeeded in obtaining a serious pay rise for younger officers and much increased funding for recruitment as a whole from the
government. He also had the advantage that the newly formed Police
Authority and the Mayor, Ken Livingstone, who were to assume office
that summer, took time to find their feet and how to deal with the Met.
But the mood was difficult. John had the idea of holding mass meetings
so that he could talk to staff and hear their views. These were blindingly
unpleasant at first, enough to justify the concern he expressed to me
backstage at Westminster Hall as we waited to go on for the first of
the events that he was not 'sure this was going to work'. Despite all this
and the normal string of events – from a catastrophic Mayday in 2000,
which left the Cenotaph defaced, to Aaron Barschak gatecrashing
Prince William's fancy-dress twenty-first-birthday party at Windsor
Castle dressed as Osama bin Laden (an event which my wife always
remembers: she is used to calls in the middle of the night but this is
the only one she recalls me shouting 'he's where, he's dressed as what
and he's done what?' quite so loudly) and the prosecutorial decision
making which led to John Stevens and Paul Condon being required
to stand trial at the Old Bailey on Health and Safety charges (and be
acquitted) – crime started to fall, morale began to climb and the work
of John Grieve and the Independent Advisory Group began to make
progress, not only to make the bitter pill of Macpherson more bearable
but also to bring about many other improvements. Even the mass meetings got better.

Meanwhile, however, a major change was happening in the relationship between the police and government. Tony Blair's interest in crime
did not wane when he became leader of the Labour Party and then the
New Labour Prime Minister. This was despite the fact that, by almost
any reckoning, crime had peaked in Britain in the early 1990s. But, as
Katherine Beckett's 1999 book *Making Crime Pay* makes clear, that no
longer mattered. Beckett's argument is that public concern over crime
is the product of political and media will. Taking the United States as
her example, she argues that political elites and law-enforcement officials frequently serve as sources in news stories which focus on street

crime (and rarely the crimes of the powerful) and which attribute the crime problem to permissiveness and the loss of respect for authority. She argues that the news media prefer a more right-wing commentary on crime because it fits their habit of sensationalisation in order to sell newspapers.

During its first ten years in office New Labour passed fifty-three Acts containing criminal justice legislation and created more than 3,000 new or revised criminal offences. It discovered and legislated against anti-social behaviour, legislation which appalled its libertarian wing but was immensely popular with both the general public, especially those living on run-down housing estates, and, more crucially, with the right-wing newspapers which the Blair government courted.

Police officers of all ranks, including me, welcomed the Prime Minister's genuine interest in policing. Most of the legislation made sense to us, much of it closing loopholes in previous legislation or equipping police officers with street powers that they had needed for years. But there was a price to be paid. The police were now firmly in the realm of politics and in the long term my story and that of, for example, Assistant Commissioner Bob Quick, driven out of office after me, are direct instances of the effect of the new dispensation. In the shorter term the price was Labour's application of its theory of New Public Management to the police: central government trying to improve police performance in the same way it was doing in Health and Education. The most obvious example of this philosophy was the introduction of the literacy and numeracy hours in primary schools under David Blunkett but Labour, as well as following every other recent government by reorganising the NHS, also pursued a rigid regime of target setting for both Health and Education. Hospital waiting lists and school league tables were the result. While these do produce genuine improvements across the board, they can eventually distort the way professionals shape their services, with occasionally catastrophic results, as the Stafford Hospital scandal revealed in March 2009.

Policing was to be no different. In the first Blair administration Jack Straw had concerned himself with two of the five Labour 1997 election pledges: to reduce the length of time before youth offenders reached trial and to increase the proportion of black and minority officers in police forces. Neither was particularly successful. Because the youth justice system, particularly in London, was chaotic and pressing only the police to improve it, rather than pressing the courts and the magistracy as well, was largely ineffective, progress on the first pledge was very slow. As far as the second pledge was concerned, the Met itself was part of the problem (and if the Met didn't deliver, the country would fail its post-Lawrence recruitment targets), not only because of the continuing poor quality of its relationship with minority communities but also because of the even worse quality of its recording practices. The situation reached a farcical climax at lunchtime on Christmas Eve 2000, when the Met and the Home Office had to announce that most of the Met's recently trumpeted improvement in ethnic minority staff numbers depended on the fact that those officers declaring themselves to be 'White Irish' had been included in the overall minority figures. This announcement had been preceded by a meeting on the morning of that same day characterised by acute irritation, during which Jack Straw, John Stevens and I ended up counting the figures and making the calculations ourselves.

A later Home Secretary, John Reid, famously said that he could not depend on any Home Office statistic, as he tried to stem the fallout from the resignation of his predecessor, Charles Clarke, over the number of dangerous foreign prisoners alleged by the tabloids to be on the loose. But neither the lessons of the past nor what was to occur in the future would deter David Blunkett when he arrived at the Home Office after the 2001 election. The change from Jack Straw to David Blunkett produced an interesting contrast. They are both politicians to the end of their fingertips but Jack has the meticulousness of the lawyer he trained as – hence the counting of the statistics on Christmas Eve. He very rarely does anything without careful consideration and is an expert on the constitutional relationship between the police and the Home Secretary. You have to get up very early to steal a march on or get ahead of Jack and he may be particularly suited to his present job of

Justice Secretary, where he must be getting things right, as he is upsetting both the legal profession and the Prison Officers Association.

Jack is also a very kind man, inviting himself in to have a cup of tea with me during some particularly troubling period during my time as Commissioner. That sort of kindness is also a feature of David Blunkett's personality. He has an interest in people and a warmth that is immediately obvious. No one can be other than deeply impressed with the way in which he has so astonishingly overcome his blindness to rise from a relatively impoverished background to hold great offices of state. He was less aware of the world of the Home Office and he seems much more impulsive than Jack, as his subsequent difficulties in office have shown. But that impulsiveness probably made him the great supporter of reform that he showed himself to be over the introduction of Police Community Support Officers, against much opposition.

Being around a blind man has its moments. On the first occasion I met him after his appointment as Home Secretary, I was asked to explain to him why the Met was supportive of the decision then being contemplated to lower the official classification of the drug cannabis. Among the different reasons I gave was that this would save officers from criticism because, when they found small amounts of cannabis on people, it was not worth the hours involved in processing an arrest and officers were sometimes just, as I put it, 'turning a blind eye' to these offences. I could not believe I had said that: everyone else was aghast but David was entirely unperturbed. He also has a fierce although short-lived temper. On another occasion, when I was meeting with him to try to explain some disaster the Met had presided over, I sat at his office table with just him and one note taker. I could sense that I was about to receive a Blunkett tirade. So could his dog, Sadie. She got out of her basket and came to the table and laid her head on my lap, from which she could not be displaced. It was very comforting.

David Blunkett had presided over real improvements in education and he expected to do the same at the Home Office. However, while he was able to direct the Prison and Immigration Services as he could Education Authorities, the Tripartite Arrangement meant that, when

he pulled on the levers of power about policing from his office, there
might be a lot of clanking but little happened. He could use the might
of his position to browbeat the Chief Constable of Sussex, Paul White-
house, into resignation in June 2001 (but had to pass new legislation
to allow him three years later to direct the Police Authority of Hum-
berside to suspend its Chief Constable, David Westwood, after the
Bichard Inquiry into the Soham murders). In 2002 he could give my
predecessor John Stevens six months to sort out street crime in London
or face the consequences – and airily announce that on the front of the
Evening Standard – over rises in street robbery in London, but in fact
he had no power to do so in such circumstances (and he backed down).

What he could do, however, was to build a system of performance
monitoring inside the Home Office and apply it to every force in the
country. And he did this on the back of an intervention by the Prime
Minister, which was probably one of the most extraordinary interfaces
ever between politicians and policing and certainly one of the most
effective.

On the very evening of the day that David Blunkett had warned John
Stevens about robbery, in February 2002, I was at a seminar being given
by Alistair Campbell, Tony Blair's press secretary, during a high-level
conference on crisis management. Campbell revealed that he thought
that the worst moment in Blair's first term had been the fuel dispute in
September 2000, when concerted action by drivers and others revealed
the weaknesses of 'just-in-time' processes in a distribution chain critical
to the nation. Campbell said that Blair had discovered the powerless-
ness of government processes in such a situation and was determined
that it would never happen again. Only a few months later Blair enlisted
COBR to confront the 2001 foot and mouth outbreak, bringing the
military not only into the handling of the crisis but also into COBR,
and then used COBR in anger on 9/11. Campbell made clear that it
would lie at the heart of Blair's own response to future crises.

He was right. What became known as the Street Crime Initiative
was to follow the sharp rise in street robbery in late 2001 and was to use
a version of the COBR model. While John and I and our team were

doing a lot to turn the Met round, late 2001 and early 2002 felt very difficult indeed. With shootings and murders on the rise, there was a media and popular feeding frenzy over crime. A new crime of violent car-jacking had emerged, with the public outraged by the murder in Battersea of an estate agent, Tim Robinson, in January 2002. After 9/11 many police officers had been withdrawn from the suburbs to be deployed in central London on counter-terrorism patrols. Street robbery, which is the police term for what is more often called mugging, was on the rise but particularly quickly in the suburbs, where the crime had previously been fairly uncommon. By the end of 2001 street robbery in London was 53 per cent up on the previous year. London was the main problem but increases were also occurring in other major cities. The Prime Minister called the first street crime summit in the spring of 2002 and much changed in policing.

What the Prime Minister did was to summon, half a dozen times in the next eighteen months, the Commissioner or me as his deputy to represent London policing, together with the President of ACPO to represent the rest of England and Wales, to explain to a large part of the Cabinet what we thought the problems were which lay behind this change in crime pattern. He would then turn to various Cabinet ministers to see what their departments could do to help. Obviously the first port of call was the Home Secretary, David Blunkett, but other prominent members included Education (most robbers were youths), Transport (robberies were happening around transport hubs) and Trade and Industry (what were the telephone manufacturers doing to make stolen telephones unuseable?) but, most significantly of all, the Lord Chancellor, Derry Irving, and the Attorney General, Peter Goldsmith, were present. For the first time in my life I was at a table with representatives of the Judiciary and the Law Officers who could be told, very politely, but still told – by the only person who could do so, the Prime Minister – to get the judges and magistrates to do something, to get involved, to take notice. In this case that was to take street robbery seriously, to produce appropriate sentencing guidelines and advice on bail, advice, for instance, in the shape of 'stop giving bail to repeat offenders'.

It was a fairly daunting arena. The Prime Minister would turn first to the London police representative. 'Ian, hi,' he would say. 'What is happening in London, what's the pattern, what can we do to help?' I would have a binder of information but I always boiled it down to a handwritten page because this was not a place for verbosity or detail. To be effective, a few key points had to be got over fast. With each succeeding meeting the room got more crowded, with more senior civil servants, representatives of the Director of Public Prosecutions (DPP), the Magistrates' Association, ministers with responsibility for local government, with other police officers charged with delivery, like Chris Sims, then Deputy Chief Constable of West Midlands, or Tim Godwin, Assistant Commissioner in the Met, responsible for criminal justice liaison and delivery on street robbery. Norman Barber, David Blunkett's former guru on delivery at Education, now at No 10, gave PowerPoint presentations on trends. This was suddenly becoming one of the key events in Whitehall. Over time new directions on sentencing and bail were handed down to the judiciary by the Lord Chief Justice; the CPS was required to become involved earlier and the police told to remain involved for longer once the CPS had got the case; local authorities with particular street robbery hotspots or successes were summoned to explain; the Home Secretary and Trade and Industry ministers called in the mobile phone manufacturers. Eventually, over the course of a couple of years, through this concentration of government firepower – and, to be fair, significant development of new police tactics – street robbery began to fall and has been falling ever since. But in that achievement were laid the seeds of some real difficulties. But before the seeds, one anecdote.

Visitors to London in the 1990s stayed clear, if they could, of Leicester Square in the heart of the West End. While never reaching the notorious danger of New York's Times Square in the 1980s, Leicester Square was a seedy, ugly space, the domain of drug dealers and drunks. While there was little enthusiasm in the Met for what many commentators believed was the key to the startling reduction in crime in New York in the nineties, known as 'zero tolerance', there was enthusiastic acceptance

1. Speech thanking the team in 2008, at a ceremony to thank those who volunteer to work alongside the police, such as special constables.

2. University days at Oxford, 1972. This photograph was taken for a version of *Marowitz Hamlet*, where I was a rather young looking Claudius.

3. Hendon class photograph, 1975. I am third from right, in the back row.

4. Special Course 1978: a week long practical exercise in Lincolnshire.

5. With a Met firearms team 2008: it was this photograph I used in my last speech, after my resignation had been announced, with a caption underneath 'Just be a bit careful Boris!'

'To lose one Home Secretary may be regarded as a misfortune: to lose three seems like carelessness' (with apologies to Oscar Wilde).

6. David Blunkett and Sadie

7. With Charles Clarke outside New Scotland Yard on the day of my appointment as Commissioner 2005.

8. John Reid: As Home Secretary, he concentrated, perhaps more than any of his predecessors, on strengthening the UK response to terror.

9. Jacqui Smith, the first woman and perhaps the most unlucky of Home Secretaries in my time.

10. One of the two *Private Eye* covers of my time, both relating to the death of Jean Charles de Menezes.

11. Mac's take on the disagreements at the Yard over race. The caption, spoken by Osama bin Laden, read: 'I'm thinking of sueing Sir Ian Blair for racial discrimination.'

12/13. Two takes by Brookes: first on Tony Blair's possible reaction to the appointment of a namesake, 2004: then on my response to a vote of no confidence by the Greater London Assembly, 2007.

14. With Richard Chartres, Bishop of London, at a Remembrance service for the dead of the Commonwealth, 2006: working with faith communities was a significant part of my role.

15. Talking to a Police Constable and a Police Community Support Officer, East London 2007: part of the roll-out of the Met's Safer Neighbourhood teams.

16. Comforting the mother of a fallen officer 2007: at the annual Met Service of Remembrance.

of another of the elements of that achievement, the theory of 'broken windows', developed in 1982 by the American criminologists George Kelling and James Wilson. This posits that crime and anti-social behaviour occur more in areas where neighbourhoods are allowed to decline physically. I later based the revitalisation of local policing on London on a variant of this theory. Close liaison between local authorities and police was seen as vital to design out crime by making public space more pleasant for people to use and therefore less comfortable for criminals.

Visitors to Leicester Square now have a different experience, as a combination of Westminster's own patrolling uniformed staff and an enhanced Met presence, redesigned seating and lighting, together with the use of various parts of anti-social behaviour legislation, have driven away the elements that made it so unpleasant. At one of the Street Crime Initiative meetings a combined Met and Westminster Council team briefed the Prime Minister about how they had driven down crime, including robberies, dramatically. Obviously speeches at meetings at which the PM is present are normally listened to in decorous silence but never have I heard a silence deepen quite as profoundly as when one of the Westminster Council delegates explained the troubles of the past. 'For instance,' he said, 'the area used to be plagued by groups of schoolkids who would get drunk and then wander off, abandoning one of their number ...' Nothing stirred in the room. 'Yes,' said Tony Blair after a long pause, 'I know something of that.'

The meetings lasted for about eighteen months and were very successful in helping the police and other agencies to bring down street robbery. However, they led to a period of political managerialism in the Home Office from which it is only just recovering. Despite the fact that there already was an Inspectorate of Constabulary, David Blunkett invented a new Police Standards Unit, based on his experience in Education. This was designed as a sharp instrument to express the Home Secretary's displeasure with forces which he judged were performing poorly in one way or another. Although neither John Stevens nor I would have allowed it across the Met's threshold, this would have added an edge to the work of the Inspectorate, had it been the only development in town. But the Home Office, like all other government departments, had also made what were known as public service agreements with the Treasury, as part of the funding arrangements arising out of each three-year Fundamental Spending Review. These agreements set out targets for many types of crime and spawned endless strategies and meetings, filled with earnest civil servants who had been told that they had responsibility for delivering the targets on knife crime or violent crime or car crime or whatever. The Police Standards Unit now began to pursue forces adjudged to be 'failing' against a whole range of targets: Nottinghamshire and Avon and Somerset were two forces to be early named and shamed. I have no problem with a management culture which seeks ever better performance: indeed I developed probably one of the first ones in British policing as an Assistant Chief Constable in Thames Valley Police in the early nineties and have driven performance rigorously ever since. The problem was government doing it over so many forces and such long periods. Targets were being chased which for some forces were of little local relevance (street robbery, for instance, is an almost exclusively urban phenomenon, as is gun crime) and which, for many forces, continued to be pursued long after the problem subject of the target had been overtaken by another local issue which was not the subject of monitoring by government. After David Blunkett left, the culture of targetry remained, principally because neither Charles Clarke nor John Reid was particularly interested and it was only Jacqui Smith who finally listened to the police chiefs and reduced the targets to the simple outcome of public satisfaction. The managerialism of central government was part of the context which I inherited as Commissioner.

In the summer of 2004 John Stevens announced that he would retire at the end of the following January. By this time the process for selection had become almost unbearably complicated. This was the first time that the new Metropolitan Police Authority was to choose its Commissioner – or was it to do so? Jack Straw was a great enthusiast for the concept of a Police Authority in London, which was scarcely surprising because, as a fairly new MP in 1980, he had put forward a Private

Member's Bill to create one. The legislation that finally brought one into being in the Greater London Act 2000 was of his making. That act, of course, would have been expected to take cognisance of the latest thinking on policing and the latest thinking was the report by William Macpherson into the death of Stephen Lawrence, one of the recommendations of which had been that the Home Secretary should create a Metropolitan Police Authority. Another of the report's recommendations was to give this new MPA the power to select the Commissioner and Deputy Commissioner of the Met. These are the only police operational positions the appointment to which is retained by the Home Secretary because of the national and international responsibilities of the postholders. (Formally, it is not actually his or her appointment: their task is to recommend the candidate to HM The Queen for her appointment.) This was the only one of Macpherson's recommendations which Jack Straw turned down flat. It was, of course, the very issue on which my relationship with Boris Johnson was later to founder.

By this point the selection process was beginning to bear some resemblance to a reality TV show. Pure resilience was possibly going to be the secret of success. An interview similar to the last time started it off, chaired by the Permanent Secretary, by now John Gieve, and then there was a fourteen-strong panel of the Police Authority, headed by a new chair, Labour's Len Duvall, after which the Mayor was to make representations and then and only then was the Home Secretary, David Blunkett, to interview the candidate or candidates recommended to him. Four candidates had applied, reduced to three by the first Home Office panel. Suffice to say that, after a pretty gruelling interview with the Police Authority, I was made aware that I was now the only candidate being put forward to the Home Secretary by the Authority and to have the Mayor's blessing. The Authority had decided that, if I was not to be appointed, then the post was to be readvertised.

A few days later I was informed that the Home Secretary wanted to see me. I sat in the waiting room along the corridor from his office. Police officers are entitled to retire on full pension when they reach thirty years' service and most do. This was, ironically, exactly thirty years to the day on which I had joined. One of David Blunkett's private secretaries came along to fetch me and as we walked along she congratulated me. 'How wonderful,' she said, 'to have reached the absolute pinnacle of your profession.' She showed me into the Home Secretary's office, where he sat with John Gieve. By now I had met David Blunkett many times but a surprise was to follow. After he greeted me as always, with words that were slightly disconcerting until you got to know him, 'Good to see you', he began to interview me, for which I was genuinely unprepared. He was a similar kind of interviewer to Jack Straw and my answers were rather bumbling.

At the end I was unsure quite where we had now got to, but John took me out and reassured me that the letter recommending me to the Queen had already been prepared and now awaited only the signature of Mr Secretary Blunkett, as he is formally described in correspondence with the Palace. I was to be the twenty-fourth Commissioner of Police of the Metropolis, the heir of Peel and Rowan and Mayne and of so many great predecessors. I confess that it was a great moment.

Two weeks later the appointment was confirmed by the Palace and David Blunkett and I walked over to the Yard arm in arm, with his dog Sadie, and faced the biggest crowd of cameras I had yet seen. The *Evening Standard* already had the news on its front page and I took home a copy of the paper. This was about the same period as the cartoon film *The Incredibles* had emerged as a box-office hit. My children cut out both the headline about me and the headline on another page in the *Standard* about the film. They went up together on to our fridge door, arranged to read: 'Police Modernizer Ian Blair is named as new Met Chief: Just Incredible.'

5

Commissioner

On 1 February 2005 I started early on my first morning as Commissioner. I arrived at Hackney at about 5.30am and met the shifts of officers who changed over at 6am, the departing night duty and the arriving early turn. Oddly, it did not feel very different from the sort of briefings I had attended before dawn on many occasions over the previous eleven years as a Chief Officer of police. I heard about some of the night's events over a cup of tea in the canteen, listened to the briefing of the new team and wished them well. It was only when I was heading back in the car across London to Notting Hill, which I had selected as the place to meet the first press of the day both because I had served there and because they paraded their officers for duty an hour later, that what was happening actually sank in. It was a phrase that did it. My press officer, Joy Bentley, was on the telephone and said something about 'the Commissioner wants to ....', words I had heard so many times before. I wondered for a moment why John Stevens wanted to do that: then I realised it was me she was talking about. I was the Commissioner.

As Deputy Commissioner I had been a heartbeat away from it for five years but I don't think anything can quite prepare an individual for the change between any other job in policing and this post. I had been a Chief Constable and very proudly, but the role is different. A Chief Constable is important, of course, but ultimately he or she is only the senior officer currently in charge of the team.

The Commissioner is different: the Commissioner is seen by those within it as the emblem of the Met itself, even sometimes the emblem of British policing (after the bobby, of course). During their time in post Chief Constables in most forces should be able to meet the great majority of staff who work for them and get to know most supervisory officers, perhaps down to the rank of Inspector. However hard he tries, most of the more than 50,000 people who work in the Met never meet a Commissioner during their whole career. He is – and so far it has only been a he but that will change – a figure seen only in the newspaper or on television. One of my habits was to drop into police stations without warning and I was always struck by the same expression on the faces of staff: a smile which mixed recognition, disbelief and delight. Almost always colleagues wanted to have a photograph taken of them with me on their mobile phone. When I heard about some act of bravery or an excellent result at court or about an officer who had been badly injured, I would try as often as I could to ring them up to congratulate them or to sympathise. Or rather I learned not to do that but to get someone in my office to do so, to explain that it really was the Commissioner who was about to speak to them because otherwise they would not believe it and think it was a wind-up. I remember popping in on one occasion to see a Flying Squad office and the laughter that followed when the Detective Chief Inspector to whom I was talking received a phone call on his desk which was obviously from someone more senior. 'I am sorry, guv'nor,' he said, 'I can't talk at the moment, I've got the Commissioner with me ... no, guv'nor, I wouldn't say that, I really do have the Commissioner here.'

This is a great privilege but it is a great and heady danger, an easy path to disaster, to begin to think that it is you that they are pleased to meet or to speak with, when it is the office you hold which is respected. If that can be avoided, it is still a great joy. And it is, of course, another reason why what was so casually done over my resignation was so counter to the tradition of the service, because it was distressing for the Met as a whole, irrespective of what individuals thought about me as a person.

The second difference between this particular role and any other in the police is the fascination it holds for the press, something I began to learn on my first day but would have to go on learning until the end of my time in office. As an example, during my last interview at the end of that tiring first day, I made a comment about people not understanding the true price of drugs, not just how much a wrap of cocaine cost but also the cost in blood along its journey from Colombia to the estates of north London, and I noted that some of the consumers of these drugs would not touch anything that was not organic or fair-trade and did not see the contradiction. The next day I found these comments being represented as my declaration of war on drug taking at Hampstead dinner parties. I had been a police leader for many years but, experienced as I already was at dealing with the press, I was to learn a lot more – sometimes bitterly – in the days and months to come.

A well-known theory of leadership is that it is easier to create change in an organisation which believes itself to be in real trouble: most people will see that it is better to hang together than to hang separately. The rather pleasant problem I faced in 2005 was that things had been so bad after Macpherson, six years ago, and were now so much better, that the organisation felt good about itself and did not really want further change. And yet I knew it was necessary. It had been John Stevens's task to rebuild the Met: mine was to reshape it, in terms of its mission, its structure and its culture. In two speeches on that first day I laid out the five challenges which I believed that the Met now faced, speaking in the morning to the Met's senior management and then in the afternoon to a large but representative group of the workforce.

Some of these challenges would be standard in any large organisation: that we were very effective but not very efficient and that therefore we needed to cut out duplication and improve processes, particularly in technology; that our performance on crime reduction and detection was improving fast but was not yet anywhere near as good as that of what should be seen as our competitors, by which I meant other large police forces, like Greater Manchester or West Midlands; and that we needed consistency in the standard of our service to victims of crime, not so much at the serious end but in connection with things that seemed routine to us, like a burglary, but were a once-in-a-lifetime event for a member of the public. This is a perennial problem: with an average of 6,000 calls for service per day it is inevitable that some calls will be handled less well than others. However, the variation from the astonishingly good to the truly lamentable seems extremely difficult to eradicate: there was no guarantee of consistency.

On my first morning I asked my senior colleagues to think of a test for themselves: when a friend's house was burgled in a part of the Met in which they did not work, were they perfectly content that the matter would be dealt with well or would they ring someone senior they knew there just to make sure that an eye was cast over what had been done? I knew and they knew that they would make that call and in the coming year I had the same calls made when an aide to a minister had their laptop stolen, or a newspaper editor had their car broken into. It probably got better in my time but not fast enough.

Those were the kind of matters which all Commissioners seek to improve. They are improvements, but they are not the product of the passion that really changes something with the size and tradition of the Met. I had two further goals, which I had outlined repeatedly during the selection process, to the point of saying openly to the Police Authority selectors that, if they did not want a Commissioner to pursue them, they should not select me. They did.

The two goals had been long in the gestation. First, I wanted to return to something that had faded when Peter Imbert had retired twelve years before in 1993. He had launched something called the Plus Programme, aimed at uniting the workforce. The programme had not been sustained by his two successors.

I now wanted to make another sustained attempt at cultural change in the Met, around gender, race, hierarchy and power. During the previous five years a huge investment of more than 20 per cent extra funding had been made in the Met, a larger increase in cash than had been received by almost any other body in the public sector. I thought that there would be little new money to come: improvements in productivity now needed to come from within. In addition to structural and procedural improvements, I was convinced that real change could only be unleashed if we could truly release the talent in the organisation, so that everyone was able to work to the maximum of their potential.

I was certain that, whatever successes had been achieved in the previous few years, the potential of the workforce was constrained by a monotone culture that favoured police officers above non-police officers (as an example of this, even the police staff at the very top of the organisation, on my Management Board, made it clear to me that they felt less valued than their uniformed colleagues), a culture that was patently male, white and rank-obsessed. Not only that, but I told them in these first speeches that there were too many people who were capable of bullying when they did not win the argument. That was going to stop. Additionally, I wanted to make the Met more welcoming to volunteers, including Special Constables. I was very pleased that their numbers increased dramatically during my tenure.

I was also very concerned that the Met had simply stopped training supervisors above the rank of Inspector to deal properly with personnel matters. So I sought out the most revered detective available, Deputy Assistant Commissioner Bill Griffiths, at that time leader of the homicide squads but a fervent admirer of the Plus Programme of the past, and asked him to lead a programme of cultural change. If an operational officer of his calibre would front it, who would speak against it? Thus was born 'Together', an approach which combined training at a new Leadership Academy, which for the first time placed police and non-police supervisors on courses together, with the creation of a new set of organisational values, involving nearly 5,000 staff in their development. I addressed thousands of staff on these courses during my time as Commissioner. I told them that no Home Secretary cared whether the Met was a happy organisation but I did. The Home Secretary was interested in results but I knew that those results would come best from a workforce that felt empowered and involved and was made up of people who would go home to their friends and family and demonstrate just that; a workforce that would treat the public decently because they were decently treated themselves, regardless of their own background.

Much has been written about my passion for diversity and fairness in the police service. This is not just a matter of fairness, although that matters, nor is it merely also about the business benefit of drawing talent into and through the organisation from the widest range of the available gene pool, although that is obviously desirable. Above all I was principally concerned with these issues because within them lay the clue as to how to police the capital. At present, battle lines are being drawn up over whether the concept of multiculturalism has gone too far and we need to return to a more integrated sense of Britishness. That is not the territory in which I was operating: that is for others. What I was concerned with was how to police a city with hundreds of languages and nationalities and with many faiths. In this I was particularly struck by a story told me by some of the officers who had founded the Met's Black Police Association (BPA). After the murder of the young Nigerian boy Damilola Taylor in 2001, these officers put together a group of Yoruba-speaking colleagues and went to the Peckham estate where Damilola had briefly lived and so sadly died. One of them told the story as follows. She knocked on the door and a child of about ten opened it a crack and asked in English what she wanted. In English the officer said she wanted to talk about the murder of the little boy; in Yoruba the girl relayed to someone inside what she had said. A deeper, older woman's voice answered in Yoruba, 'We don't talk to the police, tell them to go away.' The officer replied in Yoruba, 'I think you might want to talk to me' and a moment later the door was flung open and she was invited inside.

That is why I declared that the Met should look like London, why the work of the many staff associations, like the BPA, concerned to help colleagues from different backgrounds, is so important and why I was prepared to endure the way that approach was to be twisted. I learned about that on the first day. I had decided upon the word 'Together' as the symbol of what we would now attempt: 'Together with all our citizens; with all our partners; with all our colleagues.' Met vehicles already carried the logo on their doors: 'Working for a Safer London'. I ordered that this should be changed to 'Working Together for a Safer London'. These are only transfers: they cost almost nothing and were only to be replaced on existing vehicles when they were serviced. However, someone unknown to me decided that the italic script of the existing logo should be replaced with a cleaner, roman typeface. Someone then concocted a newspaper story that all this had been done because I was concerned to help the visually impaired. It was a little pinprick but an early one. Later my support for diversity would be tested almost to breaking point by the very BPA whom I had praised so often. Before that, however, my interests in it and in the multi-faith nature of London would prove advantages during the summer of 2005.

'Together' was the internal change which I believed necessary for the Met to be effective. I drove it hard but, like Peter Imbert's work fifteen years before and probably like any programme concerned with changing culture in any organisation, it had varying degrees of support at different levels. What seemed to command universal support was the principal external change which accompanied it: the reintroduction of community policing to London, in the shape of what are known as 'Safer Neighbourhoods'. This involved the intelligent and dedicated support of a whole raft of different people but also perhaps the boldest stroke of my career. At its heart was the redesign of the police workforce by the introduction of a new type of police employee: Police Community Support Officers.

Safer Neighbourhoods had many origins. The first was the pattern of preventative patrol over fixed beats introduced by the first Commissioners, Rowan and Mayne. By the time I joined the service, walking officers were still assigned to individual beats but the concept of having to stay on your specific beat had disappeared. West End Central covered most of Soho and most of Mayfair, each of which was divided up into a series of beats. You were expected to stay on one side or other of Regent Street, which divided these two areas, otherwise where you went scarcely mattered.

Most of the rest of London outside the West End had few officers on foot patrol and had largely adopted random, motorised patrol. This had begun as an experiment in Lancashire in the 1960s. The panda car, named after the Chinese bear because of their livery of blocks of blue and white, was a logical response to the increasing number of calls for service from the public which could not be dealt with by foot patrol alone. There were and are three problems with this. First, it severed a bond between police and public about which the public have been complaining ever since: you can't talk to someone driving past in a car. Second, it meant that the police had lost sight of part of their principal purpose: in adopting this approach wholesale they had moved away from a preventative to a solely response mode: solely response because by the time the British were doing this all over the country, the third problem was that the Americans had proved that random motorised patrol did not prevent crime. In an astonishingly brave experiment in 1972–3 the Police Foundation in the United States had divided Kansas City into three sections: in one, routine random patrol in cars continued, in another the number of vehicles carrying it out was virtually doubled and in the third vehicles only entered the area to respond to a direct call for assistance. The effect was precisely nil: there were no changes to the crime rates in the three areas and that is because the public did not notice and nor, presumably, did the criminals. There was no difference in citizen satisfaction.

Although senior police officers had long known of the Kansas City Preventative Patrol Experiment, no British force had ever been able to put its obvious findings into effect, which would be to get the officers out of cars, for one overriding reason. There were never enough officers available to answer calls from the public without their being in vehicles. This is because policing tasks can be rather simply divided into three types of work: responding to calls for service from the public, the handling of complex tasks and the provision of preventative patrol. Calls from the public have risen at an exponential rate: to the Met, for instance, from 1.5 million in 1996–7 to more than 2 million in 2001–2, which is when the Community Support Officers first appeared (the figure for 2008 was 2.2 million). Meanwhile the number of officers involved in complex activities out of sight of the public increased every year, as they worked in fields such as child protection, counter-terrorism, investigating organised and serious crime, surveillance, intelligence analysis or the ever-increasing demands of the criminal justice system. This meant that when the public have seen police officers, they have mostly been travelling from one call to another in a car.

It is true that forces, including the Met, never lost sight of the attachment that the public had to walking officers and all kept a small number of officers doing that, usually known as Permanent or Home Beat Officers, who were allocated to a specific area for long periods of time. But these officers were invariably the first to be called on to do other things and culturally these jobs were seen as backwaters, far from the excitement of car chases or being a detective. As always, the police came up with an acronym and Home Beat Officers, officially HBOs, were 'hobby bobbies' to the rank and file. As a result, the entire principle of preventative patrol was lost, to the point where a Home Office report proving that a patrolling officer on foot would only come across a burglary in progress once in a thirty-year career was widely quoted with approval. Foot patrol lost professional adherents as senior officers emerged who had hardly done any during their earlier careers and many senior officers expressed irritation at the constant public wish for 'bobbies on the beat'.

Yet in 1996 the Police Federation produced a position paper which stated: 'Patrolling is the basis of all policing operations, to which top priority will be given, and all other specialisms are there to contribute to and enhance the success of patrolling.' In 1995 the Association of Chief Police Officers announced that it wished 'to retain the monopoly of the patrol function' and that 'The private security industry does not have a role in the independent patrol of our public streets and highways.' Both bodies were getting their retaliation in first to a 1996 Audit Commission report, *Streetwise*, first drafts of which had been widely circulated and which had called for a change, by the introduction of a second tier of officers, just to patrol, paid less than regulars. The final version was much less radical under this pressure from the service.

But all this was flying in the face of reality, as ACPO was already learning. In 1997 a survey of forces, carried out by ACPO, found that, of the forty-three forces in England and Wales, seven were aware of private security patrols on their streets and eighteen knew of local authority street patrols – ironically, one of these, the Newport Rangers, was the direct responsibility of my brother, by then Chief Executive of Newport in Gwent. In the early spring of 1998, shortly after becoming Chief Constable of Surrey, I was awarded a brief Visiting Fellowship at New York University, where I chose to examine the relationship between public and private policing, in a world in which consumer choice and the drive of the new government to replicate it in public service provision were clearly becoming dominant. A few months later this work culminated in a speech entitled 'Where Do the Police Fit into Policing?' that I gave to the annual ACPO-APA (Association of Police Authorities) conference, in which I challenged the idea that the police had a monopoly on patrol. This was one of the very first times that a Chief Constable had stepped so clearly out of line with the position of colleagues on something so central and was regarded as very controversial. But it was not yet that brave. This was stage one in the evolution of my thinking. What I was doing was trying to protect the dominant market share of public policing in the securing of public space. My idea was to get the service to accept that there was now a variety of organisations providing patrol and reassurance and that police constables should be given the task not of replacing but of coordinating the work of them all. I was later to describe this as the 'horizontal model' of what would become known as the extended police family.

Three years later I developed an alternative: the 'vertical model', in which the police returned to those ideas in the earlier Audit Commission report about a lower tier of patrol, controlled by them. Instead of coordinating other bodies who were patrolling, the police should attempt to take back a near monopoly of patrol by delivering our own cheaper patrol service. In this there were also a number of influences: the recruitment of neighbourhood wardens by a growing number of local authorities, what I understood of Amsterdam's Stadtwacht ('citywatch'), which was precisely a two-tier police patrol scheme, but, above all, by the state of the relationship between the Met and the different tiers of London government.

On my return to the Met in 2000, I discovered that this had not been improved by the addition of another competing tier of London government, in the shape of the Mayor and the Greater London Assembly

(GLA). I have already referred to the deepening public concern about crime which John Stevens and I were facing in late 2001 and early 2002: this was the background to the emerging clash between the thirty-two London boroughs and the Mayor. Whether Livingstone or Johnson, whatever the Mayor says, his powers are much weaker, say, than his equivalent in New York. London's boroughs control most services and have their own revenue-raising powers: they viewed the arrival of a Mayor who had some influence over policing with deep suspicion but not as much as they already felt towards the Met. The history between us was one of broken promises from the Yard, of rises in precept to employ more police whom they never saw, as they were spirited away into squads at the centre. One of the implications of the Macpherson Report had been the more than doubling of the numbers of officers permanently deployed to homicide investigation, while the forthcoming report by Lord Laming on the death of Victoria Climbié was pretty obviously going to say the same about child protection (and did). Or, if the growth in officers was to be sent to boroughs, it always seemed, particularly to the Conservative-run outer boroughs, that they went elsewhere. At this point a number of London boroughs began to explore their options: they discovered an interesting gap in legislation, which was that, while there are many laws governing what a police force shall and shall not do, there is nothing to stop anyone setting up one if they want one. Newham, Wandsworth and Kensington and Chelsea already had their own Parks Police but Kensington and Chelsea now proposed to create its own constabulary to police not parks but streets, not just city centre shopping areas or its own council estates but the whole borough. This seemed to threaten the Balkanisation of the policing of London, a return to the situation before 1829, and I was determined to prevent that if possible.

I went to Kensington and Chelsea and we hammered out a deal whereby they would pay us for extra cops and for wardens which we would provide. This was going to be tricky. I had had a meeting at the House of Commons in the run-up to the 2001 General Election with Charles Clarke, then Police Minister at the Home Office. He knew of my plan and told me, laughing, that I was 'the Trotsky of the Police Service', seeking permanent revolution. The Labour government was not going to include a second tier of policing in its manifesto. It was too controversial. The Federation would hate it. Even if I could persuade the Metropolitan Police Authority to back it, it would not get through the Commons. We reflected on this conversation a few years later.

Some eighteen months later, in July 2002, a Police Reform Act became law, including the establishment of Police Community Support Officers, with a number of powers including that of detention for thirty minutes until the arrival of a constable. This was despite some opposition from ACPO, whose then president was unconvinced, and the total opposition of the national Police Federation, whose executive saw this as the thin end of a very threatening wedge. On two successive days in the preceding May I had to go first to the ACPO conference and make a direct intervention to disagree openly with the ACPO president in public and then to the Federation conference to face a hostile and silent hall. Nevertheless, the Act ushered in the first transformation of the police workforce in many generations: it introduced the extended police family. It was to make possible the development of Safer Neighbourhoods. Because PCSOs cost much less than police officers, this meant that we genuinely had something to offer to Kensington and Chelsea.

The main explanation for the difference between the moment at the House of Commons with the Police Minister and the Police Reform Act was the largest experiment in policing ever undertaken although, unlike in Kansas, it was entirely involuntary. The experiment was caused by what happened to street policing in London immediately after 9/11. Like everyone else in the world, Londoners were stunned by the events of 11 September 2001. The Met logs crimes on a daily basis and on 11 and 12 September, crime fell markedly. On the 12th the Met began to transfer hundreds – at the height of the crisis 1,500 – officers from outer London to its centre. By mid-September street robbery began to rise in the outer boroughs and go down in the centre. As I noted in the last chapter, by Christmas, the rise in street crime everywhere except central London had become precipitate, with January 2002 53 per cent up on

January of the previous year: hence, the Prime Minister's Street Crime Initiative.

By the end of 2002 crime had fallen back by 18 per cent from that peak, with 6,945 street crimes in London in January and 4,428 in December. That first year of fall was largely the result of choices: we cut back the traffic department, spent money on overtime like mad, drove performance rigorously in every borough, with the looming presence of the Prime Minister to spur us on. But the rise in street crime in different parts of London after 11 September 2001 and the fall during 2002 proved conclusively, as I entitled a speech that I made about it at Keele University in July 2002, that 'Surprise News: Policing Works'. We had rediscovered the purpose of patrol, not to detect crime but to prevent it and to provide reassurance, a reassurance that can only be provided by people in uniform on foot. However, we could not afford to do this with cops alone.

With John Stevens's slightly wary approval and with the active assistance of Tim Godwin, who by then had become Assistant Commissioner for policing in the boroughs, we began to lobby for the creation of police auxiliaries with limited powers. Even the London Federation were grudgingly with us because they did not want to see their officers being bored out of their minds by being required to guard government infrastructure and buildings, an obviously necessary task after 9/11. David Blunkett, now Home Secretary, was thoroughly behind us – indeed he thought up the title of Police Community Support Officer, which was adopted in preference to my Police Auxiliary. The new Police Minister, Hazel Blears, was also supportive, although she also favoured a system of accreditation by police forces of other patrolling bodies, a development which, in the interest of preserving market share, I admit unashamedly that I slowed right down in London to the point of inactivity. However, the key was the Tories, whose dominance in the Lords would have blocked the development. And the key person in the Tory hierarchy was the Shadow Home Secretary, Oliver Letwin. The Tories were against the idea of PCSOs in general and PCSOs with powers were anathema, probably because they were opposed by the

Police Federation. Letwin came to see me for what I recall was to be a half-hour meeting and stayed for almost two hours. He did something which I particularly respect and which, in my experience, is quite rare in leading politicians: he changed his mind. He came in opposed and went out agreeing that the Tories would back the Bill, although they would seek a position where only in some areas, including London, would the PCSOs have powers.

The first PCSOs reached the streets of London in October 2002 and were deployed to a mixture of security roles and some borough policing. Meanwhile a national experiment was underway to bring back some form of local neighbourhood policing, being driven by Tim Godwin and an Inspector, later to be Chief Inspector, of Constabulary, Denis O'Connor. The Met had a few locations and there were some encouraging falls in crime. The arrival of PCSOs transformed the situation and we started to experiment with a model of one sergeant, two constables and three PCSOs working in a team based on individual wards. We called the idea 'Safer Neighbourhoods'. Once it was well underway we explained this model to the Prime Minister and he asked to see it, so one early autumn morning in 2004 I travelled down on a train to Bexley in south-east London with him and David Blunkett. The Prime Minister was clearly tired: the invasion of Iraq and its aftermath were becoming poisonous issues. He warmly shook hands with various people and listened for a moment or two to the officers from the Safer Neighbourhoods Team explaining what was going on and I could see him drifting into automatic mode. He did not stay in that mode long, at least not after the local residents began to speak. Old and young, male and female, articulate or not, they told him of how this team had transformed their lives. I remember one elderly lady said that she had been almost a prisoner in her flat for five years but now she walked in the park most days. A headteacher told him that the school had been able to open its disco for the first time in years. I could see Tony Blair's electoral instincts come straight on alert. He listened, he thanked them, he took David Blunkett to one side and said, 'This we must have – everywhere as soon as we can' and walked out to his car.

What was going on in Bexley and our other experimental sites was the 'broken windows' theory in a new guise. Now, the police were to be the catalyst for solving local problems, whether by their own work or by spurring on local authorities or businesses to take action which would make an area feel safer, which would then make it more pleasant for people to use public space of all kinds and would thereby deny the habitat of unruliness which provides cover for criminality. For too long – probably thirty or forty years – the police and Home Office statisticians had too narrowly defined what constitutes crime. The public have a different definition. Except in particular locations or at certain moments, the public are not overly concerned about gang violence or the threat of terrorism. They are concerned about burglary, street crime and assault and understand the police response to it. However, what they are really worried about, and what they see as needing but not receiving police intervention, is something quite else: noisy neighbours, open drug dealing, drunks, rowdy teenagers, the mentally ill and the simply rude and aggressive. Because these had not been defined as crime by senior police officers or by government, the police service had not put a sufficient priority upon them.

Safer Neighbourhoods was the signal that the Met was now stating that policing for the purposes of reassurance was as significant as responding to calls for assistance or detecting recorded crime: that the rowdy teenagers in the part of the park reserved for small kids, the smell of urine, the needles and the used condoms in the stairwell, or the smashed bus stop which is passed by thousands of people every day are what define the degree of safety to people in their local community. Much of what provided reassurance in the past would have been done by other agents of social cohesion: the park keeper, the janitor, the caretaker, the bus conductor or by collective associations, concerned neighbours, the trade union, the residents' association, the church. Now, however, those agents and agencies have largely gone or are much weaker. It would have to be the police service which led the drive towards reassurance.

Not only did local people like it, as at Bexley, not only did local politicians like it – I remember one MP from elsewhere in London saying that complaints in his weekly surgery about policing had almost disappeared once the teams were at work – but so did the cops. In explaining Safer Neighbourhoods I often quoted the words of one of the early Team Sergeants, who told me: 'I have been a police officer for fourteen years, and a sergeant for six: I have been working with this team for three months and I have just remembered what I joined the police to do.' One of the clues to this was the rules. Twice before in my time in the Met there had been an attempt at the reinforcement of local policing, the intellectually coherent but geographically limited Neighbourhood Policing experiment of the 1980s and the over-optimistic Sector Policing system of the 1990s, both of which had failed because the officers involved always had to be available for other duties. This time the Safer Neighbourhoods staff could not be sent to do other tasks, such as policing demonstrations in central London or filling a vacancy somewhere else in the borough, except in extremely limited circumstances.

The job satisfaction officers obviously felt was manifest whenever they spoke about what they were doing and was revealed by the fact that, when the teams were first set up, most officers had to be ordered to take the positions, whereas very quickly their replacements were volunteers. Of course, some police officers would not be attracted to this type of work but the PCSOs had joined to do it and were clearly willing to do tasks which officers would have considered mundane and repetitious. The Police Federation inspired a whole campaign of vitriol against the PCSOs, particularly taken up by the *Daily Express*, using the expression 'Blunkett's plastic policemen', but, while there were plenty of officers who expressed wariness about these new colleagues, I never met one who had worked with them who would have wanted their role abolished. The Federation's position over them was an old-fashioned demarcation dispute, which was often translated in print as me 'having lost the confidence of the rank and file'. I had not. I never did. I just took on the vested interests of the Police Federation, especially the National Federation.

Throughout 2003 we carefully monitored what was happening in the sixteen London wards where the Neighbourhood teams were in place. Crime was falling faster here than elsewhere and we determined on expanding as rapidly as we could. By April 2004 there were forty-six teams and by the autumn, as I entered the selection process for Commissioner, there were ninety-six, three in each borough. Ken Livingstone had promised in his manifesto for the 2004 mayoral election to provide a team for all of London's 630-odd wards by the end of 2007. The next stage was to see what happened if we provided a team for every ward in a borough and we agreed to do this in Tower Hamlets in early 2005, which was not a popular move with other boroughs. Immediately Tower Hamlets became the borough where crime fell fastest.

The Police Authority Chair, Len Duvall, and Ken Livingstone were increasingly impressed and I began to discuss with them how fast this could be expanded. Then, one afternoon in the summer Parliamentary recess of 2005, my wife and I had lunch in Norwich with Charles and Carole Clarke.

Although David Blunkett selected me, Charles had become Home Secretary even before I was actually appointed. At our first meeting he recalled what he had said before the 2001 election about two-tier policing, with the words 'Well, Trotsky, things haven't turned out too badly: I'm the Home Secretary, you are about to be the Commissioner and, as far as PCSOs are concerned, I will say what no politician ever says, I was wrong and you were right!' Charles is a big man in every sense, physically, intellectually and in terms of political courage. He fills a room with his presence, and often with his laughter. He was a great Home Secretary in one particular way. I think that, like only Willie Whitelaw before him, whom I never met but heard much about when I worked in the Home Office, Charles really wanted to be Home Secretary rather than have any other job in the Cabinet. Had he remained in post, British policing would have been greatly improved through the force amalgamations he was subsequently to propose.

At that lunch I told Charles that, with a little more cash from the government, I believed we could roll out Safer Neighbourhoods across the whole of London within eighteen months. He nearly fell off his chair and went on talking about it as we wandered through Norwich Cathedral. He offered his firmest support and in the autumn Len Duvall and Ken and I announced the the full rollout of Safer Neighbourhoods would be brought forward. There was a fair of bit of funding from government, Ken raided the budgets of some other parts of his London empire and Len and I pledged money from the efficiency drive I had launched on my first day.

But it was not to be easy. There were complaints from other parts of the country about too much money going to London, not necessarily helped later on when the Police Minister, by then Tony McNulty, himself a London MP, explained to an ACPO-APA meeting that London was being favoured because it was doing neighbourhood policing right and others had better catch up. The Federation was still being difficult, as were those unions who represented PCSOs because the Federation would not admit them. The unions did not like us because we were brutally determined to use the introduction of PCSOs to clear away the accretion of allowances that many non-police officer jobs had acquired, because we were going to phase out a number of job types to accommodate them (specifically traffic wardens) and because we resolutely rebuffed union pressure to create a hierarchy for PCSOs.

This was also connected to traffic wardens. Years before, I had been driving into a police station yard behind another vehicle when a man got out of the passenger seat, dressed in traffic warden uniform, with many silver bars of rank on his shoulders. I said to the officer driving me, 'Who on earth do you think that might be?' 'Supreme Allied Commander, Traffic Warden Service,' was his telling reply. The police service, certainly in London, had neglected the traffic wardens, treating them as a species apart, scarcely acknowledging them, being largely uninterested in assaults on them, caring little about their truly shocking and indefensible sickness rates, leaving them to their own hierarchy and often in separate buildings. That was not how PCSOs were to be: they were to be part of integrated teams, supervised by police officers.

And there was one extra good reason for that: over 30 per cent of the PCSOs were coming from minority communities and I saw this as a wonderful opportunity to increase the number of minority staff in the main force. Having no hope of advancement as a PCSO and being exposed to the greater variety and promotion prospects implicit in the work of police officers, some of them would seek to become constables. It worked and as a result minority recruitment of police officers soared from a paltry 5 per cent to nearly 20 per cent during my term of office. And what skills they brought. It was as if we had mined a new vein of people who wanted to be in policing. I was always struck by their languages. I remember walking with one PCSO through a street market in Wembley, listening to him switch from Cockney to Urdu to Punjabi with the different stallholders, and another one in Victoria who had left Lebanon during the civil war and who spoke, to my memory, Arabic, French, a number of north African littoral dialects, Portuguese and Romanian. His English was not good enough to allow him to be a police officer but without PCSOs we would never have had such skills among us. I suggested he be made the first PCSO attached to Special Branch.

There were two further reasons why the Safer Neighbourhoods programme could be driven through against such odds. The first was simply that it worked. During the three years and ten months I was the Commissioner, recorded crime in London fell faster than at any time in recent history, with total crime down by 17.8 per cent and violent crime down by 12.8 per cent, including robbery by 15.6 per cent and murder by 19.5 per cent. While there are many reasons for the public to be sceptical about individual parts of police crime statistics, there is nothing to suggest that anything changed in the way they were collected during this period. The second reason was that all my senior colleagues could see one further great advantage, which arose when the distant echo of 9/11 became the reality of 7/7: the Safer Neighbourhood teams became the first defence against terror, the eyes and ears of the Met on every street.

In both of my speeches on my first day, I had said of the Safer Neighbourhood teams that:

These teams will be the visible manifestation of a changed relationship between the Metropolitan Police and the community over the years ahead. They will be the hallmark of this term of office of the Metropolitan Police Authority and of my Commissionership.

However, as I have made clear, this is only the first part of a widening mission. We have to deliver policing across a huge range: from trying to help kidnap victims in Baghdad and Kabul to handling anti-social behaviour in Barking and in Kingston.

The key point, however, is that our mission is widening in both directions towards seriousness and towards the need for reassurance and we have to deliver on all of it. There are no longer any 'ors' in our external delivery, only 'ands': we cannot do safer neighbourhoods *or* counter-terrorism, meet our targets for volume crime *or* deal with Trident killings. We have to do it all and do it all well.

That was nearly at the end of the speeches but I ended both of them with something much more personal about the hope and the passion with which I began my term of office. These I never lost:

I joined the Metropolitan Police over thirty years ago and, while I have served in two other forces, twenty-four years of my working life have been spent in this organisation. I started as a police constable at West End Central and have served in both uniform and CID at Wembley, Chelsea, Notting Hill, Shepherd's Bush, what is now Charing Cross and Belgravia, Paddington, Kentish Town, Kensington: I have served at the Yard, I have travelled all round the service: I have done earlies, lates and nights, Christmas and New Year, Eid and Divali and, as much as any person ever can, I know this organisation. Perhaps most importantly, I love this organisation. I am passionate about this organisation. I think it is the greatest of police services imaginable, with a history of triumph and disaster, of courage and of sacrifice. I am proud to have served in it and I am proud to serve in it, and I am proud to serve with you all.

The Met is currently enjoying some of the greatest successes it has ever known. We can go further: we can go further together. I want you all to be part of that future.

I want you to feel part of the finest police service in the world: a world-class police force serving a world-class city. I want you to be part of an organisation that is striving to be the organisation that you want it to be. I want you, whatever your role in this great service, to know that the Management Board, the Metropolitan Police Authority and I are hugely grateful to you for what you do and what you aspire to be. I look forward to every day of my Commissionership and to having the honour to serve with you and, indeed, serve you in that role. Together, we can go forward. Together, to get there. Together, the good can get better. Together, we can be the best.

But there were to be two further challenges, which I did not mention because I did not foresee their impact. Those were the changing nature of both the press and politics, particularly in London. I had had an unremarkable relationship with the press, with my first major encounters at the Newbury Bypass, as Chief Constable of Surrey and to the limited extent that the Deputy Commissioner does press interviews. But I was to be the first person to undertake the post of Commissioner as the twenty-four-hour global media came of age. I used to explain the difficulties this created by referring to the afternoon in January 2006 when a whale got up the Thames nearly as far as Battersea Bridge, well west of central London. For hours there almost no other news and both twenty-four-hour channels in Britain had experts on the couches giving newscasters their expertise. This continual commentary and the almost endless repetition of the same clips of film was to be a feature of the years ahead. And if a whale could do it, the Met or I could do it most weeks.

However, I should have taken more notice of one particular straw in the wind, which might have indicated how politics and press would coincide. My selection as Commissioner was formally announced on 31 October 2004. More than two weeks beforehand, on 14 October, the *Daily Mail*, having had the result of one interview in the process leaked to it, ran a story under the headline 'Yard's top job is lined up for

"Labour's favourite cop". The opening paragraph contained a number of clues as to what was apparently wrong with me from a particular perspective. The italics are mine: 'The policeman once *accused* of being Britain's *most politically correct officer* is set to become head of the Metropolitan *force*. Scotland Yard Deputy Commissioner Ian Blair will succeed John Stevens in the New Year. *Oxford-educated Sir Ian*, 51 – *no relation to the Prime Minister ...*'

It went on to mention that I had been outspoken about the 'canteen culture' of the police service, that I wanted it to be more caring and gentle to ethnic minority and homosexual officers, that I was a reformer with close links to New Labour and that I had shaved off my beard in order to become Commissioner, an appointment for which I had applied five years before in an 'opportunistic' manner.

This was to be a pattern for the next four years: innumerable articles in an array of newspapers sought to shape my image, refining this early portrait of an intellectual, upper-class, diversity-obsessed, unscrupulously ambitious Labour fellow traveller. The first direct hit of this kind, after I had become Commissioner, came again from the *Daily Mail*, at the end of June 2005, in a front-page headline one morning with the banner 'The Police Chief who hung his officers out to dry'. This was its reporting of an Employment Tribunal hearing at which three white officers had sued the Met because they had been disciplined for either making racially offensive remarks at a diversity training event in front of a minority colleague or because, in the case of the supervisory officers, they had not intervened. They had been found guilty of this by an internal inquiry but had subsequently been cleared on appeal and now, with the support of the Federation, were suing. They won and received damages, but what was interesting to me was that, in answer to a question from one of the barristers, I had said something to the effect that 'If you are suggesting that I wanted them hung out to dry, that is emphatically not the case.' It was to be this phrase that the *Mail* picked up without, of course, the second part of the sentence.

This is the norm for public life. But it is dispiriting. Sometime, early in 2008, I think, I was sitting at a meeting of an Olympic Steering group, jointly chaired by Ken Livingstone and Tessa Jowell. A major consultancy was reporting to the group that its work showed that there was an 80 per cent probability that the London Olympics would be delivered within the budget available. It had been promised that the results of this work would be made public and this should have been an unremarkable but good story. For nearly half an hour the politicians and officials present tried to decide how to deal with the presentation of the announcement, convinced that the media would report the findings as indicating that there was now a 20 per cent chance that the budget would be insufficient. A very positive press release was eventually constructed but the story ran exactly as predicted. It is very notable that, when individuals holding such positions talk together, the press is the subject of their most bitter complaint. This is not normally because they want to suppress information but for two reasons: first, the amount of time involved in handling the press has risen exponentially and second, it is so cumulatively depressing that the journalists and editors almost invariably look for the worst slant that can be put upon the story. This is a part of living in the public square but it is exhausting.

It was to be the connection of press reporting to politics which was to bring the real pressure, however, and which makes London as an environment in which to be a senior police officer so different from anywhere else. While I had been in the Inspectorate I had met with many Police Authorities and had worked closely with those of Thames Valley and in Surrey for more than six years. Wherever I went and wherever I served, it was the boast of almost all members – and certainly Chairs – that Police Authority members left politics at the door: policing was to be regarded as a non-political matter. In the postwar period there had actually been two or three famous political squabbles. In addition to the Northumbria baton-round incident in the early 1980s, the Labour Chair of Merseyside Police Authority, the redoubtable Margaret Simey, clashed openly during the same decade with the strong-willed Chief Constable, Ken Oxford. Events in Derbyshire had reverberated widely in the early 1990s when the Labour Chair of the County Council, David Bookbinder, presided over the running-down of the police budget to such a point that Her Majesty's Inspectorate of Constabulary declared the force 'inefficient', a course of action that had not happened anywhere for decades.

After that event the composition of Police Authorities was changed so as to reduce the number of local authority councillors significantly, although they still remained a majority. Furthermore, the small number of magistrates who had made up the balance of the previous authorities were joined by a larger number of independent members, who were neither elected nor representative of any particular block. A typical English Police Authority has nineteen members, with the smallest, Warwickshire, having seventeen. A majority must be local councillors.

And this was to be the model for London. Jack Straw implemented Macpherson's recommendation for the creation of the Metropolitan Police Authority, including it within the new London structures contained in the Greater London Act 2000, notably the Greater London Assembly, the new Mayoralty and Transport for London. But the MPA was never going to be the same as elsewhere. First, the Home Secretary did not relinquish all leverage: uniquely, the Home Secretary retained the power to appoint one individual to the MPA, neither of whom, in my time, particularly appreciated the unofficial title of the 'Home Secretary's member'. To reflect its additional size, there were to be twenty-three members of the MPA, more than anywhere else, but, far beyond this kind of detail, there turned out to be a number of perhaps unforeseen but certainly distinguishing characteristics when a body like this was set up in London. The first and the most important was the politics, which was not left at the door.

Politics in London has always been characterised by a combativeness, a sometimes studied viciousness rarely seen outside the capital. Furthermore, the local authority politicians who formed the majority of the MPA, the members of the Greater London Assembly, almost without exception had much more substantial experience of politics than is commonly found elsewhere: a number had been leaders of significant London councils during difficult times and there were members of the House of Lords and at least one former MP. Four members went on to become MPs during the first two sessions. This meant that, as they effectively chose the independent members, they had no qualms about ensuring that the majority of them were closely aligned to whichever was the majority party or, perhaps more accurately, were definitely not aligned to the main opposition. Set against this, none of the members, except the very few who had been on the MPA's predecessor, the almost entirely powerless Metropolitan Police Committee, had any experience of the way in which a Police Authority normally operated. Finally, particularly but not exclusively the GLA members proceeded to work in the way with which most of them were familiar, as in a large London council, combative, aggressive to officers, always in public, usually looking for party advantage and media notice.

The second difference was precisely this last point. Although all formal Police Authority meetings in England and Wales are open to the public, it would be fair to say that there are few during which the public areas are very full or at which there is more than the odd local reporter. The MPA was completely different. There were often members of the public there for individual items but the media – not just the London media but the national media – were there always, in force. And their number increased after the London bombings, when it was not unusual for up to five different television cameras to be present, sometimes showing proceedings live. This was reinforced by the decision of the MPA to require a verbal report from the Commissioner, which included the opportunity for members to ask any question of him they wanted, an agenda item which increasingly dominated the three-hour meetings during my time in office. All this had the effect of turning a meeting into a live and unstructured press conference on whatever anecdote a member wished to raise, a situation unique not only in policing but also in British public life. It enabled the MPA to fulfil the first duty it had given itself, always displayed at the meetings on a banner explaining the role of the MPA, which was 'rigorously to hold the Commissioner to account'. It also was some part of the difficulties I faced at first in my Commissionership when inadvertently I said something during a session which could become a story that I did not want. Much worse than that, however, the combination of these seriously experienced politicians and a London-based national media produced a culture from all parties of leaking and briefing, to the complete despair of Catherine Crawford, Chief Executive of the MPA and a fine public servant. There were too many Sundays when we would ring each other up to discuss who was the most likely source for a particular story.

The third difference was the other structures with which the MPA found itself in competition. The Greater London Act 2000 was apparently the lengthiest Parliamentary Bill since the Indian Independence Act of 1947, which might be considered a more consequential piece of legislation. When it came to the issue of the police, it was fiendishly complicated and was nicknamed the 'stop Ken' Bill. The whole idea of a London Mayor had been a New Labour creation, directly associated with Tony Blair himself. The election for Mayor was supposed to be won by a Labour candidate. As the 2000 election loomed, however, it was obvious that Ken Livingstone looked certain to defeat Frank Dobson, the Labour candidate, together with everyone else. Ken was now an independent, precisely because, contrary to what he had previously said he would do, he had decided to stand against Frank and had left the Labour Party. At that time I had never met Ken and could only remember the 'Red Ken' of the eighties, when he presided over the fundamentally antagonistic Lambeth Police Monitoring Group. I had named my cat after him, so that at least I could boss something called Ken around.

What I did learn, however, in the months leading up to the creation of the London Mayoralty and the MPA, was that Ken was uniquely admired and loathed in equal measures by members of the Labour Party and the government. There were Cabinet ministers who hated him. There was no way given this attitude towards him, along with his defection from the ranks and his track record of anti-establishment gestures and policies, that he was going to be allowed any real control over the Met. He knew this. I first met him when we sat next to each other at the inaugural meeting of the new Police Authority on 1 July 2000. 'Ah,'

he said, 'you are the man on the substitutes' bench: we should meet –
perhaps in time there can be a better arrangement than all this?'

This meant that the members of the new Police Authority found
themselves in a structure of labyrinthine complexity, of which the
budget-building process is perhaps the most symbolic part of the
absurdity. After much negotiation each autumn, the Commissioner
proposes a budget to the MPA; after discussion the MPA, the majority
of whose members are members also of the Greater London Assembly,
vote on the proposals and forward their budget to the Mayor; after
consultation the Mayor sends the MPA budget, as part of his overall
London budget, back to the Greater London Assembly, in which – wait
for it – the majority of members are also members of the MPA, who
engage in major political battles to overturn or alter the very budget
which they have already approved. Additionally, throughout my time
at the Met, those members of the GLA who were not members of the
MPA felt frustrated and set up committees to scrutinise events in the
Met or its finances. The MPA fiercely defended its sovereignty against
this, as it did against the Mayor at first. While Ken was still an independent, before his controversial readmission to the Labour Party, I
went with the first Chair of the MPA, the influential Labour peer Lord
Toby Harris, to a budget meeting with Ken. He laid out his mayoral priorities for the Met, which he expected to be accommodated within its
budget. A silence followed and Ken then asked Toby what he thought.
'It adds to the rich tapestry in which we are operating,' was the response.

Principally, however, the MPA was frustrated because it was over-
shadowed by both the Met itself and the Home Secretary. The Met's
profile – and its press office – dwarfed the MPA. For many years the Met
was entirely capable of organising events or developing policy without
mentioning it to the Authority, partly through poor forethought but
sometimes out of sheer frustration. Meanwhile it seemed to many of
us that Jack Straw had quite quickly forgotten that he had created a
Police Authority for London, carrying on, for instance, with his regular
bilateral meetings with the Commissioner and Deputy Commissioner.
It was some years before Toby Harris got an invitation to these. And, of

course, unlike any other Police Authority, the MPA could not choose its police chief. And because London is a dominant feature of British policing and of British politics, that police chief is always going to be wrapped up in national affairs. What was to happen in the years ahead in national politics would play out across the office of Commissioner and across the MPA.

I have always thought London should have some form of Police Authority and it is important to record that the MPA did much that was valuable, particularly in connecting the Met and people of London after the bombings of 2005. I am equally sure, however, that the present structures are unfit for purpose and always have been. A part-time group of people, however well meaning and diligent, are not capable of overseeing the work of an organisation with more than 50,000 staff and a budget in excess of £3bn, particularly one that takes so many controversial decisions; they are certainly not if they are not capable of deciding what kind of authority they are – not fully agreed whether they should be concerned with geographic constituencies, or only with particular hobby-horses or with strategic decision making.

That does not mean that I was not impressed by Len Duvall, who was the Chair throughout my time as Commissioner, and the amazing job he did in corralling together these different views of the work to be done. He is a classic street fighter of a Labour politician, brought up in the school of hard knocks, who eats, sleeps and breathes politics. He has a strong south London accent and left school pretty early. I really enjoyed watching people underestimating him. It was a mistake.

Nor do my criticisms mean that all the work that one member did, for instance for matters in Lambeth, wasn't valuable, only that it made the work of the MPA unbalanced, in that few other members behaved in the same way and therefore other boroughs got short shrift. It doesn't mean that the endless scrutiny by one member over matters of HR policy or another over the Met's property portfolio did not produce useful changes (as well as frustration for officers), but it just seems a pity that, at different times, whole other policy areas were largely neglected.

Nor did it mean that there were not some wonderful characters, such as Jenny Jones, a Green member of the Police Authority of whom I grew very fond but who was capable of denouncing the Met in an authority meeting for the way an early May Day had been policed – it had been the first use of the police tactic which later became known as 'kettling' – and then going outside to join the demonstration against the Met. And then there was Peter Herbert, an urbane black lawyer but whose interest in human rights made him victim to a form of MPA bingo; the winner correctly guessing the time he would ask his question about Guantanamo Bay or extraordinary rendition or visiting tyrants of one sort or another. And there was the one I could have hugged who, when a member of his own party began yet another acerbic question with the words 'I may be stupid, but', quietly said, 'Yes, you are'. There were some fine people who stood away from the spin and the briefings and the politics, particularly but not exclusively among the independent members, and who carried out the various scrutinies that I believe to be the most valuable work done by the Authority.

As I stood on that stage on my first morning, however, when many members of the MPA were part of the audience, I almost loved them, all of them. Sometimes emotions are misplaced.

6

21 and 22 July

At lunchtime on 21 July it all happened again. At least, that is what it felt like. Once again Caroline Murdoch, my chief of staff, and Moir Stewart, my staff officer, came into my office and said that there had been further explosions. Within minutes different attacks were being reported, between 12.20 and 12.50pm, at the underground stations at Shepherd's Bush, Oval and Warren Street and on a bus in Hackney. We know now that they were unsuccessful but that was not immediately clear. Some of the devices had partially ignited and we had to assume further mass casualties. As before, I called a meeting of Management Board in crisis management mode and, as before, COBR was called for mid-afternoon. Again I gave a short announcement to the media asking for calm and for people to stay where they were.

My mood was much darkened by an early report that geiger counters had sounded at the Oval scene and officers were being dispatched in radiological protection suits, which sounded like an echo from the earlier conspiracy headed by Dhiren Barot. This felt like disaster and my main concern remained the prospect of serious disorder, if again there were numerous casualties. Our discussion focused on force mobilisation if necessary. However, by 2.30pm it was clear that there had been no casualties because, whatever had happened, no complete explosions had occurred and the radiological scare had passed. There was a moment of farce when it was discovered that I had go back on air and state that the request for people to stay where they were did not apply to tube drivers, otherwise London would be shut down again.

I then went to COBR with Andy Hayman. I don't think we were

sure by this stage whether what had been left behind at the scenes were or were not viable devices but that was emerging by the time I held another Management Board meeting at 4pm. Given what we knew about the quantity of explosives in the house in Leeds and the viable devices left at Luton railway station, and given that we knew the 7/7 bombers had been determined to kill themselves, we had to assume that that afternoon's bombers had intended to do the same. It seemed almost certain that they would be returning to somewhere to get more bombs and to attack again imminently. We braced ourselves for the most urgent manhunt in the history of the Yard.

At 4.30pm I went on to a further meeting in the Cabinet Room at No 10 with the Prime Minister, the Home Secretary and the Security Services Chiefs. The meeting had been arranged some time before to review the intelligence picture and to consider whether any further legislation was necessary. Our discussion was dominated by the events of the day. The conversation about the intelligence picture was short: it had suddenly become starkly clear that the country was under the most severe of threats. How many more attacks were being planned and how many could already be near delivery? In that room, at the very centre of the British state, the simple answer from the security services and everyone else was that we had no idea.

The review of legislation had been intended to cover gaps and was part of a continuing discussion of matters such as the outlawing of attendance at terrorist training camps, subsequently introduced the next year. These were under consideration because it had become obvious that we were trying to deal with twenty-first-century terrorism with nineteenth-century legislation. Kamel Bourgass, for instance, charged in connection with the plot involving the deadly poison ricin, had had to be charged with the nineteenth-century statute of public nuisance in attempting to administer a noxious substance. It was also a fact that for some time English jurisprudence had been moving away from wide conspiracy charges in favour of what are known as substantive offences, conduct specifically banned by individual sections of individual acts, and these weren't always obvious when it came to the people on the periphery of terrorist conspiracies. The main Act dealing with bombs had been drafted to deal with the Fenians.

This was important but I was concerned with something else. A manhunt was now on, seeking men (and perhaps women, I didn't know – the Tamil Tigers specialised in those) who were prepared, indeed determined, to die. I had been looking for some time at the position of firearms officers, following the case of Harry Stanley who had been shot dead by police in September 1999 in north London. Officers had been called to a pub by a member of the public who believed he had seen an Irishman inside with a shotgun, wrapped in plastic. Having been challenged outside the pub, Harry allegedly turned towards the officers and raised what he was carrying towards them. The two officers fired: one shot killed him. He was not Irish and he was carrying a table leg. He was entirely innocent. Whatever the rights and wrongs – and I am now sure the officers thought they were doing the right thing – what followed was a judicial and personal disaster for all involved. Another force investigated the case. It took three years for an inquest to occur, at which the jury returned an open verdict, then a second inquest was ordered, which returned a verdict of unlawful killing in October 2004, five years after the incident. The officers were suspended. That verdict was overturned at the High Court and a further inquiry ordered, which led to the officers, who had been released from suspension, being arrested. Finally, in February 2006, six and a half years after Harry had died, with absolutely nobody content, the Independent Police Complaints Commission (IPCC) concluded that the officers should not face any disciplinary action.

Unfortunately this was not untypical of processes concerning deaths involving police officers. The drawn-out case of Roger Sylvester was similar: he had died in 1999, probably of what became known as positional asphyxia after being restrained by police. In both cases I had been aware throughout of the traumas being faced by the officers involved (and their families) but in the Stanley case there was another problem: the threat that some of their firearms officer colleagues, who are all volunteers, who believed that the two officers involved had been treated

shamefully, including by the Met, were considering action tantamount
to refusing to carry weapons any longer. That had been averted for the
time being. I had also looked at the judgements concerning the case
of Trooper Lee Clegg, who had been convicted and then cleared of
murder in a shooting incident in Northern Ireland. The Law Lords had
expressed unease at the state of the law, which provided no alternative
to murder and manslaughter as the basis for the investigations which
are launched when soldiers or police officers kill someone in the course
of their duties.

I reminded the meeting briefly of these cases and suggested that,
given what we now faced in the pursuit of those who had attempted
further atrocities earlier in the day and remembering the officer killed
in Madrid, it was now time to reconsider the legal framework under
which firearms officers were operating: not to free them from the
responsibility they carried but to see if the law and investigative and
judicial processes were any longer fully appropriate. I did not wish to
exempt police officers from scrutiny but the threat we faced was so
acute that we needed to do everything we could lawfully to protect
and reassure those officers prepared to carry firearms. It was agreed that
this was an important matter and that I would write the next day to the
Home Secretary, setting out my concerns and asking for such a review.
The meeting broke up and I went off to give a press conference with
the Mayor about the events of the day. It was that letter that I was considering when I arrived at work on Friday 22 July and I sent a first draft
across to David Hamilton, the head of the Met's legal department and
the Commissioner's solicitor, early that morning. I have no doubt that
the train of thought involved in composing this letter influenced the
mistake I was about to make, a mistake which set off a train of consequences which made a very difficult day for the Met even more difficult
in the long term.

Within eight days, the four bombers of 21 July, Muktar Said Ibrahim,
Yassin Omar, Ramzi Mohammed and Hussain Osman, were all
arrested, one in Birmingham, one in Italy (claiming through his lawyer
there that the bombs contained only flour) and two, dramatically and

on television, in west London. A further bomb was found on waste ground in Shepherd's Bush, indicating the existence of a fifth bomber, Manfo Kwaku Asiedu, who had abandoned it in the minutes before the attacks. He was arrested in north London on 26 July. He was charged and convicted in the name of Asiedu: again, like Kamel Bourgass, his real identity remains uncertain. The recovered bombs made clear the deadly intent: they were made of hydrogen peroxide, again wrapped with nails to cause maximum injury. They had failed only because the hydrogen peroxide mixture had been incorrectly prepared. Although it appeared to be a copycat attack – and the selection of a bus may have been a late development after 7 July – this had probably been months, if not years, in the planning.

Ibrahim, Omar, Mohammed and Osman subsequently received sentences of forty years and the man known as Asiedu one of thirty-three years. Capturing them was a brilliant operation with many twists and turns. Nobody knew what these individuals would do when finally tracked down or whether they had access to firearms. A gun had been found in a car left by the 7/7 bombers at Luton. The stakes could not have been higher.

I am aware that those who planned and commanded the operation to arrest Ibrahim and Mohammed in west London were deeply concerned that they might be sending colleagues to their deaths. Eleven further people were also later convicted of assisting the bombers, before the attack or after it, to evade capture.

Speaking on BBC TV's *Question Time* in the week after these attempted bombings, I expressed my astonishment that a firearms officer in Birmingham had used a Taser during the arrest of Omar, when he was found holding a rucksack, still dressed in the woman's burka in which he had fled. I know that my astonishment was shared privately by the then Chief Constable of West Midlands. Firing the Taser was a very brave act but entirely contrary to firearms doctrine because the Taser darts themselves might have set off a bomb. However, it provided a stark contrast to the event which was to overshadow all these arrests and so much bravery, an event which led one member of

the audience during that *Question Time* to speak about police officers 'executing' someone on the streets of London. That event, was the
death of Jean Charles de Menezes just after 10am on 22 July, less than
twenty-four hours after the failed bombings.

Jean Charles de Menezes was entirely innocent of any wrongdoing
connected to terrorism and yet he was shot and killed by the Metropolitan Police. From the first moment I understood his innocence, I have
tried never to forget it. Many bitter allegations were subsequently made
about the Met and about me but all of that pales into insignificance
beside the fact of his death. There are not many days on which I don't
think about it.

The circumstances have been subject to lengthy investigation, a trial
under Health and Safety legislation and an inquest and most of the facts
are well known. Three things about this case are particularly difficult
for the Met: first, that a public perception emerged, fairly quickly, of an
attempt by the organisation to present a different account of the circumstances of the death and of who knew what and when, a perception that
the processes of investigation and trial failed to substantiate but certainly
did not dispel; second, that the investigation and public commentary
inevitably centred on a police firearms operation and it became clear that
the doctrine and practice which underpin such operations are not understood outside professional circles, which made getting the police case
across much more difficult, even to the point that some of the conclusions reached in the Health and Safety trial were thrown into question by
testimony given at the inquest; and, third, in the long term, it provided
an opportunity for the opposition on the MPA to seek to remove a Commissioner whom they disliked because of his closeness to New Labour, as
they perceived it. The death itself became a political issue.

Given what they thought they were dealing with, the officers who
killed Jean Charles, whom I will continue to refer to by their call signs,
Charlie 2 and Charlie 12, in running towards and getting within a
few feet of a suspected suicide bomber, together with the surveillance
officer, known in court as Ivor, who sprang on him and pinned his
arms to his sides on the tube train, should each have been awarded the

George Medal. Instead – and I have met all three – they live for the rest of their lives with the knowledge that they took part in the killing of an entirely innocent man. Had he been a suicide bomber and they had not shot him and the train had blown up, then, if not dead themselves, they would have faced investigation for manslaughter. As the Coroner implied by refusing to allow the jury to consider a verdict of unlawful killing, their decisions were reasonable decisions on what they themselves knew and perceived at the time. The great difficulty is that this is a case in which it appears that so were the decisions of everybody else. Jean Charles died because of a ghastly combination of circumstances.

First and most important, as explained in Chapter 1, while the Met had developed plans for dealing with suicide bombers, all these plans were predicated on prior intelligence, either that a particular individual was a suicide bomber or a particular event was to be targeted by a suicide bomber or bombers. By definition suicide bombers die or are killed. No one had ever thought about, or practised contingencies for, a set of failed suicide bombers who were on the run and might attack anywhere in London. So the operation which began early in the morning of 22 July, deploying a number of surveillance teams to cover a number of addresses, was broaching entirely new territory. The addresses had been identified from documents found in the abandoned rucksack bombs from the day before. There was no certainty that the rucksacks had not been borrowed or stolen but it was a start. Second, there seemed every reason to suspect that the bombers, once having tried and failed to carry out one such attack, would be determined to die and attack again and they were also likely to try to kill police officers if they were discovered. Third, there is something uniquely awful about a suicide attack. Seneca said, 'The man who is not afraid to die will always be your master.' The mood of fear in the capital was profound, recalled by Toby Harris, the first Chair of the MPA. He was on a bus in north London that lunchtime. It was very quiet and edgy. Suddenly someone shouted that the police had shot one of the bombers, which was the breaking news of Jean Charles's death. The passengers on the bus broke into applause.

Jean Charles lived in the same block of flats as one of the would-be bombers, Hussain Osman: Jean Charles in flat 17 Scotia Road, Osman in 21. There seems to have been some resemblance between the two men, although this would, in the course of subsequent enquiries, become a crucial point of disagreement. Jean Charles left the front door at 9.33am. He boarded a bus and then got off it at Brixton tube station and then got back on the same bus, a classic anti-surveillance tactic. Surveillance officers reported him as appearing agitated.

Following suspected terrorists requires surveillance officers who are armed. At this time the armed teams were of two sorts: the Special Branch teams, who are used to targeting people with established identities and then identifying new ones during long-running operations, and the Specialist Crime teams, who are more used to assessing whether the person they are following in a fast-moving operation is or is not the person being sought, although that can never be an exact science. The team at Scotia Road was a Special Branch team. When Jean Charles came out of the address, the team were in contact with a control room at Scotland Yard. That particular control room did not have recording facilities for radio transmissions and, in the few minutes during which Jean Charles was under surveillance, there was a considerable amount of radio traffic. Those in command, Commander Cressida Dick and Detective Superintendent Jon Boutcher, in charge of the manhunt, were and remain quite certain that a positive identification of Jean Charles as Osman was given and repeated. It was on that basis that Cressida Dick made her decisions. However, when the surveillance team was asked how positive an identification this was on a scale of one to ten, they were unable to answer because they were not familiar with such a process.

Jean Charles got off the bus and went into Stockwell tube station, the same station as had been entered by three of the attempted bombers of the previous day. Cressida Dick had already weighed up her options, rejecting, for instance, the possibility of confronting him on the bus as much too dangerous. She could have let him run on the tube system, in the hope that he would lead the police to the other bombers, but she assessed that as risking a catastrophe. She therefore ordered that he be stopped. There was momentary confusion as to whether the fire-arms team were there but some of the team were – a fact which did not feature in evidence at the Health and Safety trial, which may have led to some unwarranted criticism of the Met – and the firearms officers ran down the escalators towards the platforms. What Cressida did not do was to issue a Kratos codeword, which would have required the firearms officers to shoot the suspect. Nor did she issue an order, as reported in some parts of the media, to stop him 'at all costs'. She expected him to be detained at gunpoint, although she knew that if the officers felt that he posed an immediate threat to life, they would shoot.

In effect the operation now passed out of her hands, a situation made more absolute by the fact that Met radios did not work on the Under-ground. The codewords for firearms operations are completely different from Kratos and are based on traffic-light colours. They are in regular use. Codes amber and red can only be given if a suspect is positively identified: amber represents firearms officers moving into position, red is taking control. Red had been called. In these kinds of operations fire-arms officers are not in uniform. Charlie 2 and Charlie 12 ran into the tube station, vaulting over the barriers as they did so. The firearms offic-ers make clear in their statements that, as they approached the train, they were certain that the suspect they were about to confront was one of the failed suicide bombers of the day before. They expected to be able to detain him. As they arrived in the train, Ivor, the surveillance officer who had followed Jean Charles, pointed him out. He was seated in the carriage. Jean Charles got up from his seat. The officers were adamant that he kept coming towards them, with his hands in front of him. They had already drawn their weapons. Ivor jumped at him and pushed him back into the seat. The officers fired. It was 10.06am.

Questioned by counsel for the Coroner at the inquest, one of the officers who fired answered as follows:

I have brought the weapon up into his facial area, hoping that it would have been seen or whatever, but he's continued on his forward momentum towards me, and it was at that stage then I just formed the opinion that: he's going to detonate, he's going to kill us, and I have to act now in order to stop this from happening.

Q: You say in your statement: 'I thought, "He's going to detonate. He's going to kill us." I had no alternative. I must shoot him before he kills. In my mind I had no choice.' That's what you say in the statement.

A: Yes, sir.

Q: Is that the truth as to your state of mind at this time?

A: Yes, it was.

I find it impossible to conceive that this officer, with his long years of experience, is not telling the truth in this account, although I have to acknowledge, for their part, that the jury did not accept, for instance, that Jean Charles, having stood up, moved towards the officers (a question specifically asked by the Coroner).

The officers in command at the time of the Stockwell incident were part of the absolute 'A team' of the Met. I have rarely worked with a more professional and competent officer than Cressida Dick, who is widely regarded as one of the finest officers of her generation, with extensive experience of firearms operations. Despite all the issues surrounding Stockwell, the MPA has twice promoted her further and she is now arguably the most senior woman police officer in Britain. The key issue was identification and she and her team were convinced that Jean Charles had been positively identified. She faced a dynamic, rapidly changing operation in a timeframe which was diminishing quickly, with a genuine risk of catastrophe. Many of the things that different commentators have suggested could have been done would have been unwise in the extreme. Stopping everybody who came out of the building where Osman was suspected to live would have risked alerting terrorists who might have still been inside. Suspending all buses and tubes would have been impractical as well as being another indication to terrorists that police were suspicious of somewhere nearby. Once 'red' had been called, the matter was in the hands of the firearms team.

The fact that the Met radio system did not work underground merely made the end seem more dramatic.

Ironically, this was a result of another part of the story of the King's Cross fire: at that time, not only did the Met's system not work underground, but the British Transport Police (BTP) did not have an effective radio system below ground. The report into the fire by Desmond Fennell QC had forced the then London Underground to install one but it only worked on BTP frequencies. Over the past seven or eight years all police forces in the UK have taken on a completely new radio system known as Airwave: as Deputy Commissioner I spent many hours trying to persuade the Home Office to widen its scope to cover the Underground. It was like pushing water uphill because the Underground was now funded by a public–private partnership, the financial rules of which meant enormous extra charges for changes like this. The events of 7 July had changed all that but it would take a further three years to install it throughout the system.

The firearms team had not been far away from Jean Charles's flat when he left it. Most of them were parked up, out of public gaze, at a nearby Territorial Army centre. It is vital that these vehicles and the men in them are not in public view near a scene (like Scotia Road) in case they are spotted. They left as soon as a positive identification appeared to have been made. Some of the firearms team got to Stockwell tube station before Jean Charles.

Jean Charles de Menezes died because the time between what was at one stage believed to be a positive identification and his descent into the tube system was simply too short to get the firearms team to him in a manner in which they could contain him above ground and yet was just long enough for the surveillance team, who could, in an emergency, perhaps have stopped him, to be told not to because the firearms team were taking over.

As a number of police witnesses testified to the inquest, policing is full of risk and no guarantee can ever be given that something like this will never happen again. Changes have been made to the training and command of the Met's surveillance teams, particularly around identification, but sooner or later another set of operational circumstances will arise and another single component in those circumstances will be found to be wanting and another tragedy will occur. Both the firearms officers and Cressida and many others expressed their deep sympathy for the family at the inquest, as I did many times on other occasions. This is not mere gesturing or politeness: there will rarely have been days when those of us involved have not thought about Jean Charles and his family and wondered whether something could have been done differently which would have saved his life. He was killed by the Metropolitan Police Service but, in a very profound way, Jean Charles de Menezes was truly the fifty-third victim of the bombers of July 2005.

Meanwhile, back at Scotland Yard, I made two mistakes. The first and most obvious one was to ignore the first rule of major incidents, which is not to believe the first report of what has happened. I was told that there had been a positive identification of one of the failed bombers of the day before and that he had been shot dead. This was so clear and unambiguous that all of those I gathered together for the emergency Management Board meeting worked on that basis in the hours ahead. The second was connected to my promised letter to the Home Secretary. That letter never got sent but I adapted it – and traces, including the wrong date of 21 July, are visible from the first one – into a second letter, this time addressed to the Permanent Secretary at the Home Office, John Gieve. It is worth setting out in full.

New Scotland Yard
21 July 2005

Dear John
Operation Kratos: suicide bombers
In the meeting we had with the Prime Minister yesterday, I raised the issue of maximising the legal protection for officers who had to take decisions in relation to people believed to be suicide bombers.

This is clearly a fast-time decision-making process, in which officers cannot risk the kind of containment and negotiation tactics that would normally be the case. Put simply, the only choice an officer may have may be to shoot to kill in order to prevent the detonation of a device. In due course, I believe we need a document similar to the military rules of engagement but time does not permit its creation at the present time.

The officers have the protection of Section 3 of the Criminal Law Act. I do not seek to exempt them from investigation (and ultimately therefore prosecution, if evidence of deliberate malfeasance was available). However, I am confident that prosecuting authorities will take cognisance of the pressures under which the Service operates in terrorist scenarios.

The current urgency, however, is over the role of the Independent Police Complaints Commission. There is much concern about revealing either the tactics that we have and/or the sources of information on which we are operating.

I therefore believe that, in a fast-moving, multi-site terrorist situation, in which suicide bombers are clearly a very strong possibility, a chief officer of police should be able to suspend S.17 of the Police Reform Act 2002, which requires us to supply all information that the Independent Police Complaints Commission may require. The IPCC has a dual role in the sense that it, itself, is under duty to provide as much information as it can to the complainant or to members of the deceased's family. This could put further lives at risk in these circumstances.

I have therefore given instructions that the shooting that has just occurred at Stockwell is not to be referred to the IPCC and that they will be given no access to the scene at the present time. The investigation will be carried out by the Met's own Directorate of Public Standards. This investigation will be rigorous but subordinate to the needs of the counter-terrorism operation.

I have spoken to Nick Hardwick, Chairman of the IPCC, and informed him of this decision. I am grateful to know that your office had already contacted him.

Clearly, this is a developing situation but for the time being I seek your support for this measure, which may form the basis for amending legislation in the future.

A copy of this letter goes to Nick Hardwick and to Len Duvall, Chair of the Police Authority.

Ian Blair
Commissioner

Section 17 of the relevant Act provides for automatic referral, as it is known, of any death caused by contact with police to the Independent Police Complaints Commission for investigation. My view was that the Met was in the middle of a terrorist emergency and that handing over the control of any part of such an investigation to another agency was a recipe for confusion. About 10.45am I spoke to both the head of investigations at the IPCC, Roy Clarke, and then to the Chairman, Nick Hardwick. Nick is a very decent, honourable man and was actually pretty sympathetic. My view, however, was blunt, as this part of the conversation reveals, which, unusually, I recorded at the time:

> **IB**: All I am saying to you in this scenario where I have got three more potential suicide bombers out there I need a provision [The proposed suspension of s17 of the Police Reform Act re referrals] which just allows me to get on with the job in whatever way I need to and the idea that we treat this in the same way as we would treat another police shooting is not possible. We are not going to be overly sympathetic to officers or anything else, we have got to be completely clear that this is an ongoing terrorist attempt at atrocities and I have just got to deal with that in whatever way I need to.
> **NH**: I don't have any difficulty with that at all and that is what I would expect from the police force that protects me as a citizen to do but I am not sure that suspending powers is the answer.
> **IB**: That is what I am asking the Home Office to do and for the time being I am going to assume that they are going to do that. Then we can discuss it further. What I am saying is there is no role for the IPCC in this shooting at this time.

It was not an offer but a statement of intent. The plain fact is, however, that there was no legal power to take this course of action and, although John Gieve and Len Duvall were both very polite and sympathetic in their responses, the Home Office refused to suspend the legislation. As I made clear later, there would no doubt have been a better way, which might have been to agree with Nick that the investigation would begin with a joint IPCC and Met team and that the needs of the counter-terrorism investigation would initially be paramount. I didn't think of that. I just knew that I did not want the IPCC crawling all over a life-or-death Met operation which in the next few minutes could see other terrorists attacking the city. The order got changed in the telling so that those on the ground received it as an order from both me and the Prime Minister, which probably made it sound rather grand, but it was my decision and he was not involved: that's the trouble with the surname.

In fact my decision made no difference to the practicalities of the investigation. By the Saturday evening it had been agreed that the IPCC would take over and we would meet on the Monday in the Home Office to discuss the arrangements for handover: in fact the IPCC team did not formally commence work until the Wednesday, five days after the shooting. Much later on, at one of the preliminary hearings before the Coroner, Mr Sampson, an IPCC investigator stated that the Met had handed over 'a full and comprehensive package'. It made no difference then to the practicalities but it made a significant difference to public perception.

When this letter emerged into public view in very difficult circumstances in the middle of August, it was rapidly portrayed as an immediate attempt to cover up the circumstances of Jean Charles's death. I made clear that it was not, on the grounds that it is not usual to seek to cover something up by writing to the Home Office Permanent Secretary and informing the Chairs of both the IPCC and the MPA of my intentions. But the release of the letter in August came at the end of a series of subsequent developments about the shooting of Jean Charles which were to create a very uncomfortable mixture. These were, in turn, on the first day, an innocent mistake in the first of the Met's press releases about the shooting, which was repeated in the subsequent press conference and then in a third press release and then the revelation, on the second day, that I had not been informed of growing doubts as to the identity of the dead man before it was confirmed that he was entirely unconnected to the attempted bombings. This was followed by a continuing failure by the Met to correct wrong information about the circumstances of the shooting in the days that followed and then, finally, the leak of parts of the IPCC investigation to ITV News in mid-August.

Much later on, all this was compounded by allegations about who knew what and when, made by a disenchanted senior Met officer, revelations at the Health and Safety trial about tampered notes and allegations that counsel instructed by the Met tried to smear the reputation of Jean Charles at the same trial. It also deeply damaged the Met's relationship with the IPCC and mine with Nick Hardwick, primarily because both he and I knew that one of the reasons behind my action, as I had explained to John Gieve in the letter and Nick himself in the phone call, was concern about the duty of the IPCC to provide information to the families of the deceased, which would not be helpful in the case of a terrorist. Furthermore, I did not say in that conversation but Nick, I think, suspected, what also lay behind my decision was that the IPCC was having difficulty in attracting high-class investigators and those they had were very much finding their feet in a new organisation, particularly in relation to counter-terrorist tactics. This fact was made apparent later by the variable quality of the IPCC investigation into all aspects of the Stockwell shooting.

Given all that transpired afterwards, a real problem in the months and years that have followed has been to get across what our mindset was on that day. Of course, we were worried that a man had been shot but we had been informed of a positive identification and unfortunately the Met does sometimes shoot people dead, albeit rarely. But, during the following hours, our concentration was not on the shooting but on the manhunt. We had to find these people before they struck again. We had excellent CCTV images of the four men involved and we needed to get those images into the public domain, but this was now the largest story in the world and the Met was worried, just as in the case of the casualty bureau two weeks before, about its capability to handle the large number of calls from the public which would follow the showing of those photographs.

At 11.41am the first Met press release stated that a man had been challenged by police officers at Stockwell Underground Station and subsequently shot. It was later discovered that a press officer had just typed in the standard line for a press release concerning a police shooting because police officers never shoot without issuing some sort of challenge. In fact there was to be a great deal of controversy at the inquest as to whether the police officers had or had not shouted 'armed police' before firing. I find the account of Charlie 2 convincing, which is that he did not issue a challenge at all but did shout 'armed police' just before he fired, not to challenge the suspect but, being in plain clothes and about to kill somebody, to tell the public who he himself was. Shouting 'armed police' at a suicide bomber close by is to invite instant death.

The press conference which followed was repeatedly delayed until about 3.30pm. In the meantime, just before 2pm, I had another briefing with Andy Hayman and pressed him for information about the dead man and whether we could find any link between the attacks on the two Thursdays. He was unable to provide any answers, which, given how little time had passed, did not surprise me. I walked down to the press conference at about 3.10pm. It was held in the main room of the Queen Elizabeth II Conference Centre opposite Westminster Abbey, about two hundred yards from Scotland Yard. In another room the Met's head of press, Dick Fedorcio, who did a great job all through that extraordinary summer, and a whole raft of other people were going through the proposed press statement I was to make before Andy made the appeal for information. At the same time as making an appeal we could not remain silent about the shooting and, having seen a number of previous drafts, I was now content with the wording because it contained a number of caveats. It is worth repeating most of the press statement in full because, perhaps together with that telephone call with Nick Hardwick, it gives a real flavour of what were our thinking processes at this time, not only about the gravity and immediacy of the threat but also the need to provide reassurance to a badly shaken city. Andy and I walked into the press conference and I imagine that we both breathed in deeply. I had never seen so many cameras and journalists. Dick introduced the two of us and I began:

As you are aware, there is a lot of police activity going on today in relation to the underground and bus incidents of yesterday. This is a very, very fast-moving investigation.

Andy Hayman is going to make an appeal for information. I have a few points that I would like to make to begin with. As I've said before, this is the greatest operational challenge ever faced by the Metropolitan Police Service. The MPS and its sister services are doing a magnificent job but officers are facing previously unknown threats and great danger.

We need the understanding of all communities and the cooperation of all communities and we need calm. We know there are rumours sweeping London and I really do appeal for people to listen to the facts as they emerge. We remain resolute and will work tirelessly and imaginatively with every community in London to solve this crime. The most important message we have other than this appeal is that this operation is targeted against criminals. It is not targeted against any community or any section of the community.

I can say as part of operations linked to yesterday's incidents, Met officers have shot a man inside Stockwell Underground Station at approximately 10am this morning. London Ambulance and the Air Ambulance both attended and the man was pronounced dead at the scene. I understand Stockwell tube station remains closed.

The information I have available is that this shooting is directly linked to the ongoing and expanding anti-terrorist operation. Any death is deeply regrettable. I understand the man was challenged and refused to obey. I can't go further than that at this stage. I am now going to hand over to Assistant Commissioner Andy Hayman.

These words had been carefully drafted. It was entirely true that Jean Charles de Menezes had left a building which was under observation as 'part of operations linked' to the incidents of the day before and that this shooting was 'directly linked to the ongoing and expanding anti-terrorist operation'. However, when it became clear that the building and the shooting were thus linked to the anti-terrorist operation but Jean Charles was not, then these words were only barely capable of supporting the weight of scrutiny to which they would now be subjected.

I returned to the Yard and a series of meetings and briefings. At 5pm there was a further meeting of the Management Board, at which we were joined by Len Duvall and Catherine Crawford from the MPA, together with John Gieve from the Home Office. This was unusual but I wanted them to understand the pressures we were under and the plans we had. In the light of subsequent events, it is worth noting that Andy Hayman arrived late at this meeting from a meeting with a number of journalists after the main press conference and that Deputy Assistant Commissioner Brian Paddick was there representing Tim Godwin, who was on leave. I had foreseen a difficult summer and I had insisted that senior colleagues take their main summer leave wherever possible. This could not really apply to me or to Andy, while Peter Clarke had been recalled as he arrived at his holiday villa and was now on his way back. Brian had been a main spokesman for the Met during the bombings two weeks before and it may be that he was disappointed that he had not been given that role during the current incidents. I did not give him that task because he was now the Acting Assistant Commissioner responsible for maintaining general policing across London.

The notes of the meeting make clear that we were very concerned about community tension and we did not believe we had put out enough about the Stockwell shooting. The meeting split up and a small group, including me, drafted a further press statement, which was then shown to both Andy Hayman and Alan Brown, who had overall responsibility for the investigation into the shooting. It was released at 6.45pm and read as follows:

The man shot at Stockwell Station is still subject to formal identification and it is not yet clear whether he is one of the four people we are seeking to identify and whose pictures have been released today. It therefore remains extremely important that members of the public continue to assist police in relation to all four pictures.

This death, like all deaths related to police operations, is obviously a matter of deep regret. Nevertheless, the man who was shot was under police observation because he had emerged from a house that was itself under observation because it was linked to the investigation of yesterday's incidents.

He was then followed by surveillance officers to the station. His clothing and his behaviour at the station added to their suspicions. While the counter-terrorist investigation will obviously take pre-eminence, the investigation into the circumstances that led to his death is being pursued and will be subject to scrutiny through the IPCC in due course.

At no time in either meeting did anybody raise the possibility that the man was not a terrorist or suggest that he was probably not one of the four would-be bombers. The facts of what happened next are fairly clear. During the course of the night, contact was made with a friend of Mr Menezes, Gesio de Avila, who identified a photograph found in a wallet on the body as that of Jean Charles and was very clear that he had no connection with Islamic or other terrorism.

All that had happened then became subject to two IPCC investigations. The first of these became known as Stockwell One and concerned the death of Jean Charles de Menezes, which became the subject of, first, a prosecution of the Met (technically of the office of the Commissioner) and then an inquest. The second, Stockwell Two, inquired into complaints by the de Menezes family that I and others had put false information into the public domain, not only in the press conference and in subsequent press releases but also in newspaper interviews. The two reports are lengthy documents already in the public domain. The second is covered in Chapter 7 but given full exposure in Brian

Paddick's book *In Line of Fire*, which, given that many of its pages concern the shooting of Jean Charles de Menezes, is probably the most tasteless title imaginable: it was co-written with an investigative journalist and its publication coincided with Brian's 2008 campaign as Lib Dem candidate for London Mayor.

Central to Brian's account of what happened in the hours that followed Jean Charles's death is that he was told by my staff officer, Moir Stewart, even before I gave the main press conference on the afternoon of 22 July, that the Met had 'shot a Brazilian tourist', that either I must have known of Jean Charles's emerging identity during the evening and that I had therefore misled the public over an extensive period of time, or I had been seriously let down by my personal staff. It was his public duty to confront me and then to work with the IPCC in their investigation. This stance, of course, was to be accompanied by the conversations with journalists that he recounts in his pages. I do not believe that gossiping with journalists is an appropriate activity for a senior police officer but then nor is appearing, as he did subsequently, on *I'm a Celebrity: Get Me Out of Here* an appropriate retirement activity for a former senior police officer.

There are a number of components in what went wrong and why it became such a perfect storm. Two were undoubtedly the shocking nature of Jean Charles's death and the fact that it emerged only subsequently that the British police had developed the lethal Kratos tactic for dealing with suicide bombers, which had never been made known to the public, although it was not used in this case. However, the main issues were, first, that for too long I had no idea of the emerging identity of Jean Charles and, quite simply, I should have done and, second, that the whole affair became tainted with allegations that there had been an attempt to cover up what had happened.

Certainly by mid-afternoon a number of individual Met staff knew that identification documents in the name of Jean Charles de Menezes had been found. That in itself was not particularly significant. False identities are a staple of terrorist tactics: as an example, while Kamel Bourgass is serving life imprisonment for murder, this is believed not to be his real name and it is certain that Manfo Asiedu is not the real name of the fifth bomb carrier of 21 July. Moreover, there was nothing to suggest that a Brazilian could not be a member of a terrorist gang: there had been a recent terrorist incident involving a Venezuelan national at Gatwick Airport.

I do not blame any specific person for not passing the information on to me but it was most unfortunate that it did not happen. Except for expressing surprise at and refuting what Brian Paddick had said, I refused to criticise any of my colleagues in the interview I had with the IPCC, as part of Stockwell Two: I do not criticise judgement calls. In particular, I completely understand the decision making of Alan Brown, who, although fully aware of the emerging information, was completely au fait with the use of false identities by terrorists but also knew that counter-terrorism officers were not ruling even an identified Jean Charles out of their investigation. He knew during the latter part of 21 July of an emerging name for the dead man of Jean Charles de Menezes, but he did not believe that it was appropriate to inform me until he had more certainty. I am not sure he was right but it was a thoroughly professional approach.

On the other hand, even at this distance, I remain completely puzzled by Andy Hayman's behaviour. During the day, I repeatedly pressed him for information as to the connection or otherwise of the dead man with the bombings of the previous day and, long into the evening, he did not provide an answer. At that stage, I was not particularly surprised. Yet a number of witnesses, both Met staff and journalists, gave statements to the IPCC investigators dealing with Stockwell Two, to the effect that, at a briefing earlier at about 4.30pm with a loose media grouping known as the Crime Reporters' Association, he had made clear to them that Jean Charles was not one of the four bombers. Andy has always denied this but the IPCC found the allegation substantiated and it has to be said that, on my side, doubt entered into our previously close relationship that autumn when I began to hear that story, a story given credence by the fact that, by just after 5.15, BBC Television News reported the following from outside Scotland Yard: 'We don't know any more than the police have said for sure that he was challenged, he refused to obey instructions, he was subsequently shot and he was not one of the four people whose images were released by police a little earlier.'

Eight floors up in Scotland Yard our meeting was in progress. Andy was late. I do not know whether he had arrived by 5.15, when those words were being spoken outside, but he did not give the same information to me, the Deputy Commissioner, the Chair of the MPA and the Permanent Secretary. Whatever happened, though, while Andy would always maintain that he had not said this to journalists and did not know that the dead man was not one of the four bombers, the IPCC subsequently found, in the words of their report, that he had 'briefed the Commissioner, MPA and senior colleagues ... on lines which he must have known were not consistent with what he had told the CRA.'

The case of Brian Paddick is even more puzzling. Brian makes clear in his book, which is apparently based on his statement to the IPCC, that he had been told, first by Moir Stewart and Caroline Murdoch, of the existence of Brazilian identity documents, which they accept happened, although Brian puts this in the colourful phrase about a 'tourist', which Moir categorically denies saying and Caroline certainly does not remember hearing. He is then very clear that, at two linked meetings around about 4pm, he was told of de Menezes's identity and that he was not thought to be one of the bombers. At an early point in one of these meetings he told a colleague about the possibility of the man being 'a Brazilian tourist'. He then attended, in his capacity as Acting Assistant Commissioner, my 5pm meeting. As I have already said, I wish Assistant Commissioner Alan Brown, also at the meeting, had been professionally less cautious concerning the emerging identity for the shot man during it but at least he explains why in his statement to the IPCC. At this point, he is talking about the moment he did tell me, the next morning:

> Although the deceased had still not been physically identified, address checks were still precluded [because police could not enter de Menezes's flat without the risk of alerting the terrorists, possibly in the flat above] and therefore the opportunity to obtain comparative data for DNA, fingerprints and odontology testing to confirm identity were

not available. The items that had been recovered the previous day were in themselves inconclusive but added to the account given by Gesio Avio [de Avila], I concluded beyond reasonable doubt that the deceased was Jean Charles de Menezes. I asked for an urgent meeting with the Commissioner ... I briefed the Commissioner fully regarding the sequence of events in the identification and the rationale behind my decision making ... By close of play on 22 July I could not be certain of the identity of the deceased and that I had only been certain of the identification on receipt of the information ... relating to Gesio Avio [de Avila] at 0930 hours that morning.

I did not tell the Commissioner about the findings of documents on 22 July until the morning of 23 July when I was certain of the identification. I had been tasked as Gold London which meant that I had ultimate responsibility for that part of the investigation. Other officers had responsibility for the terrorist investigation. The Commissioner has ultimate responsibility for the Metropolitan Police Service and I therefore did not need to advise the Commissioner until the identification was certain or as certain as it could be and became an issue for the service. As soon as it did so, I informed the Commissioner.

Later I will contrast the wording of that statement with how the IPCC summarised it in its Stockwell Two report but the issue at this point is that I never saw an equivalent explanation as to why Brian Paddick did not say anything during the 5pm meeting about what he believed about de Menezes until that report was published, over two years after the event. His account concerning that meeting is at paragraph 16.7.44 of Stockwell Two:

[referring to Andy Hayman and Alan Brown] he did not believe it was his place to challenge either of them in the meeting. DAC Paddick states that he was present in the role of Acting Assistant Commissioner and had previously been told by a member of the Commissioner's staff that he was really only a DAC: implying that his views were not needed and he was only in attendance as an observer.

This explanation was not included in the statement by Brian Paddick that I was handed during my IPCC interview so I do not know when he first provided it. Personally, I find it hard to reconcile this with my experience of Brian: anyone who knows him or has seen him on television will quickly recognise that he is not slow in coming forward. In large meetings he would often be the first to speak up. Second, he had already told a colleague of his concerns. Third, from the very beginning of my Commissionership I made clear to all senior colleagues that I looked for an open style of meetings and encouraged participation. On this day of days, I was seeking information from anyone and everyone and I find it hard to believe that any member of my staff would say this to Brian and that an officer of his rank would accept that direction. Without the detailed reasoning process which Alan Brown had gone through, I believe it was Brian's clear duty to tell me of his concerns. I have no idea why he did not.

After the press statement was issued at 18.45 I remained at the Yard for about another hour and then went back to my London flat. I came straight back in the next morning and had a meeting with Peter Clarke, who had by now returned from his entirely truncated holiday. I then went over to the catering and briefing centre near the Yard and talked to a lot of officers about how well they were doing. On the way back I was confronted by a television crew and asked for a comment. Feeling very proud of the men and women I had just met, I replied that I thought 'the Met was playing out of its socks'. This remark was to be thrown back at me in the months to come because, of course, it was only a few minutes later that Alan Brown came to my office and told me that the Met had apparently killed an innocent man at Stockwell.

It was a profoundly shocking moment. My first thought was that this was a disaster for the Met and for all those officers involved, especially those who had fired the shots and for Cressida. As I told the *News of the World* in the interview I discuss below, I recalled the famous comment by the crew of *Apollo XIII*, 'Houston, we have a problem': you did not have to be very perceptive to see that what had been great work by the Met over an extraordinary few weeks was going to be badly damaged.

We discussed a series of actions, but first we had to make contact with and support the family of the dead man. This ended up with John Yates, later famous for his involvement in the 'cash for honours' investigation, travelling into the interior of Brazil to apologise to the parents there. I then turned to the support needed for the officers involved and for Cressida.

Once I knew that those matters were in train, the third issue was how we should release the news. This was to be the second component of the storm which broke over the Stockwell case. We got the press handling immediately after Jean Charles's innocence was established catastrophically wrong, as did the IPCC in part. In a number of statements released that day and subsequently the Met continued to repeat the comment that 'his clothing and behaviour' added to the suspicions of the officers involved. Later in the evening the IPCC requested that the Met hand over responsibility for press matters to it, which made a bad situation worse. The IPCC was very clear that press handling was now its business and was indeed cross with me for appearing in an interview on Sky Television to make the first public apology for the death on the Sunday.

Neither the IPCC nor the Met ever openly and publicly retracted or even qualified the allegation about clothing and behaviour, which was made up, I suppose, of four components. The first was Jean Charles getting off and on again the same bus, which did happen and certainly did increase suspicion, as it can be a counter-surveillance tactic. The second was the suggestion that he had jumped over the barriers at the station, which was untrue because this was a complete mix-up. What witnesses reported – sometimes on television – were the plain-clothed firearms officers in pursuit. The third arose from the description of the jacket he wore as bulky, which was certainly a matter of opinion open to challenge, although it is the word which C2 and Charlie 12 use. Lastly, Jean Charles's alleged action in moving towards the officers undoubtedly contributed to their decision to fire, although we would not have known that in the first days. I told the public meeting of the MPA on the Thursday following these events, on 27 July, that some commonly repeated statements about Mr de Menezes in the public domain had not been verified but I did not elaborate on it because the IPCC had made it so clear that it did not want its investigation discussed in public. My comments were not reported.

That MPA meeting was an almost unqualified success for the Met, almost the last we would ever have. The mood of the members was that, while Jean Charles's death was a tragedy, police action had probably been justified because of the very statements about his clothing and behaviour that they had absorbed along with everybody else. In everything else the Met had done well. The next morning, in dramatic scenes, as a result of brilliant backroom police research and the continuing bravery of the firearms teams, the last two bombers were arrested in west London. Here again the new working methods of the media were a problem. I had to get Dick Fedorcio to call the editor of one news channel to get an enthusiastic commentator off the air before she announced (potentially to the suspects as well as to all other viewers) that the police were coming through the back door.

There had been much discussion as to whether the Prime Minister and the Home Secretary could go on holiday. The Prime Minister went, the Home Secretary delayed his for a few days but I felt I could now take a short break and on the Saturday morning I flew with my family to Antigua, where I had the unusual experience of spending two long weekends, as I felt I had to be back in London on the middle Thursday of what had been planned to be a twelve-day break, in case bombers returned again for a third attack, two weeks after 21 July, as that one had been two weeks after the 7th. The press office did receive one enquiry – from the *Daily Mail* – as to whether I was in Antigua but it was too late. I was back at my desk after the second weekend. I felt refreshed and still tremendously proud of what had been done by the Met over the summer.

A few days later Charles Clarke came over to the Yard for another of the events where we congratulated the police officers and other staff who had responded so magnificently during July. Afterwards we went down to the front of the building on to the same spot where we had stood on 7 July. I said to him: 'Five weeks ago you asked me to find the fuckers. The first set of fuckers are dead. We've found the second set. I await your further instructions.' He laughed.

But the laughter quickly died away. The very next day, 16 August, ITV news ran a scoop containing material which had been leaked from the IPCC and which gave the first public account of the circumstances of Jean Charles's death: no leaping the barriers, not a particularly bulky jacket, the photographs of his corpse lying in a tube carriage and the decision to exclude the IPCC from the scene. Suddenly a bad story was becoming catastrophic. Calls for and discussions of my resignation began for the first time. I remember that I woke up one morning as the radio alarm came on, to hear an earnest discussion between two people I had never met on that very subject.

The story was growing and it was thought best I do an exclusive interview with a major Sunday newspaper to try to get our side of the story out. The *News of the World* was chosen because it still has the largest circulation on any day of the week of any single newspaper. Although I was subsequently criticised for mentioning my first thought about Houston, the interview was broadly well regarded. However, it included the following statement, although the newspaper only printed the first half down to the first use of the words 'suicide bomber'. It did not print the remaining words in the square brackets: 'The key component was, at that time, indeed for the next 24 hours or so, I and everybody who advised me, believed that the person who was shot was a suicide bomber [or a potential suicide bomber and either one of the four for whom we were looking, or even worse than that, someone else].'

The article appeared on Sunday 21 August on the front page. This particular answer became one of the matters complained about by the de Menezes family, as did a comment to the same effect subsequently published in the *Guardian*. However, that was for later. What happened next on that Sunday was, according to his book, that Brian Paddick was telephoned directly by the BBC's *World at One* to ask his opinion of what I had said – and I wonder why they had his number; they would not have had mine. He had apparently not been aware of the article.

According to his account in his book, the motivation for what he did next was to protect the force and me. Whatever his motivation, Brian must have intended to leave me with little wriggle room. Before he came to see me the next day, Monday, he had discussed his concerns with a number of people, including the IPCC Director of Investigations, Roy Clarke, Her Majesty's Chief Inspector of Constabulary, Ronnie Flanagan, the Chief Executive of the MPA, Catherine Crawford, and his own boss, Assistant Commissioner Tim Godwin, who came down to my office in a state of some concern to tell me that Brian wanted to see me about what I had said to the *News of the World* and was very agitated. I asked him to tell Brian to come down right away, which he did at about 5pm. Until this point I had been a great supporter of Brian. I think I was the first senior officer he told that he was gay and I remember him being shocked that I told him that he was not the most senior colleague to tell me that about themselves. On my appointment, against much opposition, I gave him the best job available at his rank, that of deputy to Tim, in command of more than 20,000 staff.

To my recollection, we had a very short conversation, standing up, midway between my desk and the door. After he told me what he was concerned about, I was pretty irritated. I told him that he did not know what I knew or did not know and that he should report any concerns he had about my conduct to Catherine Crawford. Not knowing how many people he had already told but remembering his tendency to seek reassurance for his actions from a number of colleagues, I suggested that, other than telling Catherine, he should keep his concerns to himself. I told him, 'We both know the penalty for not telling the truth', a comment which I was subsequently told that he apparently regarded as a threat but which was meant as a reason why I would not lie. I have no recollection whatsoever of his suggesting that other people knew more or that my immediate colleagues had let me down. The meeting, to my memory, could not have lasted more than three or four minutes. In my statement to the IPCC this conversation is covered in six lines of type: in his it lasts for twenty-nine lines of description, while in his book it runs to three full pages. When the IPCC's Stockwell Two report was finally published, two years later, its conclusions about this conversation, in which I had apparently admitted knowing the man was a Brazilian at 7pm on the evening Jean Charles was shot, are unambiguous:

> Para 21.1.5: DAC Paddick claims that the Commissioner told him that he had been through the timings with Ms Murdoch and it was about 1900 hrs on 22 July when he (the Commissioner) was told that the deceased was a Brazilian. Ms Murdoch has no recollection of reaching this conclusion with the Commissioner, although they had been over the timings.
> Para 21.1.7: The evidence of DAC Paddick and the Commissioner in relation to their meeting on the 22 August 2005 cannot be reconciled. ... The weight of evidence supports that the Commissioner did not know anything of the emerging identity by the time he left NSY.
> Para 21.2: There is insufficient information to substantiate the claim that the Commissioner deliberately misled the *News of the World* ... There is insufficient evidence to substantiate the claim that the Commissioner deliberately misled the *Guardian* ...

Unfortunately, by the time those conclusions were published nearly two years later, the crescendo of noise which was being raised about Stockwell was so great as to obscure the simple fact that, whatever mistakes had been made during those days in the summer of 2005 by me and others, I had told the truth, however unpalatable it was. Two years gave the 'Justice for Jean' campaign a lot of room. Brian was an extraordinary character, driven by a seemingly inexhaustible need to be at the centre of events. He was the only man I ever knew with an oil painting of himself on his office wall. I liked him because he was a character and all organisations need characters. But I have no idea what made Brian challenge me as he did over Stockwell. It meant that he finished his career in serious dispute with the force he had loved and had served with distinction, it damaged the Met and it certainly did me no good at all. One newspaper later described him as my nemesis: unfortunately I don't think he is entitled to that accolade.

After the summer, the first meeting of the MPA was on 29 September. It is a curiosity about this institution that, from mid-July, when members start to go on holiday, until the last weeks of September, when many of them are at party conferences, the Met is largely left alone. Len Duvall was still at Party Conference but returned for the MPA meeting. Twenty minutes before the meeting he told me that our brief summary report on Stockwell was a disaster, except he was slightly more colourful: the meeting turned into the first of many to come, a procession of members telling me and my colleagues how awful everything had been, as the television cameras rolled.

Looking back from this distance to that summer, there are some extraordinary features to it. If it had not been for the disaster and tragedy of Jean Charles de Menezes, it would have been regarded as the Met's finest hour in many generations. Personally, it was a whirlwind, which I sometimes recall as being like the film *Groundhog Day*, with the feelings and the meetings and the press conferences after the attacks on the two Thursdays blurring with one another. The pressure and the lack of sleep were mixed with exhilaration and adrenalin, pride and stubbornness. Not all of it can be recalled. For instance, even in the post of Commissioner, calls from the Prime Minister direct to your desk are not very common but both my staff officer of the time, Moir Stewart, and I know that Tony Blair phoned me one particular morning from Chequers and we think it was on a Saturday but we can't remember which one. Some of it was funny rather than sad, for example when I visited a cash machine near Scotland Yard. Thinking about goodness knows how many things, I put in my card, entered my pin number, took out my card and walked away, leaving £50 for what must have been a very satisfied next customer – and all that with an armed protection officer at my side. I could not have done what I did without the help of family and friends but I did not always repay that very well. On the middle Saturday between the two bombings, I did get home and I then announced, chock full of adrenalin, that I needed to see some friends and why didn't we have a dinner party – just what my wife wanted, I think not. Lots of people came round, all wanting to cook or bring something. We ate in the garden. I was the life and soul of the party until about 9pm, when, without any warning, I got up from the table and announced that I was sorry but I needed to sleep right then. I slept for about fourteen hours. The neighbour who had slaved for hours over his green Thai curry – which I did not stay around long enough to eat – was very surprised but very forgiving.

The support of family and friends away from the job are very important but jobs with this level of pressure would also be impossible without the support and good humour of colleagues. Shortly after the death of Jean Charles, I sat chewing over the recent events early one evening with Paul Stephenson in his office. He and I had been friends since we had been together on the Senior Command Course at Bramshill in 1993. I had been really pleased when he had approached me at a conference the previous autumn, when he was Chief Constable of Lancashire and it was known that I was in the middle of the application process to become the Commissioner. He told me that he would like to be my Deputy Commissioner. He had a tough fight on his hands, particularly facing off Tim Godwin when the running list for Deputy was reduced to two, primarily because it had been nearly thirty years since anyone had tried to do the job of Commissioner or Deputy Commissioner without having previously been in the Met. By July, Paul and I were beginning to get to know each other again and I particularly liked the way in which he used his purported ignorance of things Metropolitan as a source of humour.

A few days earlier it had been a revelation to us both to learn that Jean Charles had been shot with hollow-point ammunition, authorised for use on the tube, in a way that was unimaginable outside the Met, by an Acting Superintendent. Hollow-point ammunition is more commonly known as 'dum-dum bullets', the use of which is outlawed by the Geneva Convention. This had been bought by the Met for use after 9/11, when it was thought that firearms officers would have to be deployed on aircraft and the Home Office had accepted that this was an operational decision for a Chief Officer. The point of hollow-point, as it were, is that it does not pass through the body and cause damage to the aircraft or injury to other passengers, which other ammunition will. However, it causes massive injury as a result. When we learned of this we asked for urgent legal advice, which Paul and I were examining in his office. We were relieved to find that the Geneva Convention does not apply to police and we could not be accused of a war crime, something that Paul mentioned had not been a worry for him in Lancashire.

A few minutes later a staff officer came in and told us that the forensic scientists were so concerned about what they had found at the Leeds bomb factory that, for the first time in our professional lives, the laboratory trucks of the government's nuclear and biological centre at Porton Down were being called to the scene for real and not in one of the many exercises in which Paul and I had been engaged over the years. As we were absorbing that information the tannoy suddenly announced that a suspected suicide bomber had been spotted nearby and that all entrances and exits to the Yard were now being closed, with huge metal doors that I had never seen used before. There was a silence and then Paul said to me, 'Ian, is it always like this at the Met?' 'Not every week,' I answered and we opened a bottle of white wine and sat there in a rather companionable but amazed silence.

I needed a sense of humour at about that time because one of my other memories of the days after Jean Charles's death was the arrival in my office of a delegation from the Brazilian government to upbraid me over the failure to protect him. I refrained from pointing out that perhaps this was a case of pots and kettles or glass houses and stones. In fact I just listened politely and put it down to experience.

Next it is worth recalling how incredibly fortunate it was that the bombs of 21 July did not explode. That would have altered the security atmosphere and public confidence in unforeseeable ways. The significance of what was attempted on 21 July is often overlooked, in contrast to the bombs that did explode and the controversy of Stockwell. It is worth recalling the words of Mr Justice Fulford before he handed down the very lengthy sentences to the conspirators:

Although the prosecution have not attempted to make a direct link between the attacks of 7/7 and these defendants, the incidents are a near carbon copy and what happened on 7/7 is of considerable relevance.

It demonstrates the lethal effect of the plan, at least 50 people died, 100's were wounded, 1000's were damaged by the bombings including family or friends of the dead and injured, 100's trapped in darkness underground, hearing the screams of the injured and the dying. Each defendant in this case knew what the effects of their actions would be. Their plan, on the scientific evidence, came close to success.

It is my firm conclusion that these were not isolated events but co-ordinated no doubt by an Al-Qaida inspired group.

It is no coincidence in my view that Mohammed Saddique Khan and Shehzad Tanweer (7/7) were in Pakistan at a similar time to Ibrahim (21/7) and this attack was conducted not only with a full knowledge of what had taken place on 7/7 but also organised as part of a parallel cell under the overall control of Al-Qaida.

The last reflection is the fact that, after our appeal for information on 22 July, during which the CCTV images of the failed bombers were shown, a council worker from north London identified a flat which he said three of the men had frequented. He was right: this turned out to be the bomb factory for 21 July. However, he also told police that he had noticed that a large number of empty bottles of peroxide had been being left in the bins that he emptied. At that stage we did not have one of our neighbourhood teams yet in place on that estate. If we had had then the likelihood is that the story of 21 July would not have happened – and, therefore, neither would that of the 22nd. National security depends on neighbourhood security.

7

From Charles to Jacqui

On Wednesday 9 November 2005, four months and two days after the bombs exploded on the tube and a bus, Tony Blair was outvoted in the House of Commons for the first time during his premiership. It was to be his heaviest defeat. Almost every opposition MP rejected a proposal to which he had attached significant personal prestige, as did forty-nine Labour MPs, the largest rebellion he had faced. The proposal was to raise the length of time during which those suspected of terrorism could be held after arrest by police from fourteen to ninety days. A compromise was reached which raised the limit to twenty-eight days. From that moment, the length of detention in these circumstances, while an issue of conscience for many, became a political football to some or a statement of political machismo to others.

There were many debates before the vote in Parliament, not only across the media but also in the Home Office, in No 10 and in police circles. The analysis from the security services of the threat faced by Britain was both bleak and imprecise. Of course, we had known before July that, as well as those already in custody awaiting trial for other conspiracies, there seemed to be a large number of groupings of people acting suspiciously in the British Muslim community. These were not necessarily very well organised but some were clearly raising finance, and some were travelling abroad frequently or were in contact with individuals who were already of concern. What the July bombings had then shown us was that there were yet other groups of whom the security agencies had not been aware and who had carried out attacks. We believed but could not yet prove that both sets of attacks in London had been orchestrated in some way by central Al-Qaida and we were appalled at the ambition for mass carnage in the United Kingdom that Al-Qaida seemed to possess.

We faced the terrible dilemma of when to take action against those who seemed likely to attack. Nearly 3,500 people died in the UK as a result of 'The Troubles' in Northern Ireland. As a young officer I had seen the results of the Provisional IRA (PIRA) attacks myself and had no illusion that they were anything other than a murderous and very effective terrorist organisation, but there were striking differences between them and the threat we now seemed to face. With rare exceptions, Irish Republican terrorists (and their less effective but still deadly Loyalist opponents) did not seek to die in the attacks they were planning; most of the time they gave warnings of attack; especially towards the end of the campaign, their organisation was almost entirely penetrated by British intelligence; negotiating positions, however unpalatable, were available (PIRA were bombing their way to the table, not just blowing it up); and these two last points are the most important: most of the time they did not deliberately seek mass casualties and their quarrel was of almost no interest to anyone else.

None of these factors applied to what had happened in London that summer. These people wanted to die and a suicide bomber is the ultimate intelligent bomb, as the Tavistock Square bus bomber appeared to show: frustrated at one venue, he went to another. Al-Qaida never gave warnings. We had almost no idea who they were and there was no one at a less than international level who could negotiate anything. And research published by Diego Gambetta in his book *Making Sense of Suicide Missions* showed that Al-Qaida missions were characterised by a greater appetite for more casualties per attack than even the previous front runner, the Tamil Tigers. And lastly, their recruitment campaign was practically worldwide. This is of real significance. To most people outside the areas in which specific nationalist terrorist groups operate, the quarrels of Basque separatists or the arcane distinctions of South Ossetia or the Tamil Tigers are opaque and very specific to their locality. So too with the quarrel in Northern Ireland. Writing soon after the end of the First World War, Winston Churchill described Ireland under British rule in the following terms: 'But as the deluge subsides and the waters fall short, we see the dreary steeples of Fermanagh and Tyrone emerging once again. The integrity of their quarrel is one of the few institutions that has been unaltered in the cataclysm which has swept the world.'

No one else cared, except the Irish diaspora abroad, and the British, who did not know how to answer the agony for nearly another century. But Al-Qaida is different. In the years after 9/11 central Al-Qaida has suffered many reverses: its leaders are in hiding, those who survive, but its inspiration and its message remain vibrant and universal, resonating across the world, across continents and through national borders. It can reach not only its adherents, not only those criminally attracted to extremism and violence, but also some of the lonely and the unbalanced, using new methods of communication, outlining new causes for anger and despair, suggesting new dreams of fulfilment and offering new tools of attack.

In 2008, Jonathan Evans, by then the head of MI5, said publicly that there were about 200 groupings in Britain, comprising nearly 2,000 people who were cause for concern. In the autumn of 2005 we would not have been that certain but all who heard those kinds of briefings were deeply concerned. At the meeting in the Cabinet Room on the day after Tony Blair had lost the vote, when we heard yet another grim assessment from the security services of what we did not know, the Prime Minister turned to Charles Clarke and asked him what more could we do to get the proposals through on another occasion. 'Broadcast that briefing,' was Charles's half-humorous but slightly despairing reply.

The Prime Minister was struck by the dilemma the police outlined. In previous years, when the police and security services had been fortunate enough to discover IRA active service units in operation, it was sometimes possible to weigh up the dangers inherent in following them for a long time, even if that got near to the point of their planting a bomb, because they would not instantly detonate it and there was little risk of mass casualties. This made for the best intelligence gain and for the best evidence for prosecutors. In 2005, however, we were not in that position. The intent of these people was so terrible, as was made clear by what we knew about their search for radiological, chemical and biological material, that we believed we would, in future, have to make arrests much earlier in the trail of suspicion, often of more people than we would want because we would not fully understand what was intended and who was involved. Already, in the major cases we had already seen, such as the fertiliser and ricin plots (which at that stage were largely unknown to the public or MPs because they had not yet come to trial), evidence had been gathered internationally, not just in the UK. Forensic material was being retrieved from computers, much of it needing translation, much of it encrypted. It had taken more than two weeks fully to secure the bomb scene at Leeds. Peter Clarke, the National Coordinator of Terrorist Investigations, gave evidence at a subsequent session of the Home Affairs Select Committee examining the issue. He recounted details of a case in which a particular forensic technique led to the discovery of crucial evidence but it was a technique that took fourteen days to develop the necessary images. If, in any of these cases, we had had to make early arrests, the then current fourteen-day limit would have been insufficient. This line of reasoning was prescient: the airliner plot of the summer of 2006 had almost all these features.

In the months and years of argument ahead, one of the points that was missed was how other countries deal with such matters. The Napoleonic system of continental Europe empowers examining magistrates to place individuals suspected of grave crime in 'investigative detention' without formal charges for months or years. The large paedophile ring in the French town of Angers or the alleged murderers of Meredith Kercher in 2008 in Perugia in Italy are cases in point. In such circumstances the US authorities would treat someone as a 'material witness' and set bail at an impossibly high figure. In Britain the police have a more significant role in the criminal justice system than in many other countries and so pre-trial detention is a police rather than a prosecutorial function. This appears to make it particularly objectionable, probably again as a result of ignorance based on class. There should be no doubts about its Human Rights compliance, as the longer suspects remain in police custody, the more rigorous, regular and senior becomes the judicial scrutiny of that detention. If it exceeds fourteen days the subjects will move into the prison system and only be moved back to a police station for interview. The statement used by opponents of the measure that this represents the most draconian powers in the world is to compare apples not with oranges but with goats.

Benjamin Franklin said, 'Any society that would give up a little liberty to gain a little security will deserve neither and will lose both.' Almost a century later Abraham Lincoln remarked, 'The dogmas of the quiet past are inadequate to the stormy present. As our case is new, so we must think anew and act anew.' The ninety-day figure was first suggested by Ken Jones, then head of the ACPO terrorism committee, during the course of another earlier meeting with the Prime Minister and other senior Cabinet ministers. It had been canvassed within his committee and informally with some people within the security services. It was not seen as an absolute requirement but as an outer limit for the rolling series of seven-day periods of judicially approved detention which would be used in the event of the time limit (then fourteen days) being extended. It was felt that beyond ninety days, it would be difficult to refute an allegation that this was detention without trial, as had failed so disastrously in Northern Ireland – and for which I never heard anyone argue. Nor, given limited resources, would the police ever want to hold lots of people for far longer than was necessary.

Ministers and the Prime Minister accepted our position and announced that it would be included in the forthcoming Terrorism Bill in mid-October 2005. I do not know precisely what happened next but my best guess is that Tony Blair, learning of the opposition he faced, believed three things: it was the right thing to do, the majority of the population would support such a measure and, if the Conservatives opposed it, whether he won or lost, he would be able to outflank them politically by making them look weak on terror. He had deployed Charles Clarke to negotiate and a cross-party consensus was emerging around a figure such as forty-two or possibly forty-eight days. Then ACPO in my view made a serious mistake. The vote was due on Wednesday 9 November and, on the 4th, the Friday before, a letter was sent to all Chief Constables, urging them to lobby their local MPs in favour of ninety days. For some reason this letter did not reach us in London. Ninety days was already a matter of huge controversy but the letter produced a storm of protest from all around the country, not only from opposition MPs but privately from some police chiefs as well. The letter crossed the line of what was acceptable.

I had thought a lot about this issue following two events earlier in the year. On the first I was unrepentant, which was allowing a car owned by the Metropolitan Police to be covered in Labour Party posters as the Prime Minister toured the country during the election campaign. It was an unmarked, armoured vehicle. You can't hire or borrow those and he was still the Prime Minister, under threat of assassination. This had been negotiated with the offices of the Conservative and Liberal Democrat leaders but was still criticised later by Conservative spokesmen, including MPA members. Three years later, this was to reappear as one of my errors of judgement in the *Daily Mail*'s leader on the day after my resignation. During the same campaign I had backed the introduction of identity cards, with some caveats, during an interview with David Frost. The criticism that followed was justified, because I had commented in the election purdah period, particularly given that I was not an expert on ID cards, which were themselves a topic of political controversy. November 2005 was not an election period and Ken Jones could claim to be an expert on terrorism, as could Andy Hayman and, to a more limited extent, so could I, as the man with the ultimate law-enforcement responsibility for counter-terrorism. But bringing all chief constables into the fray was wrong.

Things got difficult. The Prime Minister and other ministers, including the Police Minister, Hazel Blears, denounced the criticism and stated that the police were entitled to give their opinion about their operational needs. I had already made this point, arguing that, when the country faced a health emergency, the public were entitled to hear the opinions of the Chief Medical Officer, as they had heard from the Chief Veterinary Officer in the face of the foot and mouth epidemic, and so it should be for the police in the face of the dramatically increased threat from terrorism. Later, Shami Chakrabarti, the Director of Liberty – together with the then Shadow Home Secretary David Davis – would be very vocal in suggesting that this was inappropriate. I have always disagreed with that argument. But for now, the Prime Minister was staking his personal authority on the issue and stating that he was doing so on the advice of the police and making the actual number of days, at ninety, the pre-eminent issue. It was ninety days or defeat: he ordered Charles Clarke to stop seeking a consensus.

Charles could see defeat looming. He asked Andy Hayman to come with him and address MPs on the threat and the operational difficulties. Andy asked me if he could and should go and I could see no other course: I still can see no way out of that decision. Unfortunately, MPs from most of the parties other than Labour declined to attend, so that it was subsequently alleged that I had permitted Andy to brief the Parliamentary Labour Party, which was far from his, mine or Charles's intention.

In the same way, by the kind of unpleasant coincidence which occurs, I had long before agreed to address a lunch for the Parliamentary Press Gallery on the Tuesday, the day before the vote. It was a well-attended lunch and I could scarcely not talk about the issue. It would have been impossible for the two of us or Ken Jones to have withdrawn our support for a proposal which in large part we had ourselves initiated. However, what was thrown at Andy and me ever afterwards was that we too had crossed the political line. I do not think we did but we were swept up in the general commentary and, from now on, a battle line was drawn between me and the Tories on terrorism.

The Prime Minister lost. It was yet another coincidence that the meeting on terrorism, which I have just described, the one at which Charles Clarke had made his somewhat sceptical suggestion as to the way forward, was the very next morning after the vote. The Prime

Minister asked the meeting for any comments about the vote. John Reid, then Minister of Defence, was and is a great Celtic supporter (and is now the club's Chairman). Celtic had lost the night before. He began by sadly relaying that fact to a rather puzzled Tony Blair and then said, 'Of course, I still have faith in the manager,' to much laughter.

It was after these developments that the regime of control orders had to be brought in to deal with those believed to be a danger to the United Kingdom in connection with terrorism but on the basis not of evidence that could be given in court but of secret intelligence that could not. The previous system of indefinite detention unless the suspect agreed to leave the UK had been struck down by the courts. The control order regime – termed house arrest as shorthand by the press – has been fiercely criticised by the Conservatives and Liberal Democrats and many others ever since, and has slowly unfurled over the subsequent years. What puzzles me most about those who attack the system, however, is that they never see any need to suggest an alternative, except the future in the introduction of intercept material as evidence in court. I have always supported that suggestion, put forward trenchantly by the Conservatives, but at the moment there appears no likelihood of such a system being successfully developed for use in the peculiarly adversarial criminal legal system of England and Wales.

Meanwhile, whether or not I supported that aspect of Conservative policy, some Tories were gunning for me. While most of the Conservatives on the MPA were pleasant enough, with Bob Neill, now an MP but then their leader, promising me his support on the way into the Commissionership, it seemed to me that an individual GLA member, Richard Barnes, had very much taken against me. In part this may have been because he had unsuccessfully stood to be Chair of the MPA in 2004 and he saw my inevitably close working relationship with Len Duvall as further evidence of my closeness with New Labour. He had some reason to be bitter, although it had nothing to do with me. The rules of the GLA are that its members should be allocated to its four constituent bodies, such as the MPA, according to the political make-up of the GLA itself. However, Ken Livingstone decided that this meant that he had to do this only in overall terms and that he could separately decide the number of members of each party that should be allocated to each individual body. He therefore arranged the numbers so that there were more Tories on the Fire Authority and fewer on the MPA.

This kind of politics then collided with the press. Completely out of the blue, at an MPA meeting a couple of months later, in January 2006, Cindy Butts, whom I described in Chapter 1 as being very involved in our Trident programme, asked me to comment on the way the press treated murders of members of different races differently. This was a subject in which I was very interested and on which I had previously commented publicly. In this particular instance, the murder of a young, white lawyer, Tom ap Rhys Pryce, in the course of a robbery while he was on his way home in Willesden, north London, had received a great deal of publicity. This was street crime hitting the middle class and the story had the additional detail that he was about to be married and that he had dropped some of his wedding plans in the street as he died. Nothing I said then – I described it as a 'terrible' crime – or will comment now takes away the senseless and distressing nature of his death. But, in the same few days, there were three other murders: a young black woman dismembered in south London, a young black man shot in north London and an Asian man, Balbir Matharu, murdered in east London as he tried to prevent his van being stolen. These murders had received very little publicity. I said, as I had said before, that media organisations appeared themselves to be suffering from institutional racism. I mentioned the exceptions, such as the extensive coverage of the murder of Damilola Taylor and that of Stephen Lawrence, or the murders of Letitia Shakespeare and Charlene Ellis at a New Year party in Birmingham, but made clear my view that in general the murders of minority citizens were of much less interest to the press than those of white people. This made the investigations more difficult and was obvious to and distressing for the families of the victims. So far, so good but what I said next was going too far. I then commented on the iconic murders of Holly Wells and Jessica Chapman at Soham, saying that few people could understand why these murders – although I described them as dreadful – became the biggest news story in Britain and that it was to do with the gender, age and race of the victims. The comments were largely regarded as unexceptional by those members still present. At the end of the meeting Cindy and Len congratulated me on what I had said but Joy Bentley said she was concerned that some journalists were really angry and that this could be a bad story. I should have remembered the old adage that dealing with the press is like picnicking with a tiger: it is exciting but the tiger always eats last.

The Met press operation, although working twenty-four hours, was much reduced between about 9pm and 7am. There was no night editor. There soon would be. I was pretty bullish about what I had said because I believed it to be right. At about 1.30am Richard Barnes rang me at my London flat and told me that he thought he ought to let me know that my comments about Soham were on the front page of *The Times* and the *Sun*. He seemed to indicate that he had not spoken to the media until he had been rung at about 11pm. He ended the call with the rather chilling words: 'Nothing personal, Ian, just politics.' I rang Dick Fedorcio. He had not been aware either but by about 5am it was obviously the main news of the day. At the much happier MPA meeting in the previous July I had been invited to criticise the press over some of its misreporting during the events of that month. I had reminded them of Voltaire's words on his deathbed, when asked if he abjured the devil and all his works: 'This is no time to make new enemies.' Now, I had not only made new enemies but I had given significant ammunition to some old ones and I had to go on to Radio 4 to defend my position.

In addition to the appointment of a night editor, there were a number of other consequences. First, just like the letter to John Gieve, this was added to the 'list' of my mistakes, whenever they were compiled. Second, I wrote a letter to the parents of both of the murdered girls to apologise if I had added to their distress, and had it delivered that evening. Third, a few days later I confronted Richard Barnes, in the presence of Moir Stewart, suggesting it was odd that he had not spoken to the press before 11pm although the first edition of *The Times*, printed I understand before that time, apparently contained quotations from him. He arrived in the room as a critic: he left, with his shirt drenched in sweat, as a real enemy. Fourth, a few weeks later a police constable from Kentish Town emailed me. He said that he had started serving there shortly after I had left and had heard that I was a good bloke. He said that I ought to look therefore at a particular page of *The Insider*, the book by the former editor of the *Daily Mirror*, Piers Morgan. I found the entry, which reads:

> SATURDAY 17 AUGUST 2002
>
> The bodies of the two missing school girls, Holly Wells and Jessica Chapman, were found today after a two week hunt since they disappeared from near their school in Soham, Cambridgeshire. It's a story that has gripped the nation and dominated the news every day, fuelled by a painfully evocative photo of them both smiling in Manchester United shirts hours before they vanished. Someone raised an interesting point today, though. Would we all have been quite so gripped if they had been two black girls? I think the answer, and it is a shameful one, is no.

Almost lastly, for the rest of my time as Commissioner – and even after I left – black and Asian people would and do come up to me and thank me for what I said. Beyond that, it is worth noting that, while writing this passage, I Googled Balbir Matharu and Tom ap Rhys Pryce: one came up with about 350, the other with some 2,500 hits.

The knives were now out and they came flashing in again two months later, in March. I was away on a four-day skiing trip with my son Josh. As part of its investigation the IPCC had taken away the recording machine on which I had recorded my conversations with Roy Clarke and Nick Hardwick. As far as I know I had inherited possession of such a machine from John Stevens and I imagine he did from his predecessor. In the few months that I had it I used it six times: those two calls, another one to the IPCC on another occasion, one to a journalist with his consent and one to a family member by mistake and once during the previous September when I was in my office later than normal, about

7.30pm. I think I was going out to dinner a bit later on. I had let all the staff go except for my protection officers. The telephone rang on my desk and a young woman announced that she was ringing from the office of the Attorney General, Peter Goldsmith, who wanted a word. At this time a debate – probably the fifth during my career – was underway about the admissibility of intercept evidence, that is what is said in telephone calls that are listened to by the police or the security services, which can only be done with the authority of the Home Secretary. Unlike in most jurisdictions, in the UK intercepted material cannot be used in court as evidence. In the major corruption case which I had dealt with, Operation Gallery, the police officer defendant tried to produce the actual records of intercept material as part of his defence, so I had more knowledge of the intricacies of intercept law than most. However, at this stage some of the proposals were getting very intricate indeed.

The Attorney General knew that I supported the introduction of intercept material as evidence and wanted to explain his current thinking about different forms of warrantry, a warrant being what the Home Secretary signs for the interception to take place. At this stage of his thinking he was beginning to talk about, I think, three forms of warrantry, some of which would be subject to Public Interest Immunity, some of which ... At this stage I switched on the recorder because I felt I would need to listen to this again, which I did the next morning and wrote down some notes to discuss with colleagues. Out of politeness I should, of course, have asked Peter if he minded but it did not strike me as an odd thing to do as I expected that he had someone listening to the call in his private office so that a note could be made; this is an entirely common but not universal practice for ministers and senior civil servants and sometimes they mention it and sometimes not.

Suddenly, somewhere on the ski slopes in Austria, I got a call that the existence of this recording was in the hands of the press and before I got back home it was front-page news. Richard Barnes called for me 'to consider my position'. I apologised to Peter Goldsmith and made clear that I had not used the recording in any way to his or anyone's detriment. Of course, the question that I was considering was not my position but who had leaked the existence of recorded calls to the media. And for that, I looked in the direction of, but could not prove the involvement of, the organisation which had taken away the machine on which they were recorded: the IPCC. As so often, there was one amusing consequence. The fact that I knew its editor, Rebekah Wade, had not stopped the *Sun* from running a front-page headline about this affair, reading 'Blair is Doomed'. That evening my wife and I had been invited to a dinner at Claridge's by a media group, where I was to be the principal speaker. The very first person we met on arrival was Rebekah. My wife greeted her with a broad grin and the words 'Great headline, Rebekah'. It is the only time I have seen Rebekah lost for words. She subsequently sent me a presentation copy of that day's front page.

A series of shocking leaks about Stockwell followed. During April the nature of Brian Paddick's testimony became public knowledge via the BBC, as recounted in Chapter 9. In May the *News of the World* ran further anonymous leaks about the investigation, including the ludicrous charge that I had not been told about the identity of Jean Charles de Menezes because I 'took bad news badly'. Catherine Crawford very decently and publicly stated that this was simply not true. The need for a night editor became absolute in June, when, listening to *What the Papers Say* on the radio, I heard that I was to face manslaughter charges. 'Met Chief could face charge over Menezes,' read the headline in the *Observer*, with 'legal sources close to the CPS' noting that 'prosecutors are considering whether the command team are ultimately responsible, a decision that could give rise to a charge of gross negligence manslaughter against Blair and two other senior figures.' I have to admit that it was a fairly shocking moment. It didn't take me long to work out that it would be highly improbable that anyone could be prosecuted for something as serious as manslaughter without being interviewed by the investigators but I felt very sorry for Cressida Dick because she knew she could face such a charge. Roger Alton, editor of the *Observer*, subsequently apologised to me.

I had also had real concerns about the way a *Sunday Times* article the

17. The shell of the bus which exploded in Tavistock Square, 7 July: what we were looking at was not the result of a power surge.

23. Jean Charles de Menezes: the shrine to his memory at Stockwell underground station. A genuine tragedy and perhaps the fifty-third victim of the London bombings of 2005.

24. Andy Hayman

25. Brian Paddick

26. Tarique Ghuffur

*Turbulence at
the Yard*

"we hoped you'd make things easy for us, Sir Ian."

27. September 2008: As Mark Twain remarked, 'the report of my death is an exaggeration': a cartoon view of my statement under the famous revolving sign at Scotland Yard.

28. Boris and Ken: the only two politicians universally known by their first names: Ken always polled ahead of Labour but not when the polls were so grim for the national party. Perhaps he was premature to announce at the Party Conference that he was 'giving the Boris Johnson memorial lecture'.

previous October had been constructed. This alleged that I was considering resigning over de Menezes. It emerged from a question-and-answer
session following a speech to the charity, the Windsor Leadership Trust.
The questioner asked me about resignations in public life exactly as follows:

> It's an interesting thing that public figures are very often, when some-
> thing goes wrong in the organisation there is a baying for blood. What
> makes it for you, and I don't mean to personalise this because I really
> want to avoid the personalisation, but you've actually thought about it,
> what makes it right or wrong to decide to resign, in any walk of public
> life, when that baying for blood goes on?

The main part of my reply was:

> In a particular interview, I was asked a question, had I considered
> resigning? And it was a point I almost made earlier which is, I think
> you would be arrogant to the point of you know absurdity not to
> reflect on what people were saying around you.
>   But where does resignation end?
>   Well of course it might end fairly soon, but where does resignation
> end [*laughter*], where does resignation begin and end? It seems to me
> about whether the organisation has behaved so poorly, so deliberately
> over a period of time that your leadership, and you have been in charge
> of it for a length of time. I mean I think there's an issue about difficul-
> ties aren't on day two you know, so – the – that really frankly it's time
> for you to take that decision.
>   It's a rare decision. I think for people to do, but I am always
> impressed by somebody who decides to make that decision. If it's jus-
> tified. I would not respect somebody who just resigned because the
> heat was getting too much which I think is a different piece. We will
> see where this leads, but I can tell you that I have absolutely no inten-
> tion, on the knowledge that I have of the events around that, of going
> anywhere near it.

The *Sunday Times* headline and opening part of the article ran:

MET BOSS: I MAY BE FORCED TO QUIT

ROBERT WINNETT AND DAVID LEPPARD

SIR IAN BLAIR, the Metropolitan police commissioner, has admitted he may soon be forced to resign over the shooting of an innocent Brazilian man on the London Underground.

Britain's top policeman told a private gathering of business leaders and officials last week that he might have to go 'fairly soon' over the killing of Jean Charles de Menezes.

Describing the pressure he faced over the botched operation, he said: 'Where does resignation end? Of course, it might end fairly soon.'

When Dick Fedorcio, my head of press, played a tape of this exchange to the editor of the *Sunday Times*, John Witherow, he apparently accepted that I had some cause to feel aggrieved. However, what I had done, by complaining to him was make an enemy of another journalist, David Leppard, who had been in the audience and who would go on to write a number of other hostile stories about me even well after I had resigned.

It was sometime around this time that I first spoke to Gordon Brown, then Chancellor. He had been giving a speech in Victoria when he spotted me as he was leaving. He came over and sympathised with me over the level and nature of the press coverage I was receiving. 'Now you know what it is like to be a Cabinet minister,' he said as he walked away.

But that was part of what was wrong. The media had started to treat the Yard in a new way. Stories about it had moved from the middle pages to front-page splashes (something that has continued under my successor, as Damian Green, the G20 and the *News of the World* taping stories show). In part, this stemmed from the openness with which I had tried to deal with the media, in part from the controversies on my watch, but it was also a reflection of the way in which crime and terrorism had become such a central political and therefore media issue. The days of the crime correspondents were ending and they were being replaced by Home Affairs and Security correspondents, men and women who saw the Yard as another part of Whitehall, in the same sense as the security services have always been. But the security services don't hold open public meetings and I was not a Cabinet minister. I did not have – and the Commissioner should not have to have – the kind of press machine designed to support ministers. The pressure of these kinds of stories was very wearing and certainly impacted not only on me but also on my family and particularly my wife.

Much later, in the summer of 2008, Felicity and I were invited to lunch at Chequers by Gordon and Sarah Brown. I had known Sarah before she married Gordon and it was a very pleasant lunch of about eight people. The press were being very critical of Gordon and it was obvious that Sarah was hurting for him. At one point Sarah and Felicity were talking about the media pressure and Sarah said, with a wry smile, 'But we all signed up to this, didn't we?' But in many senses Felicity hadn't: she had married a young police Inspector, not the Chancellor, who was almost certain to become Prime Minister. Nor had Jane Williams, who had married an academic not an archbishop; nor Katherine Gieve who had married a graduate student not the sometimes embattled Deputy Governor of the Bank of England; nor Pippa Dannatt, who married a young officer not the sometimes much praised but sometimes fiercely criticised head of the Army. Of course all had married partners who they knew were capable of high achievement but none could have expected the level of press comment that they have had to endure. All of these are our friends and conversations with them and many others make clear the toll that modern public life now takes on families in a public service world subject to such scrutiny and sometimes such trenchant criticism. None of us was prepared for the extent, and sometimes what we perceived as the unfairness, of the media coverage we received. Not that politicians are immune: Michael Howard's wife has spoken publicly about the anger she felt over press criticism of her husband and Cherie Blair's dislike of the press was well known: but, to different extents, they had signed up first.

In every dealing I had with Gordon, he was interested and informative and committed. He laughs a lot and is far more at ease with people than is generally portrayed. But it was obvious to me that the criticism he had received in the year between taking office and that lunch was taking a brutal toll. It is a cruel profession. I suppose I never saw that at such close quarters as I did in the case of Charles Clarke, who had been such a support to me in my first year as Commissioner.

Suddenly, at the very end of April 2006, Charles discovered just what kind of a disaster the Home Office can produce. It was reported that more than 1,000 foreign nationals imprisoned in Britain, including three murderers and a number of other serious offenders, had simply been released in recent years instead of being considered for deportation, nearly 300 of them since the problem had been discovered at a time when Charles was already Home Secretary. David Davis, Shadow Home Secretary, scenting his second Home Secretary scalp, called for his resignation. Charles fought back, held a press conference and briefed MPs in the House. However, his was just the worst of the disasters afflicting the Prime Minister at the time: the Health Secretary had been booed at the nurses' annual conference and John Prescott's affair with his secretary had been uncovered.

Charles's problem was that nobody could tell quite how bad the situation was or when it could be sorted out and, after a very poor showing in the European elections, Tony Blair decided upon a reshuffle. Charles had been at the centre of the Labour Party for nearly three decades, being Chief of Staff to Neil Kinnock for nearly ten years. He was very loyal to Tony Blair and had driven through many difficult policies in Education and the Home Office. Because I liked him so much I took the chance to see him as the afternoon before the announcement of the reshuffle wore on. There was no laughter now as he paced his room in his socks. He made clear that he feared but could not really believe that he would be asked to move in the reshuffle. He had so much he wanted to do in the Home Office. It was like seeing a great beast at bay. I felt so sorry for him and hoped that he would prevail but it was not to be. I know now that he was offered other posts in government but he turned them down and returned to the back benches.

With Charles Clarke went the one chance in generations of restructuring British policing. He had grasped the nettle that had slowly developed since the 1960s: the completely illogical structure of British policing. There are forty-three forces in England, Wales and Northern Ireland, which will remain far too many for as long as they all have the responsibility for delivering a complete range of policing services and vary so widely in size between the two extremes of the Met and the City of London forces at more than 50,000 and under 1,000 staff. The range of sizes of other forces lies between many not much larger than the City and the two 13,000-plus organisations of West Midlands and Manchester. Individually the smaller forces may or may not deliver a good local policing service but all of them must struggle to deal with organised crime, terrorism and even homicide. Their overheads are necessarily a larger proportion of total costs than those of the bigger forces, with the exception of the Met, which has additional senior staff to deal with some of the complex issues it confronts. Charles would have changed this patchwork arrangement and so persuasive and determined was he that astonishingly the majority of Chief Constables agreed, although the majority of Police Authorities did not. I doubt this opportunity will return in my lifetime.

Charles was replaced by John Reid, whom I met in his House of Commons room a day or two after his appointment. Reid is a fascinating man; a sixteen-year-old school-leaver who subsequently obtained a PhD. But he did not know much about policing. His first question to me was whether the Commissioner was the Chief Constable of London and his next comment, in his strong Scottish accent, was 'You're not my problem, Commissioner.' Fortunately the emphasis was on the word 'You're' because John's view of his problem was, famously and publicly, that the Home Office was 'not fit for purpose'. He was very polite and very supportive but he abandoned the restructuring of police forces, split the Home Office in two through the creation of a Ministry of Justice and concentrated almost all his time on counter-terrorism. His drive in this field dramatically increased the amount and seniority of Home Office involvement in counter-terrorism, providing a great deal of assistance to the Met in its national role, but it did mean that other areas of policing were neglected and one of them, in particular, was starting to worry me: the Olympics.

A new urgency arose in the Home Office and then across government to produce a coherent narrative about terrorism. This emerged as a strategy called CONTEST, with a series of strands, Pursue, Prevent, Protect, Prepare, dealing in turn with the investigation of terrorism, the prevention of extremism, the protection of the national critical infrastructure and preparation to mitigate the effects of successful attacks. In 2006 John Reid, probably like all of us, was more interested in Pursue than Prevent, sometimes for reasons of personal experience, like his confrontation with a member of Al-Muhajaroun in east London. Reid was addressing a community group in September 2006 when a gigantic man, white robed and bearded, a convert to Islam, began to heckle him. Reid would always give as good as he got but this was getting very disruptive. Later I saw the news broadcast of the event and watched as the smallest, youngest PCSO I had ever seen tried unsuccessfully to remove this enormous figure from the room. However, I also have no doubt that Reid was motivated less by such events and more by what we all came to refer to as Operation Overt, the large-scale investigation of a plot to blow up airliners flying from Britain to the United States, certainly the most serious terrorist plot yet uncovered in Britain.

Throughout the late spring of 2006 the security services and ourselves began to become very concerned about a group of fairly young men and women largely but not exclusively based around High Wycombe. When I first went to Thames Valley I remember assuming, largely because of its name, that High Wycombe would be a Cotswoldesque town. Apart from the fact it is nowhere near the Cotswolds, it is nothing like that and has more poverty, crime and racial tension than might be expected in this prosperous part of the country. Nothing, however, would have suggested that a group of young people there, mostly born or raised in Britain, would become involved in a plot of ingenious audacity. One of the individuals under observation kept making purchases of hardware and was seen disposing of empty bottles of peroxide, both of which seemed incompatible with his lifestyle. A huge operation was mounted under the codename Overt. Intensive and intrusive surveillance went on into August, both in Wycombe and in London. The Americans knew of the plot and were very nervous, as there were indications that transatlantic flights could be involved. The Pakistani authorities also knew something and we were all concerned about a man called Rashid Rauf, long suspected of being an important link between central Al-Qaida and the UK. The briefing went to the highest levels of government on both sides of the Atlantic. Then, crucially, Rauf was arrested in Pakistan and orders were given to make arrests on Wednesday the 9th. This was earlier than we wanted to because the exact details of the group's intentions were not yet clear.

The threat assessment against the UK was raised to critical and there was mass disruption to airports because no passenger was going to be allowed to bring liquids on to aeroplanes. The plot that was uncovered was a brilliant way of getting past airport security after 9/11: to create bombs out of a number of components each of which would be carried separately, each of which would look completely normal and all of which would then be put together on the plane. Security personnel would not look twice at bottles of fruit drinks with unopened tops, at disposable cameras or at AA batteries but this was the combination which was to be used: fruit juice which was actually hydrogen peroxide, and batteries and flash cameras, which combined together in a particular way would detonate the explosive. A list of flights was found on a pen drive, to San Francisco, Washington, Chicago and New York, to Montreal and Toronto: the martyrdom videos had been made. Had this plot succeeded and all or even some of the planes exploded, either over the Atlantic or worse over American and Canadian cities, then as one colleague said, 'No plane would have flown out of Britain for months and when they did, every passenger would be flying naked and without luggage.'

It was no wonder that John Reid announced that the government would again bring forward legislation to increase the length of detention in terrorist cases and no wonder that my Deputy, Paul Stephenson, whom I asked to front the press for the Yard, described the plot as being to commit 'mass-murder on an unimaginable scale'. By chance the head of MI5, Eliza Manningham-Buller, herself was caught up in the draconian airport security that now descended over the Western world. She watched all her make-up being thrown away and told me that, for the first time in her professional life, she was really tempted to say 'Do you know who I am?' (she didn't). It has so far taken two trials, the latest ending in September 2009, to convict the main conspirators with their offences. It therefore took three years before the public could be told about the astonishing scale of this conspiracy: the British 9/11. Sentencing the ring leader, Abdulla Ahmed Ali, the trial judge who, by coincidence, was Mr Justice Henriques, who two years earlier would preside over the Met's Health and Safety trial, told him that he had been convicted of 'the most grave and wicked conspiracy ever proven within this jurisdiction'. He received a minimum sentence of forty years.

Operation Overt had begun only a few months after the raid at Forest Gate, in which one of the occupants was accidentally shot by one of the officers entering the premises. There was a great deal of public concern about the shooting and the overall character of the operation, although the subsequent IPCC investigation declared the Met's action in entering the houses in the manner and at the time that we did to be 'necessary and proportionate'. For those of us involved in the operation our concern was much more that this was the first time that armed officers had had to enter premises in chemical and radiological protection suits. The stakes were getting ever higher and it was the events of this summer, coming so soon after the drama of the summer of 2005, that really proved that the UK now combined being the foremost Al-Qaida target of any country except the USA and Israel, with being apparently much easier to penetrate than either of those. The significance of the Pakistan connection was also becoming acutely worrying.

That July I had decided to take my family for the kind of last great holiday you have together before the children travel independently. We were to have a two-centre holiday, the first week on safari in Tanzania and the second on a beach in Zanzibar. I never made it to Zanzibar. In the middle of the first week my office contacted me and I was asked to contact Paul Stephenson at a certain time. I had been given some special kind of encrypted satellite telephone but, when I telephoned, that did not work. As I stood in the middle of the bush in irritation, my daughter Amelia called from the back of the truck from which we were looking at the wildlife for me not to worry, she had a signal on her mobile. So I used that to learn that the Crown Prosecution Service had finally decided to announce what it was going to do about the death of Jean Charles de Menezes and to agree with Paul that there was no choice but for me to return to the UK. I flew back to await the CPS announcement.

When it came, I felt great relief for Cressida Dick and the two officers who had fired the shots but utter disbelief at the idea of a prosecution on Health and Safety grounds. Health and Safety had been a vexed issue for my two predecessors Paul Condon and John Stevens, who had faced charges under the Health and Safety Act after a young police officer chasing a burglar fell through a roof and died. They were acquitted but had gone through a time-wasting and humiliating experience: the law was changed, so that the prosecution to come was against the office of the Commissioner not the Commissioner in person. But, in a sense, the earlier prosecution had been in the right territory, prosecuting the police as employers, not in terms of operations. It is appropriate to prosecute the police on Health and Safety grounds if officers are injured on a motorway at night because they did not have reflective jackets, but to use that legislation to prosecute the force for the manner in which officers carried out operations opened up a complete nightmare. Policing is, by definition, about emergency situations and I had spent years giving commendations to officers who had risked their lives taking guns from armed men or rescuing people from burning cars which exploded seconds later, while my senior officers were continuously planning live firearms operations entailing significant risks. The Bill which brought the Police Service belatedly into the remit of Health and Safety in 1999 was described in its opening summary as being intended to 'make provisions about the health, safety and welfare at work of members of police forces, special constables, other persons having the powers and privileges of a constable and police cadets: and for connected purposes'. This prosecution certainly extended the meaning of 'connected purposes'. The indictment was a legal labyrinth:

> A failure to discharge a duty under section 3(1) of the Health and Safety at Work Act 1974. The particulars of the offence are that between 20th July 2005 and 23rd July 2005, the Office of the Commissioner of Police of the Metropolis, within the meaning of the Health and Safety at Work Act 1974, failed to conduct its undertaking, namely the investigation and surveillance of a location believed to be connected with a suspected suicide bomber, in the planning and implementation of the surveillance, pursuit, arrest and detention of a suspected suicide bomber, and the prevention of a suicide bombing, in such a way as to ensure that persons not in its employment, namely members of the public, including Jean Charles de Menezes, were not exposed to risks to their health and safety in contravention of the duty imposed by section 3(1) of the Health and Safety at Work Act 1974.

I believed that the prosecution should be resisted as a matter of principle, a decision in which I was supported by every police officer I ever met, as well as from the left in the shape of Ken Livingstone, who remarked that he doubted whether 'Al-Qaida will be considering the implications for health and safety legislation when they are planning their terrorist activities', from the right in the shape of Alasdair Palmer, writing in the *Telegraph*: 'It seems that an Act whose intention was to protect ordinary people will actually end up exposing them to mortal danger' and, finally, by most of those quoted in the October 2007 edition of *Safety and Health Practitioner*, which carried an article about the case during the trial, one of the contributors to which stated that: 'An inquiry found no evidence of culpability amongst the officers involved – either those carrying out the operation or those directing it. To substitute a breach of the HSWA for some form of charges for unlawful killing looks suspiciously like stable door-bolting.'

One of the few detective writers I enjoy is the Swedish author, Henning Mankell. In his 1999 novel *Sidetracked*, one character puts the case succinctly. "Against regulations," he said, smiling. "But if you had to follow all the regulations that exist, police work would have been forbidden long ago by the Health and Safety watchdogs.' Some things apparently cross the North Sea.

My decision to defend the case, after advice from leading counsel, was declared by many who wanted to bring me down to be a bad call when the Met lost the case when it finally came to trial the following autumn. I have never believed it was: the bad call was the decision to mount the case at all, not only because of its implications for policing, which have since been the subject of many discussions with the Health and Safety Executive (unusually, this was not its prosecution decision but that of the CPS), not only because it delayed the actual inquest, to the great detriment of the interests of the family as well as the Met, but also, crucially, because the firearms officers themselves were not called, it provided only a partial examination of the circumstances which led to the death. All that was some time away.

The year 2006 ended with yet another extraordinary, Al-Qaida-inspired plot being uncovered, this time to kidnap and behead a Muslim British soldier in the Birmingham area and then post the beheading on the internet. Houses in the West Midlands were raided in early 2007 and those involved subsequently received long prison sentences. A major concern about this case was the speed with which the media learned of the story so that some early editions ran with screaming headlines about the plot, before all the suspects had been arrested and the local police had had time to alert local community leaders.

It is not always the gravity of particular allegations which brings them to the attention of a Commissioner: it can also be the question of who is involved in them. The 'Cash for Honours' inquiry had begun with a letter to me from the Scottish National Party MP Angus MacNeil in March 2006. It opened: 'You will be aware of the provisions of the Honours (Prevention of Abuses) Act, 1925 ...' It went on to allege that four wealthy businessmen who had lent the Labour Party large sums of money were subsequently nominated for peerages by Tony Blair. They did not get them because they were refused by the House of Lords Appointments Commission. I was just about aware of Maundy Gregory and the honours abuses of Lloyd George but this particular piece of legislation did not feature significantly in my detective training. MacNeil's letter, which I passed on to the Specialist Crime Directorate, was to be the cause of an investigation which brought Scotland Yard detectives into No 10 and was, in a sense, a triumph for the kind of force which Peel had founded. There are many countries in which it would be unimaginable or unlawful for a sitting prime minister or president to be interviewed in a criminal inquiry, although it did happen in the United States to Bill Clinton. As the scope of the case was mapped out by John Yates and his team, Paul Stephenson, John and I sat down to consider how to handle the case.

The story is well known but there were a number of features about it that made it particularly difficult. The first was that it was bound to be protracted and I had to work with a number of the protagonists, including the Prime Minister, other ministers and senior civil servants who would be bound to come within the scope of the inquiry. There was also the significant difficulty that I knew a central character, Lord Levy. My wife and I had been invited to his house for Friday Sabbath and had got on very well with him and his wife. He is a very likeable man. My wife was involved with some of the charity work such as the women's interfaith network, which Gilda Levy runs, and they had had dinner with us in return. We therefore agreed that I would 'recuse' myself – a word I learned from this case – and would only be included on a 'need to know' basis. This was the same approach as that taken by the Director of Public Prosecutions, Ken McDonald, who also knew many of the potential players. John would lead the case, while Paul was to act as a sounding board and source of advice for him. I gave John only one instruction: that, whatever he did, the investigation was to be so thorough that no one could allege a whitewash and there could be no prospect of the Yard being shamed by a second investigation being ordered.

The second source of difficulty was that this was to be a case fought out in the media. Within the Met there has long been an apparently unstoppable culture of leaks but I believe that the Met played nothing but a straight bat over this case. All the officers involved knew the penalty which would fall on them in the event of their being found to have leaked anything, and much of what appeared in the press was either inaccurate or surprisingly limited. Part of the process of investigation involves pre-interview disclosure of evidence, which passes through many hands on its way to those who are to be interviewed. The timing of a number of revelations appeared to be linked with this process. Whatever the sources, and whatever the accuracy, however, it was obvious to us that, as in the case of David Kelly, the formidable briefing machine of central government – and indeed Labour interests on the MPA and at City Hall – was at work, rubbishing the inquiry.

For the first time I had ever seen, John Yates was clearly strained and uneasy. As well as the press pressure, he was uneasy for three reasons. First, he had made clear to the CPS and to counsel that, whatever proof was found, short of a smoking gun, this case was going to rely on a weak foundation: it was likely that most of the people who could have known what had gone on would have to be treated as suspects themselves. Were the case to have a chance of reaching court, it would probably therefore be necessary for one witness to turn Queen's evidence against the others or to force any defendants into what is termed 'a cut-throat defence': it wasn't me, it was the others. While this was true, counsel still advised that the investigation should continue, as it always remained possible that documentary or other evidence would be found. Second, the case was taking an inordinately long time because some of those involved were, quite properly, invoking the concept of 'legally privileged material'. Third, John, Paul and I knew that the Prime Minister was being interviewed in the status of a witness; we also believed that, if the investigators decided that something they found or something he said in interview changed this status into that of a suspect for the commission of a criminal offence, Tony Blair would immediately resign as Prime Minister. This had never been made explicit but there was innuendo all round us and the press continually asked about the Prime Minister's status in the inquiry. We therefore faced the prospect that an inquiry about the chances of success of which we were already uneasy might lead to the premature resignation of a Prime Minister. We also believed that, if this happened, the vengeance of the government and the political classes on the Yard would make Alastair Campbell's treatment of the BBC look tame.

However, Tony Blair's status never changed and on 20 March 2007 the police dossier was handed to the CPS, just over a year after the investigation had begun. It was over 200 pages long and had more than 6,000 separate supporting documents. As well as offences involving the abuse of the honours system, the report dealt with possible offences of attempting to pervert the course of justice. John and the team believed that they had carried out a first-class investigation. Silence followed for a long time. Two things became clear. First, no announcement was going to be made until Tony Blair had left office at the end of June. Second, the very aspect that had caused concern from the beginning was to be the undoing of the case. The smoking gun had not been found and it was determined that there was insufficient evidence to justify criminal charges against anyone involved. John Yates had, however, done what I had asked him to do: no one suggested that the Yard's investigation had been anything less than thorough.

Given the nature of the allegations and their connection to the heart of government, I can see no choice in the decision – of which I think the Met can be proud – to investigate 'Cash for Honours' but the investigation was only the first, although the most high-profile, of a new form of political case. It had an echo of another new phenomenon, complaints from the public about comments made in the media on matters that previously would have been considered fair comment but were now classified as, for instance, homophobic. For example, ordinary detectives at Hammersmith, because that is where the BBC's headquarters are, found themselves investigating comments made on Radio 4 that homosexual couples were not fit to adopt children. As Deputy Commissioner, I had taken steps to prevent these wastes of public money. Now, as opposed to members of the public, politicians were calling in the Yard for what sometimes appeared mainly to be for political advantage instead of using their own processes. And then the Yard found itself tripping over Parliamentary procedures and privileges. The spectacle in 2009 of politicians defending 'the system' over expenses was to be prefigured the year before by the case of Derek Conway MP, in which what would have been a perfectly proper investigation of apparent fraud involving expensive but dubious payments to his family members was totally compromised by the way in which the authorities of the House of Commons had investigated the case and then published their conclusions. In the 'Cash for Honours' case, John Yates had constantly to defend his investigation against being compromised by the House of Commons Public Administration Committee. As with the Electoral Commission and allegations of electoral fraud, there needs to be a review which brings the police in at the right moment, neither too early, as in most electoral matters, or too late, as in Conway.

The eventual and unconnected resignation of Tony Blair was followed by the appointment of the new Prime Minister, Gordon Brown, and a new Home Secretary, Jacqui Smith, the first woman ever to hold the post. And their appointments were to be followed by more bombs. I had been rung by John Reid one Sunday morning with the news that he would be stepping down from the Cabinet when Tony Blair left office. I believed the reasons he gave me, which were that he wanted to give Gordon a clear run and not be seen as the leader of a putative opposition within the new Cabinet and that, after a series of bruising Cabinet posts, he wanted a rest. But his departure left his department in disarray. I believe that his decision to split the Home Office was insufficiently thought through, however difficult the situation he had inherited: splitting police activity from criminal justice policy seemed unfortunate and erecting departmental barriers between the respective missions of police and probation would make joined-up delivery on the ground more difficult. Whatever the position, John was the architect of the change and it was a problematic time to depart.

Worse, this was my fourth Home Secretary in less than four years. It felt a bit like an Oscar Wilde situation: to lose one Home Secretary may be regarded as a misfortune; to lose three seems like carelessness. The top of the Home Office had long seemed short of senior civil servants but in recent years it had also seen significant changes of personnel. I had been around longer than almost any of its policy makers.

I had worked for senior women in the police before and I was pleased to be working for the first woman Home Secretary. What I was to find was how difficult it is for a woman in such a high-profile position. I was horrified at the treatment that was meted out to her by commentators and cartoonists. It started with her cleavage and got worse: it is hard to imagine a man getting similar treatment over his body shape.

Jacqui Smith's previous role in government had been as Chief Whip, although she had also served in Education and Health. I knew of her but we had never met. With John Reid going, there had been much speculation as to who would be the new Home Secretary. When I heard about Jacqui's appointment I expected to be asked to come in and see her in the next few days. I did not expect to be telephoning her and introducing myself before breakfast. I was not the first to call her. Andy Hayman had done that, about the same time as he had called me. The bombers had wanted to mark Gordon Brown's first day in office.

I was called at about 3am on that Friday morning and told that a large car bomb had been found outside a nightclub in Haymarket in central London. I asked to be collected from my London flat just after dawn and visited the taped-off scene in the early light. Once again the abiding impression was of the silence in the centre of a city that is never normally silent. Haymarket slopes down from near Piccadilly Circus to the entrance to Trafalgar Square. Looking down from the top end, I saw an old green Mercedes saloon partly visible under a tarpaulin on the left side of the road and parked directly outside the open doors of a night-club called 'Tiger Tiger'. The officers on the scene told me that smoke had been seen inside the car by an ambulance crew, who had called the police. Hundreds of revellers had been inside the club at the time. The bomb had been disabled by Met explosives officers.

As the long day unfolded, the scale of the intended attack, the luck of the escape, the bravery of the bomb-disposal officers and echoes of Iraq all became clear. First, there was not one car bomb but two: a second, blue Mercedes had been parked at the bottom of Haymarket. It had been ticketed as illegally parked and removed to a car pound in nearby Park Lane by a parking contractor who is surely a very lucky man: like the first car, it contained many gallons of petrol, gas cylinders and bags of nails. Had the first bomb gone off a huge fireball would have rushed straight into the club and there would have been very little chance of escape for those inside. The second car is likely to have been the classic terrorist secondary device, used often in Ireland and Iraq. The car was parked at just about the distance from the first scene at which the emergency services would set up their forward reception point, and an explosion here, while not in the contained space of the night-club, would have killed and injured not only police, fire and ambulance officers but also many of those who had been rescued from the first explosion, had there been one. It would have stopped any further rescue attempts for hours, as every vehicle in the vicinity would have had to be searched. The bombers had tried to initiate the explosions by the use of mobile telephones. Each car contained two telephones and all four had been called a total of fifteen times, but the improvised detonators they had used had only partially ignited. I recalled that during the PIRA campaign a police officer had become suspicious of a parked van in central London when he heard a noise from inside but could see no one in there. He went on to another call and only later was it discovered that the noise had been a detonator exploding without igniting the main bomb. I can't think of another parallel.

It would be wrong to make public what prevented successful detonations but it was a very simple mistake. In the trade, this kind of device is known as a Boiling Liquid Evaporating Vapour Explosive or BLEVE. They are capable of detonating in a massive explosion. The simple but utterly callous construction of these bombs was one commonly used by insurgents in Iraq. Baghdad had come to London. It will not be the last time.

When the first explosives officer got to the scene, however, much of this was not known. He could see the phones and wires and was able gingerly to remove the main coverings obscuring some of the gas cylinders. It was his sole responsibility to decide how to make the car safe. Whereas other forces rely on the Army bomb-disposal units of the Royal Logistics Corps, the Met is unique in having its own explosives officers, all of whom have come from the services. An expo, as they are known, works in a long-time partnership with a police officer and is well equipped, using devices to disable bombs remotely if possible. However, in some cases he has to do it manually and this was one of them. Having been assured by his partner that the area was clear, the expo went forward alone: after much deliberation he cut through the correct wire to disable the device entirely. That is ice-cold courage because the system could have had a further loop designed to set off the bomb if the wiring was disrupted. In addition he did not know that the telephone might not ring again as he worked on the car. The courage of his colleague who disabled the bomb in the underground garage in Park Lane was little less, although he had the advantage of knowing what had been done a few hours before. I telephoned them later on that day and congratulated and thanked them. They would subsequently receive well-deserved national awards for gallantry.

The detonation of a BLEVE outside the open doors of a crowded nightclub would have sent a fireball inside and would probably have caused the greatest single loss of life in modern British criminal history. Later that day I received an email from the desk of Lord Lloyd Webber complaining about the closure of three theatres in the Haymarket, including one showing *Phantom of the Opera*. I sent him a reply which pointed out that, had the bombs gone off, the casualties would have been sufficient to fill a London theatre. I heard no more.

In the afternoon I went to No 10 with Andy Hayman and we spoke with Gordon Brown. Dreadful as the events might have been, the fact that they had happened less than thirty-six hours after he had become Prime Minister had given him an opportunity to present himself very early on as the new leader of the nation. He was focused and full of thanks and made clear to us that he understood the gravity of the threat and would return to the question of length of detention, so closely associated with his predecessor. He wished us well with the manhunt again underway. At about 4pm the next afternoon, Saturday, I was called at my home out of London, about another attack: this time at Glasgow Airport. The Prime Minister was convening COBR in an hour and he wanted me there. I invoked the arrangement I had with Thames Valley Police and a few minutes later a traffic police car, siren wailing, came the wrong way up the one-way street in which I live. My children were deeply impressed. The arrangement was that Thames Valley would take me nearly to the M25 and my own car would then pick me up and take me into London. I had fifty-five minutes to complete the sixty-five miles into Downing Street and, of course, the London half of the journey would be slower, sirens and blue lights notwithstanding. This was the second time I had been called in like this, the other being two years before, during the summer of 2005. The car screamed along the motorway and I read papers in the back. The police officer in the passenger seat said to me, 'You are very cool, sir, reading correspondence at this speed.' I looked up, saw the needle was showing something like 140 miles per hour and replied, 'Not cool, I am just not sure that going this fast I particularly want to look out of the window.' We all laughed but this wasn't funny. How many more attacks would there be? The sixty-five miles took forty-seven minutes and once again I went into Downing Street and then into COBR, but with a new Prime Minister.

By now it was clear that the two men involved in the attack in Glasgow had been captured and that no one else had been badly injured. It was also a reasonable assumption that these men were in some way connected to the London bombs of the day before, as we traced suspects to somewhere in southern Scotland. It also looked as though this incident, as opposed to the previous day's, had elements of a suicide attack. What we did not know was whether there were about to be more attacks elsewhere. The alert state had been raised to critical the day before, which means that an attack is no longer just 'highly likely' but 'expected imminently'. Once again, the mood was sombre.

Halfway through the meeting a unique feature of this new case emerged before our gaze. Today's attack had happened in Scotland where the Scottish Nationalist Party had been in power for nearly two months under its long-term leader, Alex Salmond. Gordon Brown had been Prime Minister of the United Kingdom of Great Britain and Northern Ireland for less than three days. Their relationship was widely compared to permafrost. Scotland Yard detectives were already in Scotland and the National Coordinator of Terrorist Investigations was on his way as fast as possible: I had come by car to Downing Street but Peter Clarke turned out to be heading to Glasgow in a Chinook helicopter – one up to him. The whole rationale of the National Coordinator's post was that we had long ago learned the folly of different police forces investigating PIRA attacks separately: it was doctrine that, in terrorist campaigns, the whole country was a single crime scene. The Chief Constable of Strathclyde Police, Willie Rae, had already called in the Yard. Alex Salmond appeared on a video screen with his chief legal adviser. There was a terse discussion between the two leaders: the Scots were claiming or, perhaps more fairly, exploring jurisdiction over the incident. The Prime Minister was having none of it. Policing might be devolved to the Scottish Parliament but counter-terrorism was not. The security of the whole country was at stake. This was UK government territory. Salmond seemed unsure but Brown was certain.

Later I discovered that all sorts of discussions had taken place until Jon Boutcher, the Senior Investigating Officer from Scotland Yard in charge of the manhunt and a very experienced and clever man, persuaded the newly appointed Lord Advocate that this was a continuous crime which had begun in England and was therefore within the jurisdiction of the Central Criminal Court at the Old Bailey. I pointed out to him afterwards that, if she had thought about it, the Lord Advocate might have noted that the bombs in London had been manufactured in Scotland and therefore the crime had begun there. Anyway, sense prevailed and when I visited Glasgow a few days later peace had broken out, although I did point out to Willie Rae that his officers might have been a bit more suspicious of the road in which the bombs had been assembled, which was called Neuk Crescent. There is now a cross-jurisdictional agreement in place between Edinburgh and London.

The two men at Glasgow Airport had been responsible for the Haymarket bombs: Kafeel Ahmed, an engineer, later died of the injuries he sustained at the airport. At trial – in England – Bilal Abdullah was given a minimum term of thirty-two years' imprisonment. The fact that, at the time he planned and executed his plot, he was a practising doctor just added to the sense of deep alarm felt by those of us involved in trying to predict where and how Al-Qaida would strike next.

It was on her very first day – the day of the Haymarket bomb – that I met Jacqui Smith, when she came over to the Yard for her first visit. Of all the Home Secretaries I served with, I think Jacqui was the most unlucky. She was given the brief of reintroducing another attempt at extending the pre-trial detention in terrorist cases, when the political moment had probably passed; she was faced with the unravelling of the regime of control orders to protect the public from those suspected of terrorist intentions and she was faced with a Tory front bench increasingly confident in its stance on law and order. Later on, she and I argued fairly fiercely over her decision not to honour in full an annual pay rise for the police, a decision which I told her was a serious mistake because all police authorities had already budgeted for it: the resulting march past the Home Office by very disgruntled police officers marked a particularly low point. But the suggestion that she was a weak minister is personally not true: she could be very direct and assertive and she obviously read the briefings put in front of her very thoroughly. As a former teacher she was adept at laying out what were her own policy proposals rather than leaving them for civil servants to present. She was also capable of great charm. I had recommended that the Head of the Met's Occupational Health Department should receive an MBE for her work after the Tsunami and 7/7. Eileen Cahill-Canning is an Irish citizen, however, and her actual award was therefore to be made by a minister rather than a member of the Royal Family. Jacqui Smith agreed to do this and went to enormous trouble to make her and her family feel very special.

All that was ahead. On this first day I decided to show her an aspect of what we had learned from the de Menezes case. It had been obvious to all of us that the briefing system for the Management Board in 2005 had been inadequate and had taken too long, even though its processes were loosely based on COBR. So we had invented a new system, called the Knowledge Management Centre, which would seek out information from all parts of the force an hour before each meeting of the Board and then deliver a single briefing at the start of the meeting, classifying the information on a scale from 'confirmed' through 'believed' to 'possible'. The Home Secretary was impressed, as indeed were those running COBR. Unfortunately the noting of this kind of learning was not the hallmark of the IPCC, which determined to return to the events of 2005 a few weeks after this latest set of bombings by finally publishing, two years after the events, its report into who knew what when about Jean Charles de Menezes, known as Stockwell Two.

8

Turbulence

In Hamlet's famous 'to be or not to be' soliloquy, among the 'whips and scorns of time' which the prince puts forward in favour of suicide, 'the law's delay' gets a prominent mention. Too many police inquiries take too long but, in the case of Stockwell Two, the Independent Police Complaints Commission really strained at the limits of what was conceivable. This was not a criminal inquiry (with the inbuilt delay involved in referral to the Crown Prosecution Service) but, as it said on the front of the final published report, 'An investigation into complaints about the Metropolitan Police Service's handling of public statements following the shooting of Jean Charles de Menezes on 22nd July 2005' or, in other words, who said what, when and on the basis of what state of knowledge. When the Home Office, itself not an organisation with the finest reputation for fleetness of foot, inquired into the processing of a visa for the nanny of David Blunkett's ex-lover, Alan Budd's report was produced in a few weeks. Even though it was concerned only with the actions of a few individuals during thirty-six hours, along with my subsequent comments about the same matters in two newspaper articles, the IPCC took over two years from Jean Charles's death (or four times the length of time it took to send its report to the CPS into the shooting itself) to publish its conclusions. It was nearly a year before the IPCC sought to interview me and, to add insult to injury, the first date suggested was 7 July 2006. The final report was published a year after that, on 2 August 2007.

What this meant was that, for two years, a shadow was allowed to hang over the most senior police officer in Britain, a manifestly false suggestion that I had set out to mislead the public over the death of an innocent man, a suggestion endlessly repeated by newspapers and other media and open to exploitation by those who wanted to damage me or, through me, the Met. For two years the only conclusion on discipline at which the IPCC had arrived had not been confirmed to me: the suggestion that one of my senior officers, Andy Hayman, on whom I needed to rely without question, had apparently briefed me and his senior colleagues on lines which were inconsistent with what he had told journalists earlier as to whether or not the shot man was one of the four attempted bombers. This matter was found substantiated against Andy and remitted to the MPA for consideration of discipline.

As the ridiculous delays went on, the effective running of Britain's largest police force did not seem as important to the IPCC as I considered it should have done, even though a mechanism for outlining emerging findings would have been straightforward to arrange. Four or five months would have been easily sufficient to establish the facts. However, I felt that facts were not all that the IPCC seemed to want in Stockwell Two: I was far from alone in thinking that it also wanted my head. And there were probably three reasons behind that. It was obvious that some of those who worked in the IPCC had been, perhaps understandably, offended by my decision to refuse it entry to the scene of the death. The second was that this was a relatively new and undoubtedly underfunded organisation. To take down the Commissioner would establish beyond question its credibility as an independent agency. The third was that I wondered if a grudge lingered on from my role in a previous case, that of Superintendent Ali Dizaei, who had stood trial and been acquitted some years earlier. I had been involved in the agreement to bring the subsequent disciplinary enquiry to an end and had not informed the IPCC's predecessor body of that decision.

Whatever the reasons, the result was a report which took every opportunity to be as unforgiving as possible, as was the press conference at which it was released. The conference was timed for midday, which meant I had only minutes after it had finished and before the one o'clock news to draw up a response to what was said, although, after two years, the IPCC had allowed me and others named in the report a full four hours to read its 134 pages. At the conference the canard was repeated that the delayed access to the scene of the shooting had hampered the Commission's investigation. There was no acceptance by the IPCC that it had had at the very least some responsibility for the failure to correct misleading information about the circumstances of the death.

In the report there were a number of places where contradicted or unsupported allegations were allowed to remain or where a particularly unfavourable interpretation of evidence was used in summary portions of the document. Obvious examples of these are the inclusion of a long passage (16.13.12 onwards) where an officer suggests that he received a telephone call from another on the afternoon of the shooting to the effect that the Met had shot an innocent man (which, if true, would have been nearly twenty-four hours before that was officially confirmed). Only later on does the report make clear that the second officer subsequently produced telephone records which proved that the call took place the next day, which makes the whole exchange utterly irrelevant. The inclusion of such a provably contradicted allegation is odd, as is the prominence given to Brian Paddick's assertion that I might have known on the first afternoon of the emerging identity when the report itself concludes that I did not know until the following morning.

Another example of the report's unusual approach concerns Alan Brown. In his statement to the IPCC about why he had not told me of the emerging identity of Mr de Menezes, he said:

I did not tell the Commissioner about the findings of documents on 22 July until the morning of 23 July when I was certain of the identification. I had been tasked as Gold London which meant that I had ultimate responsibility for that part of the investigation. Other officers had responsibility for the terrorist investigation. The Commissioner has ultimate responsibility for the Metropolitan Police Service and I therefore did not need to advise the Commissioner until the identification was certain or as certain as it could be and became an issue for the service. As soon as it did so, I informed the Commissioner.

At page 92 of the report these sentences are summarised as: 'he [Alan Brown] was Gold Commander for London and this was an operational matter for which he had responsibility and that the Commissioner had no role to play in the command of the operation.' As a way of insinuating that a man is out of touch or being kept out of touch, that is pretty neat. It is fair neither to what Alan said or what he would have believed nor to how any Commissioner could run his force.

My job on the day the report was produced was to be statesman-like on behalf of the Met, to underline the sorrow felt by all involved for the death and to lay out the many reforms which had subsequently taken place in its handling of information. Additionally, I made clear that, as I had always said, I had not lied to the public. Underneath my calm, however, I was boiling with anger. A critical, delayed and at times apparently misleading report was not enough for the IPCC.

On 30 July, three days before publication, the report was preceded by a thirteen-page letter addressed to the MPA's solicitor and copied to the Home Secretary. The last few pages of this letter alleged that the IPCC had uncovered 'possible evidence of an attack on the integrity of the investigation' but stated that, as the witnesses refused to cooperate further with their investigators, the three Commissioners overseeing the investigation had decided not to 'delay any further in bringing this investigation to a conclusion'. The paragraph ended: 'The Authority may wish to set in hand further enquiries.' I did not see this letter until 1 August. In the meantime hurried conferences were held between the Home Office, the MPA, the IPCC and the Met, represented by Paul Stephenson, who was being placed in an entirely invidious position as these were allegations about his boss which he could not discuss with me. I am told that the Home Secretary was almost beside herself with anger, as was Len Duvall, with the Home Secretary demanding to know from Nick Hardwick, Chairman of the IPCC, which was his report, the printed 134 pages or this letter. The allegations, two in number, were really serious. The first was that three journalists had been made aware of parts of the draft IPCC report when those sections had been – as is normal – sent for comment to officers potentially the subject of criticism, a process variously known as Maxwellisation or the Salmon Process. The second allegation was that, acting on my behalf, with or without my knowledge or at my behest or on their own initiative, both my solicitor (a private solicitor, not the Met solicitor) and my staff officer, Moir Stewart, had attempted to get Brian Paddick to change his evidence to the IPCC about the meeting we had had on 22 August 2005.

If these allegations were true, a further damaging investigation would follow and, if there were anything in the allegations and I were found to have been their instigator, I would have faced immediate suspension. With the agreement of the Home Office, the MPA appointed the Chief Inspector of Constabulary, Ronnie Flanagan, to investigate the matter. In contrast to the IPCC's two years and its inability to make contact with the witnesses in question, within two weeks Ronnie had contacted them all and had been able to establish unequivocally that there was no evidence that the journalists had been improperly approached, that nothing abnormal had occurred with Brian Paddick in relation to the Salmon Process, to the extent that, in the words of Brian's solicitor, 'at no time did I feel that improper pressure had been brought to bear on Mr Paddick to cooperate or the Commissioner's solicitor [name given] behaved in anything but a completely professional manner in his dealings with me.' My solicitor made clear that he believed that solicitor-to-solicitor contact had been his rather than my idea (which was my own recollection) and Brian Paddick accepted that Moir Stewart had been acting on his own initiative to prevent a public spat (when the report would be published) between two high-ranking officers, although Moir believed that the first approach had been made by Brian, when the Salmon letters were first sent to the Metropolitan Police Service.

The IPCC apologised to my solicitor, who had threatened to sue for defamation. It could never bring itself to do so to me, although a year later I did receive a letter from Nick Hardwick accepting Ronnie's findings. The first letter, which had been capable of causing such damage, was, as far as I know, unprecedented. There was a high risk of it leaking, with almost catastrophic consequences. That it did not is a tribute to all those involved – including Brian – and sits in stark contrast to the culture of leaks after the arrival of Boris Johnson. Moreover, the letter put Len Duvall, Chair of the MPA, in a very difficult position. Ever afterwards he worried that he was under some obligation to have told members of the Authority of the existence of the letter (about which they do not know to this day) and that, had it leaked, his position would have been untenable until Ronnie reported. He used to make slightly obscure remarks in Authority meetings which discussed Stockwell which, if he had been forced to explain them, would have enabled him to put the matter into the public domain but, to his dismay, no one ever picked up the hint. It is difficult to understand why the IPCC acted in this way, but it seems unlikely that it was simply a lack of time. If Ronnie could clear it up in a fortnight, the IPCC could have concluded the matter itself much earlier.

As it was the summer holidays the matter was not considered by the MPA until early September. When it did, the report's unremittingly harsh words were seized upon by the opposition members in the most strident terms. Richard Barnes led the charge by saying that what the report revealed was 'the absence of an enquiring mind' on my part, despite all the evidence of my repeated questioning on the day as to the identity of the shot man. The meeting was broadcast live on a number of channels and was an uncomfortable experience, what those in my private office were subsequently to describe as 'a flogging around the fleet'. There was little sympathy for the lethal situation London and the Met had been facing two years before. There was no understanding that, dreadful as this one death had been, our concern was the manhunt. Instead member after member, frustrated like me by the delay, expressed outrage about what had and had not happened, showing very little interest in the reforms that had subsequently occurred. The Chair could scarcely control the meeting and, although this was not to be the worst experience I would have in a public meeting – that was to come three months later – it was the first time I began to wonder if the job was do-able within this format of accountability. One of my friends described the behaviour of members brilliantly: it was as if they were teenagers, with total self-belief in their right to be shatteringly rude, in this case not to their family but to public officials who could not reply in kind, without a care as to the impact on them, to whom after the meeting they would speak kindly as if what had been said earlier did not matter and was in a different world. This is how politicians behave to one another, in their yahoo interchanges, before speaking amicably in the bar afterwards. It was as Richard Barnes had said of the Soham exchange, 'Nothing personal, Ian, just politics.' But whether it encourages people to go into public life is another matter.

It was getting wearisome and Stockwell Two was not the only cause of the turbulence. The Health and Safety trial itself was swinging into view and there were new and emerging concerns over financial controls in the Met and there was trouble beginning over the Olympics, which linked to racial politics inside and outside the force. And in the middle of all of this, the Conservatives began to realise that they had at last found a serious challenge to Ken.

Because of the public monies involved, the decision to defend the Health and Safety prosecution was not taken lightly and we instructed the same legal team that had successfully defended Paul Condon and John Stevens in their major Health and Safety case a few years earlier: Ronald Thwaites QC to lead, Keith Morton as junior counsel and solicitor advocate Mark Scoggins, an acknowledged expert in this field. While there was no certainty of success, they advised that a jury should have the opportunity to evaluate the evidence and consider whether police officers were not in an equivalent position to soldiers on the battlefield (who were exempt from Health and Safety considerations). After the case Norman Bettison, Chief Constable of West Yorkshire, wrote a brilliant article in the *Yorkshire Post* about 'the sleepwalking acceptance of the Health and Safety mantra' which included this passage: 'The Met conviction over the tragic shooting of Jean Charles de Menezes [is] a triumph for Health and Safety, a lucrative new territory for lawyers but a disaster for common sense.' It was in that frame of mind that we went forward. Ronald Thwaites is a counsel to sway juries with the emotional intelligence of his case, which is why I chose him, rather than a brilliantly forensic weigher of detail, such as his opponent, Clare Montgomery QC. At the end of the trial, the jury delivered a unanimous verdict of guilty after a very short retirement. As all of us, Ronald (and the team) were deeply disappointed, but it is possible that the explanation was simple. One of the jurors approached Moir Stewart, who had sat through the trial as my representative. 'Sorry about that,' the juror said, 'it is just that the Met had to be given a slap.'

The trial went very much as we expected, but with four twists. First, in the spirit of 'you couldn't script it if you tried', one of the jurors got caught up in a Met operation and the trial thus had to proceed with only the remaining eleven jurors. Then a prosecution witness alleged that the Met had altered the photographs of Jean Charles de Menezes and Hussain Osman to make them look more similar. This was later proved to be merely the normal way photographs are prepared for side-by-side comparison and the allegation was entirely rejected by the judge in his subsequent directions to the jury. But the headlines had already screamed their stuff.

Another unexpected twist arose from the fact that the post-mortem had revealed traces of cocaine in de Menezes's bloodstream: this had to be given in evidence by the prosecution as it was part of the post-mortem report and something the jury had to be asked to take into account in interpreting his behaviour. For the defence, Ronald Thwaites stated that he had been directly instructed by me to make clear to the jury that this was not an attempt to smear the character of the dead man. However, he might as well not have bothered: again the headlines roared that the Met was engaged in character assassination. To some extent this was because the de Menezes family had been largely absorbed by the 'Justice for Jean' campaigners, a small number of whom had experience of other protests, and had throughout this trial mounted a very effective press campaign. These just added new pearls to the necklace of allegations of cover-up and distortion: the stories fitted the narrative that the press had largely adopted.

The last twist was the evidence of Cressida Dick. Whatever Clare

Montgomery did, she could not shake Cressida from portraying the reasonableness of her actions and those of all the officers involved. Other officers, including Cressida's second in command, Jon Boutcher, gave evidence surely and imperturbably, whatever was put to them. Ronald later told me that Cressida had been the most impressive police witness that he had ever seen. Afterwards something happened of which I had never heard before: on 1 November, the jury sent a note to the judge to say that, while they had reached a verdict, they wished to attach a rider. This is very rare in criminal trials. After some four weeks of trial the verdict was unanimous: the Met was guilty of a breach of Health and Safety law in failing to protect Jean Charles de Menezes. The rider, again unanimous, that the forewoman read out was that 'no culpability attaches to Commander Dick'. So there we were: the Met guilty as charged but with the person in command (entirely correctly, in my view) bearing no culpability. This was Alice in Wonderland territory. I was in court to hear the verdict and now listened to the judge deliver his summary of the case and fine the Met £175,000. It was a balanced and legally impeccable judgement, which had at its centre an understanding of the pressures of the day, the unforeseeable threat of four failed suicide bombers at large. He acknowledged the fine safety record of the Met and made clear that 'this was an isolated breach [of Health and Safety legislation] brought about by quite extraordinary circumstance'. He praised the tremendous bravery of Ivor, who threw his arms around a man he believed to be a suicide bomber.

At the same time the puzzle which lies at the heart of Stockwell is apparent in this judgement. Henriques wondered at the fact that a number of senior officers were clear that 'they would act in the same way again'. The opening part of his speech makes clear that his main criticism was the delay in getting the firearms team to the scene but it is unclear whether that would have been his emphasis had he known what was explained to the jury at the subsequent inquest: that some of the firearms officers were only yards from the tube station when Jean Charles de Menezes arrived. The reason that this was not made clear in this courtroom was quite simply that it was the wrong trial. To the great detriment of the pursuit of the truth, the judge, jury and counsel did not have access to the full facts because the principal firearms officers were not called and their statements were not available. I stress that this is not a criticism of the prosecuting team but a fault inherent in such a prosecution. Most of the police witnesses were prosecution witnesses but Cressida together with the officer in charge of the firearms team and the two officers who fired the shots were not called by the prosecution. In its defence, the Met decided only to call Cressida, because it did not believe that the other officers could say anything useful as far as Health and Safety legislation was concerned and so as not to expose the officers directly involved in the shooting to the experience of giving evidence and being cross-examined in front of two different courtrooms and juries. But this also meant that it was not until the inquest that a decision was taken to plot the locations of the firearms officers by reference to telephone records, CCTV footage and witness accounts.

After a few words with Cressida, it was my task to face the media. I had prepared a statement but I needed a few minutes to reorder it after the judgement and then I went out into the road outside the Old Bailey. By the time I arrived, together with Peter Clarke, the National Coordinator of Terrorist Investigations, there were dozens of journalists and TV camera crews and he and I spoke and then answered questions from within a set of barriers forming a pen.

Before I went out I knew that this case and its implications had now become national politics. The Liberal Democrats were selecting their new leader and Nick Clegg, the eventual winner, was straight off the blocks within minutes: 'This guilty verdict makes it unavoidable that Ian Blair should take responsibility on behalf of his whole organisation and resign.' David Davis, Shadow Home Secretary, talked of failures in 'organisation, command and operations' which were 'systemic': my position was 'untenable'. He exempted, I am glad to say, both Cressida Dick and the front-line officers 'because this was a serial failure of organisation, training, tactics and resourcing. Only one person can be held overall accountable for that'. The fact that the judge had described the events as an isolated breach of the law did not seem to have come to his notice.

Within minutes the London Police Federation, the London Superintendents' Association and the Chair of the MPA came out in my
support but then that was expected: what was more significant was that
the Home Secretary, the Mayor of London and the Prime Minister did
the same. Even before I had finished speaking outside the Old Bailey a
new stage in policing had been reached: my continuation in office had
become a straightforward political issue. There were even opinion polls
to determine public opinion on whether I should resign: in *The Times*,
thelondonpaper and the *Evening Standard*. They were pretty evenly split.

Stepping back, it is possible to see the death at Stockwell in context.
From networked corruption to Broadwater Farm, from Michael Fagan
in the Queen's bedroom to Stephen Lawrence, previous Commissioners of modern times had faced the disasters over which the Met
inevitably stumbles without sustained and widespread calls for resignation from the media and the political classes (although the scale of
the Stephen Lawrence case brought Paul Condon some very difficult
moments). Equally, the contemporary tragedies of friendly fire, the
deaths or downing of ill-equipped soldiery or aircraft or the capture
of sailors or explosions on submarines do not lead to demands for
the resignation of either the Chief of the Defence Staff or the head
of the relevant service. This police operation was directed four levels
of command beneath mine and carried to its tragic conclusion twelve
levels below: from the first moment, I had accepted total accountability for what had happened. However, I had always declined to accept
personal responsibility for a single event about which I did and could
have known nothing. In this I had always felt quite comfortable. I knew
I had the full support of my peers for this position. We once drew up a
list of recent *causes célèbres* at the Met and calculated that Commissioners would last an average of fourteen months if they resigned over such
events. Had there been a series of such incidents, had there been other
avoidable deaths, had there indeed been a systemic failure and had that
been the Judge's ruling, my decision would have been otherwise.

What was different was politics, a politics that saw, in my removal
or defence, political advantage. This could scarcely be more clearly

demonstrated, albeit perhaps inadvertently, than by the evolution of Brian Paddick's statements. On 1 November he had said that resignation was 'a matter for Ian Blair'; and on 4 November he said that he had promised me that 'I would not publicly call for him to step down' but by 13 November, as he launched his bid to become the Liberal Democrat Mayor of London, he said that 'London would be better off without Ian Blair as the Commissioner'.

The Greater London Assembly has a series of constituent bodies covering development, transport, fire and rescue and policing: but while Transport for London, for instance, is directly accountable to the GLA and the Mayor, the Metropolitan Police Service is not. The Metropolitan Police Authority is the constituent body, which the GLA regularly calls before it. However, a tradition had grown up that, about once a year, the Commissioner attended a public meeting of the Assembly, together with the Chair of the MPA. As chance would inevitably have it, the next scheduled meeting was just six days after the verdict, on the morning of Wednesday, 7 November. In full uniform I went into the five-storey, circular chamber of City Hall and sat alongside Len Duvall. Stockwell was not on the agenda, of course, but the two of us had already agreed between us that there was no point in sticking to formal process and refusing to talk about it. The place was packed.

The Chair, the Liberal Democrat peer Sally Hamwee, with whom I had always got on well, rather shamefacedly began the meeting by introducing the topic but Len interrupted by saying that both of us would make a short statement and then take questions. The London Assembly had at that time a very wide spectrum of politics from UKIP to Green and members expressed their indignation at the events of Stockwell or their support for the force along party lines, although quite often along what might have been surprising lines if you had not known the characters. Damian Hockney of UKIP, a party dedicated to all things traditionally British, like the police, was very critical. One of the most sympathetic was Jenny Jones of the Green Party. Because the Assembly had absolutely no power of hire and fire over me, the speeches made and the motion passed were meaningless (although damaging in cumulative reputational terms). The whole event was a farce, as some of the Parliamentary sketch writers noted. Interesting, of course, that they turned up: another indication that this was now high politics. They seemed to like the following exchange, with my old *bête noire*, Richard Barnes, after I told him, 'I have stated my position. If you have the power to remove me, go on.' He asked a very long question ending with the words: 'Don't you think you should resign?'

'Is that the end of your question?'

'Yes.'

'No.'

Simon Hoggart of the *Guardian* described the event thus:

> They [the GLA members] were hostile to London's top policeman. At times, very hostile. Sir Ian's self-esteem, however, has never been in doubt. He has a rock-ribbed ego. Watching them abuse him was like seeing storm waves pounding a cliff – it's exciting, you imagine something must be crumbling, but the cliff is still there. He sat there in his full fig, medals [I don't think so. IB], poppy and badges on his chest, enough silverware across his shoulders to satisfy a South American dictator. Behind him we could see the Gherkin, symbol of the new London, and the Tower, where people were dispatched for earlier failures.

I left before they had a vote but it was obvious that I was going to lose. The votes were fifteen for and eight against the motion, which was eventually revealed to be, in an extraordinary combination of bureaucrat-speak and political decree:

> That the Assembly notes the answers to the questions asked.
>
> This Assembly calls on the Metropolitan Police Authority to take the necessary steps to bring to an end the debate on the position of the Commissioner of Police of the Metropolis, which is to the detriment of policing in London, and bring his appointment to an end, if necessary obtaining the consent of the Home Secretary.

Given the lack of confidence in the Commissioner's stewardship of the Metropolitan Police service, this Assembly also calls upon Sir Ian to reconsider his own position and resign.

During the meeting Richard Barnes made the extraordinary allegation, which he later retracted, that someone from my office had telephoned the Mayor's office, on Friday, 21 July, to tell him that the Met had shot the wrong person. I loved Ken Livingstone's pronouncement on the vote by the GLA: 'They want to run policing in London. I wouldn't let them run a bath.'

I realised, dangerously, that I had actually enjoyed the whole encounter but I knew that, two weeks later, at the next MPA meeting, the whole match was going to be replayed. Meanwhile it was Remembrance weekend. As usual, my wife and I were invited to watch the Festival of Remembrance at the Royal Albert Hall. To my amusement, we sat in the same box as David Cameron, whose party had called for my resignation only days before. He wouldn't look at me and we hardly spoke. My wife muttered rather too loudly, 'Someone in the British Legion has a good sense of humour.' Cameron grimaced and a very senior naval officer nearly fell off the balcony laughing. I loved Felicity for it but it probably did not help my cause.

Ten days later I was interested in a piece in the *Guardian* by the former editor of the *New Statesman*, Peter Wilby. He wrote, under the title 'The Blair Witchhunt Project':

How can we account for the case of Sir Ian Blair, the Metropolitan Police Commissioner? Most of the normal conditions for resignation have been fulfilled. The media have gone on about him for a very long time. There's scarcely a Fleet Street commentator or leader writer who hasn't called for him to fall on his truncheon.

The rightwing newspapers, never keen on a man they brand as a politically correct copper, became even more hostile when he accused the press of institutional racism, suggesting it gave obsessive coverage to murders of white children but ignored black victims – a charge greeted by journalists as though someone had accused the Pope of attending pagan rituals.

The liberal papers find Blair a hard case, too. He wants to strengthen anti-terrorist laws and allows his officers to go around the streets shooting innocent people dead ...

Andrew Rawnsley, the *Observer* columnist, signed Blair's death warrant on November 4th. It was no longer a question of whether Blair would resign, he wrote, but when. Against universal media hostility, he argued, public figures simply find it impossible to continue doing their jobs. 'Every step they take, every slip they make, further shreds their reputation.' They were afflicted by 'Stephen Byers syndrome'. From the government's viewpoint, it was politically vital that Blair should make the case for new anti-terror legislation. But he would not, as Rawnsley put it, be 'a persuasive advocate'.

Yet Blair remains at his post. The press has responded with fury and incredulity. 'As I wrote here a week ago,' fumed the *Daily Mail*'s Melanie Phillips, as though she were dealing with a persistently disobedient class of children, 'the case for him to go is overwhelming.' In the *Sunday Telegraph*, Iain Martin ruled 'the case for the prosecution is open and shut'. Rod Liddle in the *Sunday Times* wondered if Blair had to be 'caught in a post office with a sawn-off shotgun and a stocking over his head' before he agreed to go.

It is hard to think of a precedent for a public figure surviving such a sustained media onslaught for so long. But equally, there is no precedent for a senior police officer being a target. Other London police chiefs – Paul Condon and Sir Kenneth Newman, for example – have survived the shooting of innocent people without much trouble.

The difference is that Blair has tried to bring a degree of social and racial justice to London's policing. This, according to the press, is 'political'. Conventional demands for tougher laws and longer sentences against yobs and burglars, on the other hand, are non-political. Hence, Blair, unlike other police chiefs who make mistakes (or preside over mistakes by their officers), is fair game.

For politicians, media profile is too important for them to survive relentless hostility and a stream of negative stories, whether about their private lives or their ministerial performance. That was why Byers, Peter Mandelson, David Blunkett and others had to go ...

Do these rules now also apply to senior police officers? The government and the London mayor Ken Livingstone are clearly reluctant to accept that they do. They want to draw a line and that is why Blair remains in office. They believe that changing the Met's culture and image is vital if it is to win the confidence of London's ethnic minorities, and particularly Muslims, and they trust Blair alone to do that. Bowing to the press campaign against him, they think, would be an enormous and unacceptable victory for traditionalists within Scotland Yard. Livingstone, who has faced similar press hostility all his political life, seems unlikely to abandon Blair at this stage.

Rawnsley may be right, and so may the *Daily Mirror*'s Paul Routledge when he suggests Blair will go quietly after Christmas. But I suspect Blair will hang on and the textbook on how public figures can be brought down by press campaigns will have to be rewritten.

Wilby's magisterial conclusions did not seem as certain when a few days later, I walked downstairs from my office and across the road to the MPA offices in Dean Farrar Street. It didn't help that, in the previous twenty-four hours, the England football manager had been sacked and the Chair of HM Revenue and Customs had resigned over the loss of data on millions of taxpayers. It didn't help that, as I sat down, I noticed that in the audience there were members of the 'Justice for Jean' campaign, including some of his family.

Three Conservative party members of the MPA, all also members of the GLA, had written to the Chair, under the rules laid down in Standing Orders, to request the summoning of an Extraordinary Meeting 'as a matter of urgency to discuss the implications of the guilty verdict in the Health and Safety trial in the case of the Crown vs the Office of the Commissioner'.

The Chair had delayed calling the emergency meeting for as long as possible and had convened it just after 9am on Thursday 22 November, immediately before the regular monthly meeting of the full MPA, scheduled to begin at 10am. I knew that he was doing this in order to maximise attendance because this was a constitutionally much more important event than the GLA. A successful vote of no confidence could trigger the mechanism to request the Home Secretary to dismiss me. More importantly, I knew – and, although I had not told Len this, I imagine he also knew – that I would offer my resignation to the Home Secretary in the event of such a vote. Even so, knowing that I retained the confidence of her, the Mayor and Len, I would have been prepared to stay on if she had not accepted it: a situation different from the one I was to face some ten months later with Boris Johnson. We thought we had the numbers, partly because two or three of the members who were persistently critical of me were themselves pretty unpopular with other members.

Len's plan was, after a general discussion on Stockwell, to suspend standing orders to allow the three members to put a motion of no confidence and then to propose to debate the motion in private, as it was effectively a personnel matter. This is what happened, except that the Conservatives argued fiercely that their motion was not a personnel matter: only if it was carried would it then possibly become one. Len put it to the vote and his suggestion to hold the discussion in camera was comprehensively lost, twenty to three. I whispered to Len, 'I don't think I can do this or possibly can be asked to do this.' He looked at me in anguish and I realised that if I left the room I would not be the Commissioner at the end of the day. I nodded and sat still.

Then, for some three and a half hours, I sat while members, for and against, took the opportunity on live television to criticise me and, with increasing acerbity, one another. Richard Barnes began, quoting Judge Henriques's comment that this was 'a corporate failing'. He didn't put that remark in the context of Henriques's other comment about this being 'an isolated breach'. I was shocked to find Graham Tope, a Liberal Democrat peer, speaking in support of the motion: he told me afterwards that he had only done so under extreme pressure from his party. The eccentric but very likeable Tory member Tony Arbour opened up a different theme, that I had to go because I had become the story and I was 'a lame duck Commissioner', and then, Bob Neill, another Tory, criticised me for saying outside the Old Bailey that I would not resign. (I never got the chance to tell him but, had I not made my position clear within moments, it would have been reported as me considering my position, a place from which I would have had great difficulty coming back.)

A magistrate then criticised the Assembly for making my position a political issue, another magistrate stated that I was being undermined by a political and media frenzy, an independent member said that it was the politicians who were making me the story, Damian Hockney came in to suggest that the majority of elected members wanted me out and it was undemocratic that unelected members might outvote them and then the gloves were off as this became the divide, with members trading near insults. Cindy Butts was kind, saying:

> There are a catalogue of issues that are always raised in relation to the Commissioner which I personally believe have no basis and I personally believe are a result of a media campaign to hound him out of office. He is too politically correct. Well, what does that mean? Actually what it means is that we've had a commissioner who has been prepared to champion diversity issues whether that's in relation to women or to ethnic minorities or to the disabled. I can go on. What else do we hear? He's too intellectual. It means that – I'm not talking to you, I'm not necessarily talking to you, I'm talking about the campaign that is there in the media. I am responding to that, OK? You've had your turn, give me mine. Right, so he's an intellectual. What does that mean? Do we want a thick policeman, is that what we're saying? Well, actually I want to put on record that the Commissioner has led some reforms within the Metropolitan Police Service [and] where he has led others have followed and we are not just talking nationally but internationally.

This extract gives some flavour of the debate. The vote was taken in public: seven in favour of the motion of no confidence, fifteen against and one abstention.

After the vote there was a long silence and then I said the following, most of which was true:

> This case will live with me and my officers for the rest of our lives and I am extremely sorry it happened. Although it has not been an easy experience, I welcomed the fact we had this motion and, to my surprise, I welcome the fact that we had it in public. And I hope now this ends months of speculation. I am a man of honour. If I believed that what happened in this case was appropriate for my resignation, I would have just gone and resigned. At the end of this, I am not a lame duck Commissioner. I am not in a position of being in office but not in power – I am in office and in power.

Actually, I did not welcome the fact that it had been in public. It had been a very unpleasant experience. As Len said during the debate, 'I don't know of any public official who has faced the degree of questioning that the Commissioner has faced. It is unheard of and unprecedented in this country. I don't even believe that politicians in Parliament face this degree of questioning around their jobs.' Afterwards I learned that Len had said to someone later in the day that, 'After that, if Ian decides to resign, how on earth are we going to get a Commissioner?' I agreed with both comments. And part of my eventual decision to resign was linked to the experience of that long morning.

The reaction of the *Daily Mail* was interesting. On the day after the end of the Health and Safety trial the paper had carried a picture of me outside the Old Bailey under the headline 'Man without honour' (which is why I used the opposite phrase at the end of the meeting) and then a leading article which began with this robust statement: 'Every day that Ian Blair clings to office seriously damages the Metropolitan Police and its ability to provide safety and security in the capital. By undermining public confidence in the police force, it makes another terrorist atrocity more likely.'

The day after the no-confidence vote, the *Mail*, under the title 'Shameless Met Chief Survives ... with More Than a Little Help from

His Labour Pals', described those who voted for me as placemen. It said of the MPA:

> It is anything but the independent watchdog it claims to be. As well as five official Labour members, it is stuffed with supposedly independent members who have been appointed by the Home Office. Those vacancies, often advertised in Left-wing newspapers and police journals, are often filled by public sector veterans generally seen as sympathetic to the government.

While the suggestion that independent members are appointed by the Home Office is an oversimplification and the piece is grossly exaggerated – the juxtaposition of left-wing newspapers and police journals being a pairing indicative of the *Mail*'s worldview – there is more than a grain of truth in the point that many of the independents shared a broadly liberal perspective. Of course, twelve months later the position would be reversed, with many of the independents in the MPA formed after Boris's election coming from private-sector backgrounds. The current selection system needs to be changed because it provides an opportunity for the majority political party in the London Assembly to make its voting position on the MPA unassailable.

Nick Clegg, still calling for my resignation, said officers were 'seething with resentment ... that politics is overshadowing their day to day job'. They certainly were. Emailing the Commissioner is a pretty bold thing to do in what still remains too hierarchical an organisation but my office was receiving an unprecedented number of emails from all over the force. And they were indeed seething with resentment, although not against me but against politicians and against what they saw as the unfairness of how I was being treated as their Commissioner. One officer from Havering, whom I have never met, wrote:

> I feel that it is essential to bring to your attention how respected you are by officers who work on the streets of London. I know that I am not alone in my views on this subject as the current media attack on

you is the current topic of conversation both on and off duty. Every officer, PCSO, Special Constable and civilian member of staff I have spoken to is of the same opinion. You have the support of so many staff throughout the service and I think that now is the time to let you know the strength of feeling.

A firearms officer, an elected Police Federation representative, wrote:

Sometimes I disagree with you, sometimes I agree with you. On this matter, you have my full support and the support of my fellow constables here. I've served on both Armed Response Vehicles and the Rifle Section and know that tough decisions must be made – indecisiveness can kill. The treatment you have received from petty politicians and journalists is deplorable. I know who the public trust and it's not those who snipe at you and call for your resignation. If you need to pop down the pub for a quick pint after late turn, tell me where – I'll buy you a pint.

The loyalty of these men and women was immensely heartening, as was that I received from their colleagues wherever I went and from my personal staff. It is a pity that this was apparently not replicated by some senior officers. In the case of Brian Paddick, I had supported him for years, believing it to be essential for the service to demonstrate its ability not only to tolerate but to celebrate difference. In the summer of 2006 that came to an end. In May the Met had taken action to remove Brian Haw from Parliament Square (fairly unsatisfactorily: while his protest site was reduced, the legislation had been badly drawn up and could not be applied to demonstrations which, like his, had begun before the law was passed). This partial removal had been fiercely criticised by Jenny Jones at the next full MPA meeting. The following morning was a Friday and began with our normal senior management meeting at which Brian was present, representing Tim Godwin. I talked about the MPA meeting and Jenny's concerns, which had been raised in the general question-and-answer sessions and had concentrated on how much the operation had cost. I said to my senior colleagues that I thought we had 'got away rather lightly'. I had answered the question about cost by reading, off a briefing sheet, the figure for additional costs of overtime and some equipment, something just over £7,000. Later, as the fuss I describe next began to grow, I would have to add to what I had said, to include what is known as the opportunity costs, that is the actual wages of the officers, which was the much higher figure of more than £27,000.

But to my colleagues I was not talking about cost. That was only a consequence of my more fundamental professional concern about why we had needed so many officers to move only a tiny number of protesters in the dead of night. We had 'got away rather lightly', in my view, because I had not been asked that and, had I been, I would have found the numbers difficult to justify and indeed there had been no explanation for them on the sheet of briefing. One or two others present agreed. It was a perfectly normal conversation and it finished with me asking for a report on the thinking behind this deployment.

After the meeting was over I went to deliver a talk at the East London Mosque before Friday prayers. As my car drew up I got a phone call from Paul Stephenson telling me that press enquiries had been received suggesting that I had just told my senior colleagues that I had misled the MPA the day before. Misleading the MPA deliberately is a resigning matter and this was deadly serious. Paul and I agreed that the head of internal affairs, my previous staff officer, Sue Akers, now the Commander in charge of the Professional Standards Department, as the Met calls its internal affairs investigators, would speak to everyone at the meeting and ask two questions. The first would be whether they had spoken on the telephone to anyone outside the building and the second would be whether his or her telephone records would support that position.

It was difficult to concentrate on the speech and debate at the Mosque but I got through it. By the time I got back into the car, Sue had seen everyone. She wanted to tell me about the conversations she had had including the one with Brian. He had answered the two questions, she told me, as follows. Had he called anyone? 'No.' Would his phone records support that position? 'Yes ... er ... no.' He admitted to Sue that he had spoken to a journalist but claimed that he had not talked about Brian Haw. Sue then found out that he had, however, later called Jenny Jones herself, as he recounts in his book.

I called Brian Paddick in and put the allegation to him that he had passed information to someone outside the organisation directly out of my senior staff meeting. I told him that this was a breach of trust so impossible to tolerate that I was moving him immediately to a non-operational post, so that he would never again be required to sit in on one of my meetings.

I now understand, however, while admitting telling Jenny Jones about the matter that lunchtime, Brian has subsequently always denied being the source of the press leak which had occurred earlier than that. In *Line of Fire*, Brian confirms Sue Akers's account of their conversation. But in effect he suggests that somebody else at the meeting must have made the call which began the press enquiries. While this, of course, is possible, it matters not. No senior leader, in any walk of life, can continue to allow a colleague to attend confidential meetings if he believes that that person has revealed to an outsider what was said at a previous one. Such a breach never occurred on any other occasion, before or since, and the idea that there might be two people in the same meeting – but only ever in that one – who went outside and briefed someone outside the Met strains credulity, given the vast number of confidential matters that were discussed in these thrice-weekly meetings. If Brian thought I was saying I had misled Jenny Jones, his proper course was to report that to the Chief Executive of the MPA not to talk to the member herself.

I should explain why I moved Brian rather than arranged for him to leave the Met. One of the hangovers from the early history of the police, with each small force being controlled by the local Watch Committee, is that a Chief Constable or Commissioner does not have the power to appoint, discipline, suspend or sack one of his senior colleagues. All these powers are vested in the Police Authority, although the chief officer will always be influential about appointment and retains the power to decide which post any individual will hold. However, dismissal or discipline or the seeking of resignation is entirely a matter for the Police Authority. This is nonsensical in modern conditions. The post to which I now sent Brian was, obviously to him and to everyone else, a sharp and public reduction in his responsibilities. I am sorry that this incident effectively ended Brian's career, which had many fine features, but there could be no other course of action. In taking it, I was also aware that it was going to make the whole issue of Stockwell even more difficult because it could look as if this was my revenge for the evidence Brian had supplied to the IPCC, which is what he states in his book to be his belief.

That was not the reason. It could not have been. To move Brian for giving evidence to an IPCC inquiry would have been a serious breach of ethics, tantamount to interfering in the investigation. Furthermore, at that stage I did not know what Brian had told the IPCC because I had still not been interviewed by it or seen his statement. Nevertheless, 'love to hatred turned' produces bitterness in anyone and it was with both incredulity and foreboding that I learned that Brian was to become the Liberal Democrat candidate for Mayor of London on leaving the Met, another of the 'you couldn't script it' developments during my time in office.

In all this gloom there was still humour. The legislation which had arisen from Brian Haw's encampment was so widely defined geographically that it included Downing Street. The legislation required anyone wishing to apply to hold a demonstration to seek permission from the Commissioner but was also restrictive as to the grounds on which that could be refused, which did not include embarrassment. It was my task to explain to the Home Secretary that, on Budget day 2007, I had no power to stop a single demonstrator, dressed in a Union Jack outfit, from standing opposite 10 and 11 Downing Street in a silent protest. I also had to tell him that this protester, in the immediate run-up to Tony Blair's resignation and the likely succession of Gordon Brown, when Gordon Brown came out of No 11 bearing the famous red briefcase, would be holding a placard bearing the words 'John Reid for Prime Minister'. 'Gordon will never believe it's not my doing,' was the injured response.

If 'love to hatred turned' is the apposite phrase to describe my dealings with Brian Paddick, then perhaps 'loved not wisely, but too well' is the right description of what happened with Andy Hayman. He and I had worked together very closely indeed during the investigation into Ali Dizaei, which I describe below. In many ways he was my protégé and I helped him closely in his successful application to become Chief Constable of Norfolk. He was the only police officer I invited, along with his wife, Jane, to my fiftieth birthday party, a long weekend in France. As soon as Andy knew I was to be the Commissioner, he decided to apply to come back, either as an Assistant Commissioner or as Deputy Commissioner. He was unsuccessful in the latter application but then did become an Assistant. As the newly appointed Commissioner, I made a strong plea for his appointment. I had plans for wholesale reform of Specialist Operations, the counter-terrorism empire. I was certain that, while professionally very proud and very capable, it was inefficient, old-fashioned and elitist in some parts. I knew there would be bitter resistance to change and I needed a man whom I trusted completely and who would drive the changes through. And Andy did. So anxious had I been to get him on board that I had arranged to lend Norfolk a senior officer to be their acting Chief Constable.

But something went wrong. I began to pick up that Andy seemed to be spending a great deal of time with the press. Quite early on there were rumours that he was briefing in a careless and sometimes disloyal manner, although I never had any proof. When, about a year into my Commissionership, I made the comments about Soham, an unnamed senior source at the Yard was quoted as saying that we couldn't have a Commissioner who was a 'chump'. The only person I knew who used that word was Andy so I suspected he may have been the source although I could never be sure. Mentally I logged the comment.

In the years that followed, however, I continued to support Andy, recommending him for a CBE and then ringing him to console him for the way *The Times* broke the story of his award: 'Honours Row over Shooting Blunder Policeman' was the front-page headline. In the summer of 2006 Andy delivered the goods in the shape of a reformed Specialist Operations, combining the anti-terrorist unit with Special Branch, thus effectively abolishing the latter after more than a century of existence, agreeing to the amalgamation of all intelligence assets into a single place under a single command and taking the first steps to facilitate the eventual amalgamation of the Specialist Operations Surveillance unit into another command, something which everything about Stockwell pointed to as necessary. All of these initiatives were anathema to a great number of officers within his command and it took a toll on him. There were times that he seemed very stressed.

Elsewhere some provincial chief constables still resisted Met primacy over counter-terrorism. This is still unfinished business and needs further legislation. For now, however, while there were some difficult meetings, we finally persuaded ACPO that it was vital that the person holding the job of the Met Assistant Commissioner Specialist Operations should also be ex-officio Chair of the ACPO Terrorism Committee and we carved away the non-counter-terrorist parts of Andy's command to give him space to do this. Money was being pumped into counter-terrorism by government through the mechanism of ACPO, so we believed it was crucial to ensure that the Met got its proper share, which we certainly did: a fact which makes puzzling the claim in Andy's book *The Terror Hunters*, as serialised in *The Times*, that we did not have sufficient resources for counter-terrorism and should have slowed down the rollout of Safer Neighbourhoods. By the middle of 2007, therefore, much of what I had asked Andy to deliver was well underway. Then the clouds began to gather.

In late 2007, an inquiry had been launched into the use of corporate credit cards by Met officers and staff. It would be fair to say that this was not to be the Met's finest hour, as it became clear that the system for checking and reconciling this expenditure was utterly useless. A small number of officers were charged with criminal offences and an enormous drive was made to try to clear up the system. Particular attention was paid to senior officers and it became clear that Andy's expenditure appeared to be higher than anyone else of his seniority. An internal audit investigation began. Then it was discovered that similar questions were being raised about expenditure on a corporate card which belonged to ACPO. Further concerns were being expressed about who had authorised the amount of expenditure on the new ACPO offices which had been leased in Victoria.

Then a separate inquiry into a leak came to an end, in the course of which the telephone records of a number of people had been examined, including Andy, and it was revealed that, while there was no proof that he had behaved improperly, there was a high volume of traffic on his telephone with telephone numbers identified to be those of journalists. Moreover, there were also an extraordinary number of contacts with a former woman Met employee, then working for the IPCC (at a time when Andy had been under investigation by them). All this, of course, was coming on top of the finding against him in Stockwell Two, which was currently under consideration by the MPA.

I decided that I had to act. On the afternoon of 4 December I called Andy in to see me. My intention was formally to warn him not to use the credit cards any further for the time being, to make him aware that his contact with the former employee was now known and to ask him to consider whether his relationships with journalists were not capable of damaging his professional reputation. I wanted to keep Andy in post, because of what he had achieved and because of what we had so painstakingly negotiated with ACPO, but it was time for a serious discussion on what was going on and probably also for a warning that his position was in jeopardy if he did not clean up his act.

At first I was told that Andy was unavailable because he was having dental surgery. I was not pleased. Then I got a message that this was a mistake and he was coming in to see me. Then I learned that Channel 4 had put some questions to him that same afternoon about some of the issues on which I needed to talk to him. A little while later he came into my office. I was again with Martin Tiplady because this was a formal moment and I had notes of what I was going to say.

I was shocked. I hadn't seen Andy for a few days but he looked haggard and unwell. He had two pieces of paper in his hand. He sat down heavily at my table. I asked him if he was all right. He nodded. I started to outline my concerns. He put up his hand. 'No,' he said, 'I am going to make this easy for you, Ian.' He pushed the pieces of paper across the table. It was a list of questions from Channel 4 about the 'unusually high' amount of communication between him and the IPCC staff member and about the amount of the expenditure on the ACPO offices. A broadcast was intended as soon as possible.

'I have had enough. I am going. I quit. Now,' Andy said. Martin and I tried to reason with him but he would have none of it. We suggested he sleep on it or take sick leave but he would do neither. He announced his resignation within minutes and was gone the next day. Andy has never admitted any wrongdoing in relation to these issues. The MPA never instigated formal discipline proceedings against him.

Apart from a brief meeting the next morning, we have never spoken again. Andy has never returned the calls and messages I have left for him. In his column in *The Times* and in the extracts published from his book he has been critical of me and what appears to me to be his reinvention of some of our history together has hurt. As Duncan says in *Macbeth*:

> There's no art
> To find the mind's construction in the face:
> He was a gentleman on whom I built
> An absolute trust

So what had happened? Perhaps Andy got carried away by the power and prestige of his job, burned the candle at both ends, developed a lifestyle of late evenings and could not see the danger to his professional standing. One evening the year before, John Reid had asked me to bring the main counter-terrorism officers to his room in the House of Commons for a drink. I brought Andy, Peter Clarke and Cressida Dick and asked Catherine Crawford, the Chief Executive of the MPA, to join us. Afterwards I suggested eating together at a nearby restaurant. At the end of the meal I proposed that we divide the cost between us all. Two or three days later an article appeared in the *Evening Standard* about how 'shocked' senior colleagues were at that suggestion. Only when I realised, after he had resigned, that Andy had been in the habit of taking his senior commanders out and paying for it, at least once to the tune of more than £600, on the Met's credit card, did I surmise the source of that story.

As things closed in that December I think he was close to breaking point. Perhaps what I was asking him to achieve in Specialist Operations was simply too great a challenge. It was a great pity. I could have done with the kind of unqualified support he had given me when we worked together the first time in order to deal with the next confrontation, which was to be with Tarique Ghaffur and which in many ways arose straight out of the case which had brought Andy and me together, that of Ali Dizaei.

When I was informed in the autumn of 1999 that I was to become Deputy Commissioner of the Met, a small delegation arrived in my office at Surrey Police headquarters. It was led by Andy Hayman, then a Commander. I was to assume responsibility for internal investigations and the team briefed me about developments in the attack on corruption undertaken by the Met since I had left. Then they briefed me about Operation Helios, an investigation into Dizaei. A year later Dizaei was suspended; eighteen months after that that he stood trial at the Old Bailey on charges of misconduct in public office and perverting the court of justice. A further trial was scheduled for false mileage claims. In September 2003 he was acquitted on the first two charges. The CPS decided not to proceed with the second trial. But Dizaei had lodged an Employment Tribunal claim.

In an Employment Tribunal, the aggrieved person gives evidence first amid much publicity, often on the front pages of newspapers. This one was set down for three months and the Tribunal was not prepared to wait for discipline processes, which had had to wait for the criminal trial to finish, to be completed. With the help of the MPA, I ordered the negotiations which led to the discipline investigation being set aside in exchange for the Employment Tribunal claim being dropped.

Although as part of this agreement Dizaei accepted that his conduct had fallen below the standards expected of a police officer in one or two instances, he has never admitted any of the matters which were alleged against him.

I underestimated the impact of all this on Tarique Ghaffur. He was Dizaei's mentor and at one stage came into the purview of the surveillance on Dizaei. Because of this he was not told of the operation at that time, whereas some other officers of a similar rank were. He was even given a codename. When he was told, although it was made absolutely clear to him that he was not under suspicion, he was understandably furious. At Dizaei's trial Tarique appeared as a defence witness with little warning and it is likely that his appearance had a significant influence on the jury, who subsequently acquitted Dizaei.

The logo of the Professional Standards department was 'Integrity is non-negotiable'. I have never forgotten the angry meeting I had with the investigators, for whom I felt very sorry. Worse was to come: in our haste to find some way out of this, the MPA and the Met forgot to consult on our plan with either those of our Advisory Group who we had asked for advice or the Police Complaints Authority who were supervising the inquiry. It took a long time for some of the independent advisors to forgive me. Perhaps the Police Complaints Authority and the Independent Police Complaints Commission, which followed it, never did. Their 2004 report on the case was savage about the agreement that had been reached.

I had first met Tarique Ghaffur when he had left Lancashire Police to join the Home Office technology wing. By the time I arrived back in the Met he was a Deputy Assistant Commissioner, in charge of Westminster, the force's largest borough command. When I took over as Commissioner I was genuinely pleased that he was part of the team and I supported him wholeheartedly in his three applications to be a Chief Constable outside London, which turned out to be unsuccessful. However, he had applied to be my Deputy Commissioner and appeared to resent the fact that, while I was supportive of his application, as I had to be from someone so senior, I had obviously supported others more, as he was unsuccessful at the first of a two-stage process. But I liked Tarique and I respected the difficult journey he had had to take from Idi Amin's Uganda to high rank in the police of his adopted country. Like many who had faced prejudice in their lives, however, Tarique seemed to see slights where none were meant and a series of incidents soured our relationship, for which I am genuinely sorry, although his final actions in the force, still to come, were in my view entirely unacceptable.

For most of my time as Commissioner the Met had four operational commands, each headed by an Assistant Commissioner. The largest, with about two-thirds of the force strength, was Territorial Policing, providing the policing services delivered by officers based in police stations across the thirty-two London boroughs. The other three were Specialist Operations, dealing mainly with counter-terrorism, Specialist Crime, undertaking complex crime investigations, and Central Operations, containing traffic and many of the specialised uniform branches such as the dog and mounted sections and the Territorial Support Group, the public order officers.

When I became Commissioner, Tarique was in charge of the Specialist Crime Directorate (SCD), where he seemed to do a good job. But I saw a tendency in him to behave as if he was slightly separate from the Met. In all his commands he was a good communicator and newsletters were a feature of his style. I noticed, however, that his SCD newsletter, which always featured him prominently, did not feature a Met logo or the strapline of 'Working Together for a Safer London' and I ensured that that was changed.

The decision to roll out Safer Neighbourhoods and the need to protect spending on counter-terrorism meant that difficult cuts had to be made elsewhere, not only in support functions like Human Resources and Information Services but also in other parts of the operational commands, Specialist Crime, Central Operations and parts of Territorial Policing, other than Safer Neighbourhoods. Over budgetary matters Tarique proved to be protective and obdurate. In the spring of 2006 a newspaper report appeared that Tarique was taking legal advice as to whether, because each Assistant Commissioner is equivalent in rank to Chief Constable, he had the right not to have resources taken from his command. I asked Tarique whether this was true and he admitted that it was. This was a direct challenge, which the MPA was certain to spot and to raise, and in time it did. So I moved Tarique and I told him that I was doing so because of this and my view that he was becoming over-identified with his single command. I reminded him that, when we all met together on the day before I became Commissioner, I had made my first demand on my senior colleagues that, from that day on, they were 'to consider yourselves members of Management Board first and only secondly as leaders of your individual commands'. I exchanged his responsibilities with those of Steve House and appointed Tarique to Central Operations, actually a larger command. It might have been larger but Tarique appeared to see it as a move to something less glamorous. Steve House moved from Central Operations to Specialist Crime. One of the consequences of the switch, however, was that Tarique now became the lead for preparations for the Olympics because those had to be connected to public order planning.

Nevertheless, Tarique appeared to throw himself into his new job, particularly the Olympics. After the announcement of the Olympics in 2005, I had asked the Home Secretary to appoint one of my Assistant Commissioners as the Olympic Security Coordinator, in part to demonstrate to the rest of the UK's police that the Olympics were actually called the London Olympics and the Met, not some ACPO committee, was going to be responsible for their security. This title now passed from Steve House to Tarique. But by this time the Olympics troubled me because there were too many and not necessarily the right fingers in this pie, with both Tessa Jowell and Ken Livingstone having significant interests, while I was almost unable to get the Home Office engaged. This was going be the largest security operation in UK history and yet ministers and some officials seemed unable to see any urgency in the need to set a budget, to create a plan or a system of governance. I argued with both Charles Clarke and John Reid to no avail. So, during 2006 and 2007, Tarique and his team began to fill the gap. This arrangement was to have unforeseen and unpleasant consequences in 2008.

But there were rumblings. In early January 2007 a very odd story appeared in the *Sunday Times* without warning, under the headline 'Top Muslim officers turn on "racist" Met'. This story suggested that the three most senior Muslim officers, Tarique Ghaffur, Commander Shabir Hussain and Ali Dizaei, were 'planning drastic action to highlight what they claim is persistent discrimination in the Met'. None of the officers was quoted directly but the paper stated that Tarique was about to leave, Hussain was planning an Employment Tribunal and Dizaei was about to publish a book critical of the Met. The article went on to say that 'the three men believe that Blair is personally responsible for an anti-Muslim culture developing in the Met which is hindering the police's ability to tackle terrorism'. All three men denied that they had spoken to the paper and no other major paper picked up on the story.

Ali Dizaei did publish a book, *Not One of Us,* the following month. Unfortunately for him, he was appearing in front of the MPA promotion panel in the week that *Not One of Us* was book of the week on Radio 4 and being serialised in *The Times*. His book was critical not only of the Met but also of many junior colleagues. He was not promoted. Shabir Hussain did take the Met to an Employment Tribunal, which eventually took place in the summer of 2008. He claimed that he had been excluded from promotion on a number of separate occasions and was being passed over in favour of a 'golden circle' of white officers. The Met and the MPA took the fairly unusual step of opposing him on every count and he lost. He still serves in the Met. Tarique Ghaffur did leave but his leaving was longer drawn out and more bitter than anyone could have predicted. It was occasioned by the sudden realisation by the Home Office that all was not right with the Olympics and Tarique's evident unhappiness over this, which was of an almost Olympian scale, eventually led to his departure and mine.

In 2007 the government at last announced the security budget for the Olympics or, rather, it did not. Tessa Jowell announced that the government expected to spend no more than £600m. However, as David Normington, Permanent Secretary at the Home Office, wearily but wisely said, 'Ian, that isn't a budget: there is no budget. That is an estimate of the size of the bill. Now we have to find the money. The rest of government will look to the Home Office and we have to look to the rest of government.' And therein lay the problem for the Met, for Tarique and for me. Because Tarique had not been idle. Particularly because I had arranged for it to be a direct appointment of the Home Secretary, he was immensely proud of being the Olympic Security Coordinator and was working hard on a security plan.

In fact Tarique was working too hard on it, very personally, to the intense frustration of his deputy for the Olympics, Deputy Assistant Commissioner Richard Bryan. Richard and I had worked together in many different roles over the course of twenty-five years. But Tarique appeared to distrust him for that very reason – when the details of his Employment Tribunal were eventually disclosed, Richard was named as the only other respondent alongside me – and he began to hug the Olympics closer and closer to himself. At one stage, until I had the absolute folly of it pointed out to him, he even produced a copy of a plan marked as being the personal copyright of Tarique Ghaffur, and another time he objected fiercely when, in his absence, I ordered Richard to get whatever plan existed from Tarique's personal staff.

In a series of meetings during the autumn of 2007 I insisted that Tarique produce a costed plan, which eventually he did – but it had a pricetag of £1.2 bn, twice the amount earmarked. We asked him to make clear what was obtainable for the half of that sum which was actually available and what risks would then be outside the plan. He agreed to do so. But the security plan for the Olympics was vast and none of us was surprised that such a task would take a long time because, whatever he was doing himself, Tarique needed to get the agreement of many Whitehall departments to whatever he was going to propose. And here the insufficient grip by the Home Office became evident. It had largely left Tarique to manage the process of obtaining agreement: while other Whitehall departments would probably have prevaricated about being told what to do by the Home Office, especially if it involved money from their budgets, they resisted very stubbornly indeed being told what to do by the Met, a mere proxy for the Home Office. Of whatever went wrong, this bit was not the fault of Tarique Ghaffur.

The Office of Government Commerce (OGC) is an independent organisation within the Treasury, designed to secure value for money on all large spending projects inside government, any of which can be subject to its scrutinies, known as Gateway Reviews. In the late autumn of 2007 the OGC examined the Olympic Security Programme and sent a report to David Normington at the Home Office. It was simply the most damning of its reports I had ever seen. The OGC uses a traffic-light system to mark its findings: overall this was a double red because of the lack of clarity about responsibilities and cooperation across government. And the blame was laid firmly at the door of the Home Office for not taking a stronger lead. David found this useful because he was as worried as I was over the general lack of purpose and grip. And he moved very swiftly. He appointed his most able of lieutenants, Moira Wallace, since herself appointed as a Permanent Secretary elsewhere in Whitehall, to sort out the mess. And she did. The OGC report was received in early 2008. By the time Moira had finished, responsibility for overall coordination had been moved back to the Home Office from the Met, a senior Home Office official had been appointed as Olympic Security Director and, with the agreement of myself and the MPA, Richard Bryan and his team now reported to him. All this meant that Tarique's role in the Olympics was much reduced: the title of Olympic Security Coordinator was abolished and he was offered what he appeared to see as the less prestigious role of Senior Police User and Head of Operations.

Other than the appointment of the Director, all this could probably have been done in a few weeks but it took two or three months because Tarique was outraged. He blamed me, although never to my face, and he could not be persuaded that this was nothing personal, that what the Home Secretary could grant, in terms of a job and a title, the Home Secretary could take back. He saw conspiracy by everyone around him, including his deputy, Richard Bryan, who had a terrible time, and he fought every aspect of the change. We all spent hours in meetings and this at a time when we were concerned not only with terrorism but also a new threat, a sudden and sustained rise in the number of teenage Londoners killing one another, mostly with knives.

And the longer this went on, the more obdurate Moira Wallace at the Home Office became that Tarique should now have as little to do with the Olympics as possible. I realised we needed outside help to try to depersonalise the situation for Tarique. In late 2007, I had rung a management consultant I knew, Martin Samphire, and asked him to help sort out what was happening over the Olympics. I had used Martin on the huge C3i Programme which I had managed for the Met for many years, the transformation of its radio and telephonic communication systems. I wanted to use him in the same way initially but after the OGC report appeared, he was to be largely responsible for putting the flesh on the bones of the Home Office's plans. I believe, however, that my prior working relationship with Martin may have been wrongly interpreted by Tarique as further evidence of my hands pulling the strings. There was to be a future connection between Martin, C3i and my departure, in which Tarique apparently had a hand.

Relationships at the top of the Met got worse and worse. Tarique looked like thunder most of the time. At meetings he would say very little. This seemed an irreparable situation and a number of us, in order to restore equilibrium to the management team, explored ways of helping Tarique to leave with dignity after a distinguished career. But all the time there were persistent rumours that Tarique was preparing an Employment Tribunal case, which almost all of us believed had to be avoided at all costs because of the damage it would do to the Met.

Meanwhile all of us were distracted by the upcoming mayoral election and, by the time the Tarique situation reached the point where some payment or other solution could have been considered, the election was too near and the existing MPA therefore could not take such a decision. When the administration changed, it had one opportunity to do so but as Kit Malthouse, Boris's right-hand man, was to say, at that point, it 'no longer suits us politically, Ian'.

9

Resignation

Of all the episodes of my policing career, the one I would have considered the least likely to trigger its end was my leadership of what was effectively an engineering and IT project. C3i was the biggest change programme ever undertaken by a British police force. It had started in the mid-1990s, when I was working away from the Met, and originally had been the consideration of how and when to bring on stream the replacement for the computer system that controls the Met's radio and telephone communications, including the 999 emergency system, known as the command and control system. By the time I arrived in 2000 it had been Met-ised into a sprawling set of sub-projects and endless committees; most observers said it was never going to happen. At that stage it was also a PFI (Private Finance Initiative) project, with two large consortia of private companies bidding to undertake it.

By its end in 2007 it was regarded by the Office of Government Commerce, no less, as one of the most successful major public procurements in Britain. The MPA was also very pleased. By then C3i was firmly in the public rather than the private sector, beneficiary of an injection of £160m from the Home Office, the largest single grant for a capital project in police history. It led to the relocation of thousands of staff from every borough in London. It delivered, perhaps unusually in the public sector, largely on time and on budget, even though that budget was in the billions. Although this was obviously the achievement of an enormous team, I was, as both Deputy and for a time still as Commissioner, what was termed the Senior Responsible Officer (SRO) for C3i, so the buck for all this expenditure and unpopular change stopped with me.

In early 2006 I handed over that position to Steve House and his Central Operations command, when the first of the boroughs had successfully transferred its radio communications into one of three huge new buildings in different parts of London. These would eventually house the communications of all thirty-two boroughs, together with the central control room, which then finally left Scotland Yard. When Tarique Ghaffur took over Central Operations he inherited this responsibility. This was only for a short period, as it was to transfer again to another command, when we rebalanced Andy Hayman's responsibilities to enable him to undertake his increasing responsibilities for ACPO counter-terrorism by altering those of some of the other Assistant Commissioners. However, that short-lived responsibility was enough time for Tarique to meet Martin Samphire for the first time. At that stage Martin was working for a company called Impact Plus, co-owned by a long-standing friend of mine, Andy Miller. I had taken over the C3i programme from John Stevens, who told me he regarded it as the most awkward part of his portfolio as Deputy Commissioner. About eighteen months later and after it had been decided that the private consortia were too expensive and the Met was going to have to do this thing on its own, I realised it was too big for an SRO who had a day job. I was going to need regular reassurance that the innumerable parts of the programme were working.

By the time Steve and then Tarique took C3i over, that reassurance had, since 2002, been provided by Impact Plus and very successfully. Its role became known as the 'Programme Conscience' and it reported directly to the SRO, with Martin as the main contact. As I had feared, some parts of C3i had turned out not to be working properly and Impact Plus helped to identify and rectify them. At one stage the company was the crucial element in the recovery by the Met of nearly £20m from a defaulting supplier.

By mid-2008 I regarded C3i as a significant achievement: a long-running, immensely complex and sometimes very difficult project but one which had delivered great benefits to the Met and therefore to the people of London. It had avoided the pitfalls that had led to some of the notorious public-sector IT delays or disasters, such as the delay to the National Air Traffic Control Centre or the failure of the London Ambulance Service's new dispatch system. I was sure that Impact Plus had helped and I was equally sure that I had notified all who needed to know, including the MPA, that one of the firms who were bidding in 2002 for the role, which later developed into the Programme Conscience, was owned by a friend of mine. I had no doubts, although I had not had much cause to think much about it for six years, that the procurement had been totally proper.

So I was astonished when, in mid-July 2008, the story of my relationship with Andy Miller burst on to the front pages of national newspapers amid a slew of allegations of impropriety, even sleaze. I was even more astonished when, in the days that followed, all sorts of emails and text messages between members and officers of the MPA appeared in the press, about the possibility of my suspension from office. And I was both astonished and appalled, ten weeks later, on the day after Boris had asked me to resign and while I had yet not finally made up my mind, that another twist of the same story, false in almost every implication, appeared as the main story on the front page of the *Daily Mail*.

And here we have to return to Tarique. According to Brian Paddick's book, one day in 2005 Tarique unexpectedly came into his office and Brian – in confidence, as he puts it – told him the story of how he believed people in my private office knew on the afternoon of 22 July that the wrong man had been shot at Stockwell, the centrepiece of Brian's evidence to the IPCC in Stockwell Two. The next day, Brian states, he was contacted by Margaret Gilmour, then the BBC's crime correspondent and more recently co-author of Andy Hayman's book. They met and Margaret apparently told him that earlier that day she had had an hour-long, private meeting with Tarique, at the start of which he had pointedly told his press officer that he wanted to have this meeting by himself, and it is then apparent from Brian's account that Margaret put to him the story that Brian had told Tarique. Brian writes that he 'neither confirmed or denied the story' to Margaret but he then describes himself as waiting nervously for Gilmour to appear on the BBC's *Ten O'Clock News* that night and watching her relay to the world what turned out essentially to be his account.

All of this may or may not be true, although it is certainly true that Brian subsequently and very angrily insisted that he was not the source of the story (although he had no right to tell Tarique in the first place). To my knowledge, Tarique never denied it or threatened legal proceedings. What is certainly true is that in the summer of 2008 Tarique told the MPA Internal Audit that there was something suspicious about Impact Plus and C3i. Before I was interviewed as part of the enquiry into C3i I was shown a summary of the statement given to the investigators by the MPA's Head of Internal Audit, Peter Tickner. I never saw the whole statement but the summary made clear that Tarique had told Tickner that he ought to look at Impact Plus and Samphire.

It is impossible to say that this intervention by Tarique was the only reason why an enquiry into C3i began at this time but one of the more depressing parts of writing this book has been the unpicking of this underbelly of relationships and inappropriate briefing, so different from the bravery and straightforwardness of the cops at the front line. Unsurprisingly, the summary then goes on to say that shortly afterwards Tickner became aware that there were press questions about the procurement of Impact Plus.

All of this happened during Boris's first months as Mayor but before he became Chair of the MPA. This addition to his responsibilities had been joined with a number of other tidying-up measures about Police Authorities and was not to become law until 1 October. In the light of what happened next it is ironic that I had long argued that the Mayor should be chair of the MPA, in the same way as he chaired the board of TfL, because that might partially sort out the labyrinthine and competing accountabilities of my office. It is also fair to say that I had not foreseen – and I doubt anyone else had – what might happen if the Mayor and the Home Secretary were from different political parties. Certainly I had not thought of that when Hazel Blears, then Policing Minister, had rung me one evening to tell me that the change in the Mayor's responsibilities would be included in a forthcoming Bill. I think that call was in late 2006, at which point a Conservative Mayor – or the prospect of a Conservative government – seemed unlikely.

It was not until the autumn of 2007 that things changed, after Gordon Brown's apparent decision not to call a General Election and, much closer to home for me, the prospect of the arrival of Boris Johnson. The Conservatives had searched high and low for a candidate, with my predecessor John Stevens, the former Director-General of the BBC Greg Dyke and even Brian Paddick being mentioned as possibilities. A range of worthy but scarcely well-known characters, with admittedly unforgettable names, such as Warwick Lightfoot, Victoria Borwick and Andrew Boff, were lining up to take part in an electronic primary election, open to all Londoners, in order that one of them might have the chance to go head to head with Ken Livingstone, which looked likely to be a fairly ill-matched contest. My old critic Richard Barnes had entered these lists at one time but had withdrawn, about which I was relieved as I could easily foresee one part of his manifesto. At my occasional meetings with Ken he seemed to be preparing for his fourth term, quite apart from his third: he was very keen that, as soon after the election as possible, I should seek an extension of contract so we could undertake the London Olympics together.

Then came Boris, who, entering the primary race late, scooped up 75 per cent of the 20,000 people who bothered to vote. The established politicians were dismissive, with Ming Campbell describing the Conservative candidate as 'the blondest suicide note in history' and Ken, speaking at the Labour Party conference and joking that he was giving 'the Boris Johnson memorial lecture', saying that his rival 'proposes to add a lack of managerial competence to the Thatcherite decline and division always represented by London Tories'.

To the contrary, it turned out that an unnamed Tory spokesman was to be right, saying that Boris had 'captured the interest of the public and has helped challenge voter apathy'. He had and suddenly there was a battle on Ken's hands. In Boris, he faced the only other politician of his generation who was known simply by his first name. He was also to face an opponent who was being given direct administrative and political support by a resurgent Conservative Central Office and who had attracted to the UK Lynton Crosby, the election strategist who had guided Australia's Prime Minister, John Howard, to four election victories. At the same time the *Evening Standard* threw its weight behind Boris, with the issues surrounding Lee Jasper, Ken's race adviser, being at the centre of an anti-Livingstone campaign by its reporter Andrew Gilligan. Meanwhile the national political scene was shifting, as the Conservatives rode ever higher in the polls.

I was concerned but not by Boris personally. Our only disagreement in the run-up to the poll was when we had clashed in private correspondence when, during the Health and Safety trial, he had publicly described the Met's firearms teams as being 'trigger happy'. I had written to him pointing out that, in the previous twelve months, the Met had been alerted to over 10,000 firearms incidents but had fired weapons only three times. Meanwhile, amid all the calls for my resignation after that trial, I noticed that Boris pointedly did not join in very often. But the views of London Conservatives on policing did concern me, in part because, by and large, they represented outer boroughs and often repeated the old argument that the wealthier suburbs contributed the most money and yet the inner cities received the most policing (true, but policing resources are better distributed by need than by wish). And they seemed to be obsessed with what they thought of as the success of the US model of policing. In truth they weren't: they were obsessed with the success of New York. From the very first days of the MPA the Conservatives in London took their lead from Michael Howard and kept raising the story of the recovery of New York from its crime-ridden past, always quoting the success of 'zero tolerance'.

As a result I consumed a lot of time analysing the similarities and differences between the two cities and in the end came up with some interesting conclusions. The first similarity was that much of New York's success was based on Bill Bratton's adherence to the 'broken windows' theory, which he first tested when he was Commissioner of the New York Transit Police, a theory which would come to underpin our Safer Neighbourhoods. Second, the NYPD that Bratton inherited in 1994 had been very lightly managed beforehand, with the principal concern of precinct commanders, for instance, being to avoid the corruption that had once been so endemic. One example of this is that uniformed officers were not allowed to make arrests for drug supply: this produced exactly the kind of disorderly streets which underpinned the 'broken windows' theory.

There was little accountability for performance. Bratton introduced it very firmly with weekly 'Compstat' meetings, which replaced a fear of corruption among precinct commanders with a fear of being sacked if they did not reduce crime. I did not like the 'theatre of blood' approach adopted in New York, with the frequent humiliation of precinct commanders in front of their peers, but when I was both Deputy and Commissioner there cannot have been a borough commander in London who did not know that his or her job depended on the reduction of crime. The third similarity was the numbers of cops: Mayor Giuliani and Commissioner Bratton inherited an enormous surge in new officers from their predecessors, as did I, although even in my time the Met's strength never rose much above 32,000 police officers, nothing like the kind of numbers the NYPD had at its height, nearly 41,000 officers, or the maximum it had in Bill's time of nearly 38,500. And the Met performed duties in London and elsewhere that would be the task of the FBI and other Federal agencies in the United States.

There were also fundamental differences. Most important was just how bad New York had got. Bill used to tell an entirely apocryphal anecdote about his first morning in New York. He says that he left his apartment and asked the cop on duty how far it was to the nearest subway. 'Three blocks,' came the reply. 'How long will that take me?' asked Bill. 'I don't know,' said the cop. 'No one has ever got that far.' New York from the mid-1970s to the mid-1990s was a crime-ridden disaster. The chattering classes and the media had had enough and were prepared to back the NYPD in doing whatever it took to reclaim the city. Although Bill Bratton claims not to have used the term 'zero tolerance', this perhaps reached its apogee when, a little after Bill's time, an unarmed Liberian asylum seeker, named Amadou Diallo, was shot forty-one times by NYPD officers in 1999 and an unnamed mayoral aide declared the incident to be 'collateral damage' in the war against crime. Lastly, New York's police were aided by the fact that District Attorneys in the US need to get elected and are therefore amenable to a straightforward plan to get the bad guys off the street, in a way to which the UK criminal justice system has never been attuned.

Throughout the early life of the MPA, Conservative members constantly raised the difference between the two cities and it had been my task to take what was good from the NYPD and steer away from the bad. I knew the Conservative Party as a whole was – and is still – full of fervent admiration for US policing. (Just before my eventual retirement I was at a dinner at the Police College at Bramshill, attended by Dominic Grieve, the Shadow Home Secretary. The principal speaker was Chuck Wexler, Chief Executive of PERF, the nearest American equivalent to ACPO. As Chuck carefully analysed exactly how much better organised, trained, led and held to account British policing was than anywhere in America, Dominic's face was a picture. (Apparently he was very angry afterwards with the organiser.)

I was now concerned that a Conservative administration at City Hall would reopen the debate about the comparative resourcing of inner and outer London, in the middle of the crisis in knife crime (which, while it occasionally spilled into the suburbs, continued to be much more common in the inner city), would press for 'zero tolerance' beyond the huge increase in stop and search that I had already authorised and would be less supportive of 'Together' and the other issues surrounding diversity which I believed to be the long-term answers to making London safer. What I had not understood was that it was another feature of the American police scene on which the Conservatives would concentrate, the direct political control of local policing, by which they meant me.

It was about three weeks before the election when Ken first began to say privately that he thought he might lose, although right until the end he thought that the complex system of transferable votes might save the day, even though he was worried that Brian Paddick was not doing what he expected a Liberal Democrat to do, which was to suggest that his followers cast their second votes to an anti-Tory candidate who could win. He also could see that the 'Back Boris' campaign was very well organised and intent on getting its voters to the polls in outer London. Ken reads opinion polls like punters read form: he knew his vote and he knew that it was not that closely connected to the standing of the Labour Party. This was because of his chequered history and his standing as a Londoner: because of his political past, there were some lifelong Labour voters who would never vote for him but, equally, because of his performance as Mayor, he had a personal following among voters of all parties and sometimes of none. But he could not be entirely immune from the woes of Labour. He told me afterwards that, throughout his time as Mayor, he had persistently polled 13 per cent above Labour but he knew he was going to lose when Labour began to trail 25 per cent below the Conservatives.

So it was to be Boris and I texted him my congratulations as the result was announced and wrote him a letter the next day saying that I looked forward to working with him and continuing the cooperation between the Met and the Mayor's office. On his second day in office Boris asked to see the heads of the various parts of the GLA and held a photo shoot with each and all of us. He was, as always, very amusing. Throughout the campaign media representatives had frequently asked him whether he was going to be able to work with me, so I noticed that he went out of his way publicly to be cordial to me. He asked for a private word. We spoke for about ten minutes and, tired though he was, I thought he was listening and was interested in the Met. He asked me to bring forward plans to deal with the three main planks of his campaign in respect of policing, which were to apply even more effort to the problem of teenage knife violence, to put extra police on the buses and to introduce crime maps for the public to access. We had already given thought to all of these and, both on that first day with Boris and afterwards, the new Conservative administration were surprised at the alacrity with which the Met moved to support the Mayor's priorities. There was no immediate reprimand from the media for being too close to the Conservatives! Boris said that he looked forward to working with me and I offered him as many briefings and visits as he could fit into his schedule.

Almost immediately things got more difficult because of the effect of the new London arrangements on my relationship with the Home Office. During the course of a large meeting of civil servants and others, the Home Secretary got quite shirty when I told her that we were soon to introduce crime mapping for the public in London, as she saw this as a Labour initiative which she was shortly to announce on a national basis. I told her that I could not delay a London launch to accommodate her. The national launch came much faster than I or anyone else had expected and Boris's aides were later furious when it happened before their London event. Not long afterwards the Met launched a new development in the battle against teenage murders, which was the use of randomly placed, metal-detecting search arches. The launch was to be at the Elephant and Castle Underground Station in south London. This initiative had been long in the gestation and had been carefully designed with the consent of the local community, to the point that the Southwark Stop and Search Monitoring Group, largely long-term critics of the Met, were actually going to hand out supporting, explanatory leaflets at the scene.

When they heard about it, team Boris could not understand why this was a Met launch and demanded that their man be there. That was not a problem but it was the first indication that, as David Blunkett had been so long before with John Stevens, they were uneasy with the Met having its own personality and publicity. Next the Home Office learned about it and, pointing out that it had paid for the arches as part of its anti-knife crime work, made clear that the Home Secretary wished to support the Met's work by attending. It would be dishonest not to admit that the scenes which ensued at the launch were quite amusing. Boris was the novelty and the star of the small media scrum that surrounded us but the two press teams fought for attention and I felt like the celebrant at a shotgun wedding. The underlying message was stark, however: nobody took any notice of the community representatives and the battle between the political parties was now washing across London policing.

I needed to get to know Boris, so I went with him next to the launch of his flagship policy of strengthening policing on buses. There was a genuine problem, which was why, when Boris offered funding to strengthen the teams working with TfL, we were pleased to help. During term-time, London buses move hundreds of thousands of young people about and the main bus hubs were sometimes frightening places for both children and other passengers. Buses, bus stops and bus stations were crime hotspots. I offered Boris a seat in my car and, chatting amicably, we drove down to Croydon Bus Garage in south London.

One of the things Boris had said during the campaign was that, while he knew he could not, he believed the Mayor should have the power to hire and fire the Commissioner. It was on this journey that I took the opportunity to explain to Boris how significant a role the Mayor already had in the selection of a Commissioner, even if he did not have the final say. More importantly, I said, there had scarcely been a terrorist plot in recent times that had not been connected to or passed through London and that, if a Home Secretary of any party found that he or she could no longer appoint the London Commissioner, the Met would cease to be in charge of national counter-terrorism and London would be a lot less safe. He was affability itself during the photo shoot on a bus and pointedly supportive when a reporter asked if he was enjoying working with me. This was the longest of a number of such encounters. I found out later – because they talked so freely in front of the Met driver of another car – that his aides were furious that the two of us had spent so long alone and that they had lost control of their unpredictable front man.

In the few months I spent working with Boris, I was struck by the strong similarities and fundamental differences between him and Ken Livingstone. On meeting them in person people really warmed to both of them: they were both almost contra-politicians, as far from the mainstream type of their parties as possible, and both supremely confident. Of course, Ken was the archetypal Londoner, while Boris is not. I do not know how good a London Mayor Boris will be but the one big difference I noted was his lack of interest in detail. Ken had an extraordinary grasp of detail. I hardly ever saw him speak from notes though he would reel off lists of statistics. That is not Boris. And I remember being really worried at an early Olympics meeting which he chaired when he was completely outgunned by the representatives of those building the Olympic village. These were men who had built enormous public infrastructure projects before, across the world, and could find their way round the most complex of budgets. I hope that Boris now has someone to do that for him.

Among Boris's chief aides was Kit Malthouse, a well-educated man, with a background in finance, who, until he was elected to the London Assembly, had been a Westminster councillor and then the borough's Deputy Leader. I was aware of him from my dealings with Simon Milton, the leader of Westminster Council, and knew that in the run-up to the election he had been very critical of me in a newspaper article, as being too outspoken for a police officer. He had particularly criticised the fact that I had appeared on Radio 4's *Any Questions* and that I had given the Dimbleby Lecture, although his main charge, as ever, had been that I was too close to New Labour. Boris asked him to look after the policing portfolio and Kit Malthouse expected to become Chair at the next meeting of the MPA.

This was going to be a very odd period for the MPA. It was now a mixture of newly elected or re-elected London Assembly members but with the remaining non-elected members being from the previous MPA, as new members of this type could not come on to the MPA until 1 October, when Boris, of course, would also join them. This meant that, at the first meeting after the May election, the Conservatives did not have a clear majority. Malthouse was furious when, at that first meeting, Len Duvall refused to relinquish the Chair and this mixed membership did not support his own candidacy. For the next few months this left both MPA and Met officers serving two masters, each jealous of the other. Len enjoyed this. Kit did not. He is an imposing and intelligent man but a poor listener, appearing usually to have made up his mind before any proper discussion. We were not going to get on.

And we didn't. The next event is again connected to Tarique Ghaffur, who continued to be withdrawn and uncommunicative. As far as I knew, he was attending the annual ACPO/APA conference when a newspaper report appeared suggesting that he had decided to take legal advice on whether it was appropriate to take the Met to an Employment Tribunal. I insisted that he come to see me. While that was happening, I was told that Kit wanted him suspended at once. I pointed out that that was not a matter for me but for the MPA and it was too early to do so until I had made further enquiries. I received a message back that Tarique would only see me if it was to discuss operational matters affecting his command. I repeated that I wanted to see him one to one to discuss whatever I, as Commissioner, needed to discuss. When he came he was sullen. He denied being the source of the story but admitted that it was true that he was seeking legal advice but he did not know what that advice would be. 'It is a matter for others: I do not know,' he kept repeating. I asked him to reconsider and suggested that there must be other ways we could mend the relationship. He did not answer. I told him that his actions were a grave step which I must report to the MPA. He said that he had not made up his mind. He left and, I believe, went to see his lawyers.

I went over to see Catherine and then talked to Kit. The matter of suspension from duty was again raised and I was informed that that 'no longer suits us politically, Ian'. I was furious, not so much that they were not prepared to suspend Tarique, which would have been a tricky issue, as it concerned the seeking of legal advice about employment matters, although the challenge to my authority was flagrant: I was furious about the introduction of politics into such decision making. Later on, when we were alone, I asked Catherine what was going on. 'You must understand,' she said quietly, 'they want you gone.' I did not press her on this. She was a dear friend who, while impeccably serving the MPA, had been close to me through nearly a decade. She was now in a very difficult position, serving a new administration, whose policy towards me she had just outlined in four words. I went home that evening and, in the car, for the first time in all these long years I really thought of resignation. If the MPA was going to behave in a way that set out to undermine me, this would be unsustainable. I decided that, aggravating as this was, it was not yet sufficient to take such a step. In a radio interview earlier in the year I had said that I was a bit of a limpet. It was time to stay attached.

Nevertheless, Kit's reaction gave me pause for thought and from that moment on I worked to the mantra, which I discussed with my wife, of 'prepare, but do not presume' to leave office before the end of my term. The pressure was beginning to tell on my own family life. It was difficult to talk about anything else part from my job: holidays were interrupted and simple things like walks, trips to the cinema and entertaining friends got rarer and rarer. My mobile telephone was a constant presence, day and night.

Felicity remembered a phrase from Clarissa, wife of Anthony Eden, at the height of the Suez crisis: 'In the past few weeks I have really felt as if the Suez Canal was flowing through my drawing-room.' Felicity felt that the Met and its crises were flowing through the house and she, and to some extent our children, were beginning to be affected by the endless phone calls and the hostility of the press coverage. It was only later that I found another remark of Clarissa Eden's, from all that time ago: 'Both Anthony and I were quite naive about how the press works. Neither of us should have been, but we were.'

I was glad that Felicity and my daughter were abroad, working with a charity in Rwanda, when the next story broke only a matter of weeks later, in mid-July. 'Blair Faces Call for Inquiry after Close Friend Won Met Contract,' ran the headline on page three of the *Sunday Times*. This was C3i. The close friend was Andy Miller. The *Mail on Sunday* covered the story on its front page and it was also carried by the *Independent on Sunday* and the *Sunday Express* and Radio 4. I had been alerted to the story breaking by Len Duvall a couple of days before. I was very surprised indeed and sent for the files, which were miles away in the Met's archive. I remembered the events pretty well and I could not think of anything which would cause concern. I left others to look at the files and went home for the weekend.

In the days that followed, the MPA referred the case to its Professional Standards Committee, who immediately ordered an investigation. This lasted until December, although it was more than a year before the report into the affair was finished. It is worth quoting from the letter I received in December 2008, a few weeks after I had left the Met, from the investigator, Ronnie Flanagan, the Chief Inspector of Constabulary. He wrote:

> I now state that there is no evidence whatever of any wrongdoing on your part. I do not intend to submit the report to any prosecuting authority for further consideration of any criminal matter. There is, in my view, simply no need for this to be done in respect of you or, indeed, anyone else.
>
> So far as potential police misconduct matters are concerned, I have approached this matter as if you were continuing to serve as Commissioner of Police of the Metropolis. In this context, there again is no evidence whatever that would lead me to recommend to the Metropolitan Police Authority any further action in this regard, even if you had continued to serve beyond 1 December 2008.

There was nothing in it. There never was anything in it because the Met's Procurement Department and I had been scrupulous in the manner of the procurement. This was a story that just grew in the telling and I had to spend many months just knocking down one allegation after another.

I had rung Andy Miller when I realised I needed to come up with some mechanism for controlling the vastness of C3i. Impact Plus had already done work on C3i before I returned to the Met and he had told me, when I was appointed Deputy Commissioner, that it was in a very poor state. When I told him about the kind of support I thought I needed as SRO, he told me about the 'Programme Conscience' concept and that his firm undertook that kind of work. However, from the very first conversation he and I agreed that, were the Met to go ahead with seeking consultancy support, it would obviously have to be a full and proper public procurement.

From witnesses and documents, the enquiry which was to follow found that, before the process reached its culmination in a set of presentations by the two final bidders, I had alerted the Police Authority to the friendship with the man who ran one of those firms and that I had received professional advice to attend those presentations and no advice to the contrary. The investigating officer concluded that I had not evaluated the bids and my participation in the process 'in no way prescribed the ultimate choice [of candidate] which I have no doubt would have been made in the absence of any involvement by the Commissioner.'

By the summer of 2008 I had forgotten most of this but the facts were relatively easily available, at least to a trained eye, in writing, in the procurement file. So was the fact that, after the initial contract for some £150,000, I had handed responsibility for extensions of the contract to Ailsa Beaton, who had them approved by the MPA. Impact Plus was well known to those MPA members who supervised the enormous programme.

I could not attend the full MPA meeting scheduled for the Thursday of the week after the story hit the press in July 2008 because I was attending my daughter's graduation from university, so I wrote to Len pointing out as much as I could recall of the events and making clear my total confidence that everything had been done properly. It does not surprise me that an investigation should have been considered but, had the world been in a sensible place, that would have begun with a scoping study by the MPA's Internal Audit. That investigation could have found all of the facts above in days, as well as the truth behind a subsequent allegation that Impact Plus had won the contract despite submitting a bid for three times that of its rival bidder. This also was clear in the file: Impact Plus had applied to and had been given permission by the Procurement Department to submit an 'alternative' bid, on the basis that the work proposed simply could not be done in the timescale set out or to the budget suggested, a process expressly permitted within the procurement rules.

But a scoping study was not what was wanted. A few days earlier Len had warned me about the emergence of the C3i issue and had told me that 'they' – and I did not have to ask who – were 'after you'. The Professional Standards Committee ordered a full-blown inquiry on 28 July, even into my temerity in having had the C3i files sent to my office, in case I had interfered with them. And that was announced to the press. I was disappointed and felt sorry for the chairman of the committee, a magistrate called Reshard Aulaudin, who had also chaired the MPA body that had scrutinised C3i. In an MPA press release of 28 July he said that 'this decision does not imply any finding of wrongdoing by the Commissioner but is made to ensure that all the facts are independently and thoroughly investigated'. I never saw that reported by the press. Then the leaks began.

On Wednesday 30 July *The Times*, the *Guardian* and then the *Evening Standard* all ran stories about an email exchange between Kit Malthouse and the lawyer to the MPA, David Riddle, in which Kit complained that it should not have been for the committee chaired by Reshard Aulaudin to consider whether, after they had decided to set up the inquiry, I should have been suspended. I am not clear whether they had ever got to that point but, under regulations, it is their decision. 'There is too much decision making by committee on stuff like this and gives far too much sense of power. Essentially, it's the Mayor's decision to suspend or not,' Kit wrote, though this last point is incorrect, adding that he was 'very cross' that Len still had a role. The MPA solicitor insisted that Kit seek his legal advice, commenting that 'if there is to be action against the Commissioner, it has got to be lawful. If the nuclear button is pressed, expect it to be crawled over for legal flaws.'

Boris's spokesman neatly distanced himself from the row, noting, as reported in *The Times*, that he 'hasn't had any meetings or conversations about the future of Ian Blair and awaits the outcome of any investigation. He continues to work with Sir Ian in fighting knife crime in London.' The next day I had my regular meeting with the Crime Writers' Association. It was quite a jocular session with the holiday season coming up. Perhaps all this was some kind of summer madness. I decided that I had to say something to the general public. I expressed my concern that Boris's expressed wish for powers of hire and fire over the Commissioner was contrary to the best interests of Londoners because the Met would then lose its primacy over terrorism and suggested for the first time in public that this was 'a poor bargain'. To the question of whether people had 'got it in for me', I replied, 'I am just going to say that it appears to be a position which attracts a lot of comment.' I then went on to say, 'Most senior officers are concerned that the office of Commissioner is becoming a matter for high politics.'

But it made no difference. The joust was now in earnest and I could feel that my closest colleagues were becoming concerned for me. At one point Paul Stephenson said that he could not have borne 'the constant pressure under which you are operating'. (I fear he may have to and I know he will be able to.) In contrast to all the troubles with Andy and Tarique, the rest of my Management Board was tight-knit and support-ive. The senior ranks beneath the Management Board were the same. However, I was less concerned about them than what the men and women of the Met must be thinking about it all.

In August, determined to get away for a bit, I went on holiday, first with Felicity to the Western Isles of Scotland for a few days but then as a family to Sardinia. Halfway through that second week, Tarique Ghaffur hit his personal nuclear button. I had decided to let him go to Beijing, as anything else would look like what employment law describes as 'victimisation'. However, almost as soon as his trip to the Games was over, on 22 August, the BBC ran a story that Tarique had lodged an employment claim for racial and religious discrimination for £1.2m and, while neither the MPA nor the Met had received such papers, a spokesman for the Black Police Association confirmed that the papers had been lodged. It was a Bank Holiday weekend. On the following Thursday, knowing I was abroad, Tarique then held a press conference in full uniform to announce that he was going to launch an Employment Tribunal against the Met and centred his complaints against me. Alfred John, the chairman of the Met BPA, then spoke to the press conference and announced: 'Racism, both institutional and individual, still continues within the Met. In fact, it has not improved that much since the Macpherson Report'.

In my absence Paul Stephenson made his own press statement as Acting Commissioner, saying that he recognised Tarique's right to bring the claim but was unhappy about the issue being made public. He said he was 'very disappointed that attempts to reach a mediated settlement have failed'. He added:

> I do not think it was appropriate for this matter to be conducted in such a public way. That is a matter for him [Tarique] to reconcile with what he considers to be his proper responsibilities as one of this country's most senior police officers. The MPS will not at this time be commenting publicly in detail on the content of Assistant Commissioner Ghaffur's claims, other than to say that we do not accept the charges of discrimination against us and intend to robustly challenge them. In short, I think it is long past time that we all shut up, stop making public statements about private disputes and get on with the job we are paid to do.

Nothing like this had happened before. I returned to my office, breaking yet another holiday, and Paul and I considered what to do. Staff throughout the organisation were outraged and my office was yet again flooded with emails of complaint, many of them from black staff, on the lines of 'not in my name'. I was appalled. I could not conceive how Tarique could think that he could continue to work in the Met after the press conference. Consultation with the MPA indicated that, while almost all members, including the Conservatives, thought that his behaviour was very poor indeed and there was every prospect of an investigation, there was no appetite for suspension. I knew that Tarique had hired himself a very assertive set of lawyers, Dean and Dean, which was fronted by the high profile Dr Shakrokh 'Sean' Mireskandari. I had met him once, before I had gone on leave, when I had called Tarique in, after the first stories had appeared, and persuaded him to go into mediation. Mireskandari asked me one question, which was by what powers I was suggesting this, and I replied 'those of the Commissioner of the Metropolitan Police'. He smiled knowingly and asked for time to consult with his client.

Although I did not have the power to suspend Tarique, I decided to seek legal advice on whether I could force him to go on leave in the interests of operational efficiency. Meanwhile I ensured that all attempts to mediate continued, although this was now mediation about how he would leave the Met. In the meantime I noticed that the *Mail* had run a piece in my absence, on 30 August, intimating that Tarique's claim would include an allegation of irregularities in bringing Martin Samphire in to sort out the Olympics and that I had lied over the extent of my involvement in 'Cash for Honours'.

But legal advice takes time and, before that arrived, someone close to the MPA struck again. The fourth of September is my daughter's birthday and I had decided to take her out for lunch. My plans got delayed because that day *The Times* ran a story suggesting that a letter would arrive from the MPA that week to tell me that my contract would not be renewed. Defiantly but wearily, I stood outside Scotland Yard, alluded to a quote from Mark Twain to the effect that 'the report of my death is an exaggeration' and pointed out, first, that there were eighteen months on my contract left to run, second, that no discussion between the MPA and myself had ever been had on the matter and, third, that no one seeking a renewal would enter into such discussions until much nearer the time for a contract's eventual expiry. With a few extra details, the story was a reprise of one that the *Sunday Times* had run in mid-May and it was equally false. The sources were likely to be the same. No letter ever arrived.

Then it was time to deal with Tarique because the legal advice had arrived and it was clear. I called him in again on Tuesday 9 September. He again came with Mireskandari and with Ali Dizaei. I was struck by the sense of hierarchy. The most powerful presence in the room was Ali, followed by Mireskandari, with Tarique looking angry but puzzled. I was again accompanied by Martin Tiplady, my Head of Human Resources. It was a short meeting of which I still have the handwritten notes I had prepared beforehand. I told Tarique that I was temporarily relieving him of his command including both Central Operations and his responsibility for the Olympics, with immediate effect because our job was to preserve the safety of Londoners and I believed that confidence in the MPS and its operational effectiveness was being damaged by his conduct. I invited him to go on leave of absence. The three of them withdrew to consult. Ten minutes later I was asked whether I was asking or ordering Tarique to take leave and I said to them that I was asking but, if necessary, I would make that a lawful order to be understood by Tarique and all those who worked for him.

Tarique stormed out of the room. I have never seen him since. I am very sorry that Tarique's career ended the way it did but there was one last surprise for me about the whole saga. The Mayor issued a statement backing my actions, describing them as 'a necessary move to restore confidence so that the operational efficiency of the Met Police is not compromised'.

Again, as a number of Management Board colleagues sent messages out to their staffs supporting my action, my office groaned under the weight of emails congratulating me on standing up to Tarique. The BPA then threatened a boycott of recruiting and a march on the Yard. It also issued a press statement under perhaps the worst heading I had ever seen: 'Ethnic and Religious Cleansing in the Met'. This was an insult to the dead of, among others, Srebrenica and the Met staff who had helped in their identification. One of the emails sent to me was a copy of one sent by an Asian officer with nine years' service to the Chair of the Met BPA, who had issued the press statement. He wrote: 'The Met your organisation describes does not exist. I've never encountered racism in this job, subtle or otherwise. Neither have any of my colleagues from Black/Minority Ethnic groups.'

Despite all his blustering, it was obvious that Tarique would settle in the end. If anyone could after all this, I actually felt good. As we reached the end of September I thought that the height of the storm was passing, although the Stockwell inquest was still out there. I was completely wrong.

As I entered the Mayor's office in City Hall on 1 October, I felt proud about the Met and its achievements and good about the way Tarique had been handled, although I wished it had never happened. I knew the Impact Plus matter would be resolved in my favour in due course and regarded the noise of the BPA as no more than that. I was wary, worried by the continual leaks and conscious that Boris had again, speaking at the Conservative Party Conference, referred to the democratic deficit over the Mayor's powers to hire and fire the Met Commissioner. I was a little late when I arrived in the eighth-floor office, which is dominated by a map of London covering one entire wall. We sat at the long table, with Boris to my right at its head, Catherine Crawford at its foot and Kit and I opposite each other. I was looking towards Tower Bridge. Traitor's Gate was just out of sight. The meeting was scheduled to discuss the following Monday's meeting of the MPA, which would be the first one Boris would chair. Ironically, it was me who had pressed for the meeting.

I noticed that in contrast to his normal slightly dishevelled look, Boris's appearance was rather neat, his hair combed; he was attentive and slightly nervous. I didn't concern myself with what that might portend. I now understand that, friend as she had been, Catherine knew what was about to happen: throughout she said nothing, just looking at her feet or very sadly at me.

I began by telling them about an injured officer I had just visited and then Boris changed the subject, beginning, 'There is no easy way to say this, Ian', and then talked about a change of leadership at the Met. It took me a full twenty seconds to grasp that he was talking about me and the need for me to step down. My stomach turned over. He suggested that such a change would be best 'for the Met, for London, and, frankly, Ian, for you'. He rumbled on about all the distractions I was facing, contracts and the problems with Tarique and the BPA and that it could not be possible for me to continue to be fully effective. There was a dead silence when he had finished. Kit then said something similar to Boris, although I was not really listening as I tried to absorb what had been said and what my options might be. I eventually said 'This is very interesting but you don't have the power to do this, Boris.' He turned and looked at Kit, as if he needed reassurance as to the procedure, and then said, 'No but, on Monday, I will be asked if I have confidence in you and I will say no. There will then be a vote of confidence and this one you will lose, Ian.' That was the moment when the first intimation came to me that I might have to go: I was not sure I could go through another vote. In fact I was sure I could not.

I said again that this was all very interesting but that I needed time, I needed to think hard about my duty to the force and about my options, the Home Office needed to be informed and I had to discuss the matter with my wife. Kit said that the matter could not wait and I said it had to. I could feel myself getting very angry indeed. For the first time Boris mentioned that a financial package would be available and he would ensure that all was done with dignity. I registered that but it was not the point. My duty and my wife were the points. I got up and said, 'I am not ignoring your views and I will let you know tomorrow.' We firmly agreed that not a word of this was to reach the press until I had told them of my decision. Boris leapt to the door and asked for someone to escort out 'Sir Ian'. He had clearly and honourably found the whole process unpleasant.

The next few minutes were particularly difficult. I went down in the lift with my protection officer, with Catherine and with Nina Cope, my temporary Chief of Staff, who had been excluded from the meeting and had waited outside. I told Nina that we had not properly discussed next Monday's meeting and would have to do so at the next meeting with Kit, on Friday. We then travelled back in an awkward silence to the Yard, while I had my office cancel a lunch that I had planned that day with the editor of the *Sunday Mirror*. Catherine and I agreed to have a sandwich in her office. I went over there a few minutes after. Although I was angry, my main feeling was one of sheer disbelief. Although I had heard the phrase 'they want you gone', I had been working on the basis that I would decide if and when I believed my resignation was in the interest of the service I had loved for more than thirty years. I had not connected Boris's first day as Chair of the MPA with the pre-emption

– or the attempted pre-emption – of that decision. Closing the door, she sat down and simply said, 'Bugger.' We sat in silence and I remembered the words she had texted me on the eve of my first day: 'It's going to be fun.' This wasn't.

Catherine told me that I had behaved with extraordinary dignity and then we went through the options. It was clear that I could just dig in my heels but that that would set me on a full collision course with the MPA and, not only that, it would put the senior management of the force in an almost impossible position. I weighed the constitutional implications of staying and going and then looked forward: if they were prepared to do this now, what would they do when the Stockwell inquest finished? And there would be other disasters because the Met always does disasters. 'It looks pretty bleak,' she said. They had declared war and in the end I would inevitably lose while, in the interim, the potential damage to the effective running of the Met was incalculable.

I now determined on three things. First, no rumour of this must get out and so I must spend the afternoon as normal. Second, I needed to get someone to help me with whatever contractual arrangements would have to be agreed if I were to leave and that also had to be begun this afternoon. Third, I had to think about how I was to get home in time to discuss all this with my wife.

The first meant that I was to have the pleasure of going through the annual appraisals of two of my Management Board members, John Yates and Dick Fedorcio, with none other than Kit Malthouse, of course – and without showing any unease. For the second, I called down Martin Tiplady, swore him to secrecy and asked him to prepare 'heads of terms' for a possible departure. He was shocked but wonderfully supportive. For the third, I knew that Felicity was going out to the theatre with our daughter that evening. I had to ring her to tell her that I was coming home rather than staying in the London flat. I told her that I did not want her to go to the theatre because we needed to talk. Any wife would want to know why and what followed was a dreadful conversation to have on the telephone. Felicity had given up so much for me and the last four years had been so hard. It was not to be an easy evening.

As I drove home I was also reflecting on the conversation I had just had with Kit at the end of the appraisals. I suggested that a part of an agreement, were one to occur, would be that I should stay until my successor was appointed. It was at that point that he said, in front of a startled Catherine Crawford, 'No, that wouldn't suit us politically. We will have an acting Commissioner until a Conservative Home Secretary is elected.' The phrase was almost the same as he had used about Tarique a few months before and it echoed in my mind. It showed not only how little these people cared about the political independence of the police or the constitutional position that Peel and his Commissioners had created but also how determined they were.

At no time did I contemplate the idea that Boris and Kit had dreamed of doing this without informing Conservative Central Office. That has never been confirmed but has been frequently suggested and never denied. If it is true, then the future of the Met Commissioner and all the constitutional implications of what Kit and Boris had done were in part being used in the private tussle for influence between Boris Johnson and David Cameron. I am glad I did not even think about that possibility at this moment; the contempt for the history of my office was quite bad enough already.

By the next morning I was 85 per cent sure that I would have to resign. My wife and I had been awake for a lot of the night but, around 4am, I had made a decision. In the meeting Boris and Kit had suggested that I should give as the reason for my resignation the pressures and distractions of the past few weeks and months. That was not true and I would make clear that I was stepping down at their request. As I left the house Felicity told me she would support me in any decision I took.

Then, at the station, I saw the next piece of the jigsaw. The main headline on the front page of the *Daily Mail* read: 'Met Boss in New "Cash for a Friend" Storm' and the story went on to claim that at the beginning of my Commissionership I had used Andy Miller's firm to 'sharpen my image' in a 'so-called vanity contract', for a sum of some £15,000, and that no other company had been invited to bid. There were two things right in the report: Martin Samphire of Impact Plus had advised those who were planning the transition between John Stevens and myself, in terms of both structure and strategy, and the cost to the Met had been about £15,000.

However, the contract had nothing to do with image because Impact Plus is not in that market and it had been a properly conducted procurement, in which I had no part, with three bidders. This was a perfectly normal process: another consultancy had done something similar when I had been appointed to Surrey. The article then continued with a description of a meeting the night before at which Ronnie Flanagan had briefed key members of the MPA about this. I knew there had been a routine meeting on the previous night about the investigation but I did not know whether it had discussed this allegation. I thought it unlikely that his team yet knew about it because all of us had struggled to remember anything of the sort from more than four years in the past when the *Mail* had raised the subject of the transition contract with the press office a few days before.

So why, I thought, would an almost totally false story about as little as £15,000 be a front-page headline in a national newspaper on the day after I had been asked to resign and why would it be linked to meetings of the MPA and apparent considerations of suspension? And in whose interest would it be? When I was a young detective a sergeant warned me against believing in the Coincidence Fairy. It was, of course, possible that she had made a surprise appearance and I will never know. But with this on top of everything else, suddenly the decision was clear. I was quite calm in that it somehow felt appropriate that the finally decisive factor in my decision should be a set of untruths in the *Daily Mail*. I drafted my resignation statement on the train and then asked my secretary of eight years, Rebecca Sandifer, to type it, after telling her what had happened and was now going to happen. When she brought it back, she was almost in tears.

I rang the office of David Normington at the Home Office, and asked to see him on a matter of urgency. I got there about 11.30am and he listened to my tale and to my conclusion. He said he was very sorry but not entirely surprised because the Home Office press office had just had its first call, asking for confirmation that I was resigning. It seemed that City Hall could not even keep that part of the bargain. I was sickened but not surprised.

David pressed me on whether my decision was irrevocable. I said that it was not but seemed inevitable as the damage to the Met of a total breakdown in its relationship with the MPA would be catastrophic. He went off to brief the Home Secretary and then I was called in. She was furious, but not with me. She was decent enough to see it as a personal tragedy for me but shrewd enough to recognise it as a political defeat for her at the hands of Boris and, as we then assumed, Conservative Central Office. She thanked me for all I had achieved and then asked David to leave. She asked how Felicity and I were.

I left the Home Office and returned to the Yard, where I told Paul Stephenson and Caroline Murdoch and then called Dick Fedorcio and Martin Tiplady down separately to tidy up the resignation statement and the heads of terms for my departure, both of which had to be agreed with City Hall. Martin knew, of course, but the others were shocked and very sympathetic. The Prime Minister called me and said how sorry he was. This was 'a shoddy political stunt', he said.

There was still one more irony: that afternoon had been set aside for Management Board colleagues and me to brief the new members of the MPA, who had been appointed the day before. At about 2pm I gave the first presentation, which was about how my vision for the Met had been developed and how I saw the relationship with MPA members. I then said that I had to leave and asked the Management Board members to meet me at 3.30pm because I needed to tell them something. Paul presided over the rest of the meeting with members and then brought it to a slightly premature end, saying that they might subsequently think that my presentation had been remarkable, given the circumstances that would now unfold. I met with my colleagues and told them what was going to happen and then walked down for the last time to the press room, where I gave my resignation statement to a single pooled camera. I wore a suit, rather than uniform, because I did not want to tarnish the uniform with such a sadness, the like of which I have never felt, before or since.

The statement read:

I was appointed as the twenty-fourth Metropolitan Police Commissioner in February 2005. Since that time, it has been the proudest task of my life to lead the men and women of the Metropolitan Police. I believe that the record of the Met under my command in relation to the expansion of neighbourhood policing, reduced crime, increased detection, improved public confidence and our response to terrorism has been a worthy one.

It is the duty of the Commissioner to lead the Met through good times and bad: to accept the burdens and pressures of office and, above all, to be steward of the Service he commands. I have today offered my resignation as Commissioner to the Home Secretary, which she has reluctantly but graciously accepted.

I am resigning not because of any failures by my Service and not because the pressures of the office and the many stories that surround it are too much. I am resigning in the best interests of the people of London and the Metropolitan Police Service. I would have wished to continue to serve Londoners until my term of office expired in February 2010. However, at a meeting yesterday, the new Mayor made it clear, in a very pleasant but determined way, that he wished there to be a change of leadership at the Met. I understand that, to serve effectively, the Commissioner must have the confidence of the Mayor and the Home Secretary. Without the Mayor's backing, I do not consider that I can continue in the job. Personally I see no bar to working effectively with the new Mayor but it is there that we differ and hence I am unable to continue.

The Home Secretary has asked that I should stay for long enough time for the process of appointing my successor to be got underway. I will therefore leave office on 1 December 2008, giving the MPA time to make plans for the appointment of my successor.

I offer Boris Johnson and his team at City Hall and at the Police Authority the very best of fortune. I say to the people of London that I believe that, in the Metropolitan Police Service, they have a quite wonderful institution made up of extraordinary men and women, who daily risk their lives on your behalf. I say to those men and women and those staff who support them that they are part of one of the greatest police forces in the world. This great institution will always have a central place of affection in my heart. Thank you very much.

The rest is largely history. In the aftermath Boris never came up publicly with a coherent reason for seeking my resignation, although he was good enough to describe Kit's metaphor of 'switching the machine off' as 'grisly'. It took me a few days before I could bring myself to read the next day's newspapers and they were pretty grim even then, with the *Mail* totally triumphant. The next time I saw Boris was two weeks later, at the Service Review, an annual meeting during which Met senior officers and MPA members consider for a day the year ahead together. He seemed embarrassed, muttered something about being sorry that he had not yet written to me (he never did), and we moved apart quickly. I opened the conference by delivering what was to be my only significant speech following my resignation. I reviewed what we had achieved during the previous four years and then put up on screen a picture of me surrounded by a firearms team. There was silence. I then added a caption to it: 'Be just a bit careful, Boris'. After the laughter had died down, I used the second half of the speech to lay upon colleagues the challenge of not retreating to an older, narrower, darker version of policing but to continue the work of embracing change and diversity as the only way to police London. I left a bemused Boris and Kit having to join in the long standing ovation that followed.

Perhaps not surprisingly, almost as soon as my financial settlement (to compensate for the loss of my contracted term of office) was signed in early November, it was leaked to the *Sun*. Only half a dozen people – one in the Met, my legal advisers and some in the MPA or at City Hall – knew of its details. I was told that the journalist who wrote the story, while not prepared to reveal his source, was clear that it had not been provided to him from within the Met or my legal team. That hurt a lot: from a fairly small article in the *Sun* it reappeared on the front page of the *Evening Standard*. The settlement, of course, was subject to an agreement of confidentiality: this was smashed wide open within seventy-two hours.

It took and is taking an inordinately long time for the C3i matter to be cleared up. Even though I had been cleared in December 2008 and that that had been confirmed in a draft report sent both to me and the MPA in February 2009, it seemed that some elements of the MPA did not wish to hurry out the news. It did not surprise me that the report's contents were leaked in June to the *Observer* and that, despite my being cleared, the only person praised in the article was Boris. An article in the *Mail* from an unnamed source noted that 'some senior police authority figures are unhappy about the tone of the report and have asked Sir Ronnie to "harden it up".' In mid-July the Authority finally considered the matter officially. What it did was just astonishing. It accepted Ronnie Flanagan's conclusions that there was no evidence of dishonesty or criminality on my part but refused to accept his third conclusion:

> There is no basis upon which police misconduct proceedings (or their 'civilian equivalent') could be recommended against anyone involved in this investigation. It should be noted that this conclusion has nothing whatever to do with Ian Blair's decision to retire. It would apply with equal force, should he still be serving.

on the grounds that the investigation was not 'sufficiently rigorous.' This had been an inquiry which had occupied four police officers full-time for six months, had involved the interviewing of almost forty witnesses and had been subject to advice from a QC. The Authority declined to give an explanation as to what matters of discipline it believed I would have breached, refused either to publish the report or to let me see it and announced that the matter was now closed. My solicitor advised me that this was likely to be a breach of Human Rights law. I suggested it was also contrary to Magna Carta!

A month later they did send it to me, together with a letter outlining their reasoning which included the following: 'As the Sub Committee was not required to determine whether disciplinary proceedings should be brought against Sir Ian, it did not consider specific potential breaches of the Code of Conduct.' This took me no further, leaving me not only in the position of not knowing what I was accused of, but also apparently not permitted to clear my name, as there is no appeal against such a decision. Andy Miller is suing the *Daily Mail* for allegations it printed about him. I am not. This book is my answer.

In December the Solicitors' Regulatory Authority suspended the practising certificate of Mireskandari and intervened in the practice of Dean and Dean. In October the national Black Police Association invited David Davis, by now out of the Shadow Cabinet and operating in his newish guise as a doughty champion of civil liberties, to address its annual conference. Unfortunately it sent the invitation to David Davies, Conservative MP for Monmouth, another fish altogether, who happens to sit on the Home Affairs Committee and is a Special Constable in London. He denounced the very existence of the BPA, as having both explicitly and implicitly racist policies. A number of Met BPA members walked out of the hall. This was one of those 'you couldn't make it up' moments that had gone the right way.

In May 2009 Ali Dizaei was charged with criminal offences, which he denied. The Met BPA made a complaint against Catherine Crawford over her handling of his case. Tarique departed in late November 2008. Many newspaper reports have suggested that his settlement was much smaller than his original claim. Because of a confidentiality agreement, I cannot comment. Within days Tarique had driven a coach and horses through the confidentiality agreement in the shape of an article about our relationship in, of course, the *Daily Mail*. When the BBC made a two-part programme on my time in office in June 2009, Kit Malthouse blasted David Normington as being out of touch for quietly criticising the Mayor and defending me.

The Coroner at the inquest into the death of Jean Charles de Menezes took away from the jury the possibility that they could bring in a verdict of unlawful killing. This was on the legal grounds that, while a Coroner's jury may no longer name the person they believe guilty of causing a death, they have to be clear that a charge of murder or manslaughter could be attached either to a person or persons unknown or, at the criminal standard of proof beyond reasonable doubt, to some particular person. In this case it was manifestly the case that it could not be attached to persons unknown and the Coroner ruled that, in the light of the evidence heard at the inquest, it was not possible to do so in respect of any specific individual, either the officers who fired the shots or the senior officers who commanded the operation.

None of that is to say that that operation was not marred by difficulties in communication or that the Coroner's other observations on improvements which could be made by the Met were not valuable. It is to say that almost all of those involved did their best in an almost impossible situation but that an entirely innocent man died nonetheless and an inquest is the place where such actions should be examined. And the inquest should have occurred earlier for the sake of everyone touched by this death.

Within six months the pattern would repeat itself. In April 2009 Bob Quick, who had replaced Andy Hayman as the Met's head of counter-terrorism, was also forced to resign. He had gone to brief the Prime Minister about a forthcoming counter-terrorism operation and as he got out of his car, a briefing paper about the operation was visible to photographers standing opposite 10 Downing Street. Bob had been the officer ultimately responsible for authorising the arrest of Damian Green MP for his alleged involvement in the handling of leaked documents and had publicly clashed with the Conservatives over the affair. Even though the only implication of his mistake was that the police operation had to be brought forward by twelve hours, calls for his resignation began from the Conservatives. After the rows over expenses, the Home Secretary no longer had the political capital to save him. One of the finest officers of his generation was thereby lost to the service.

Writing immediately afterwards in the *Guardian*, Martin Kettle, a journalist and observer of the police for many years, wrote perhaps the most succinct summary of what had happened to both Bob and to me:

Quick lost his job for 100 per cent political reasons ... [He] now joins Sir Ian Blair as a senior police victim of a very recent political nutcracker. Both Blair and Quick certainly made errors – not least by letting themselves be seen as too close to ministers. But they were not sacked for that. They were sacked because the increasingly partisan nature of police accountability in London meant they could be sacked. Boris Johnson has turned Labour's decision to allow the London Mayor to chair the police authority into a weapon in the hands of the Tories. He did it again yesterday with Quick. The old idea that the police are operationally independent is draining out of the system.

I left the Met on 1 December 2008, having decided that I would stay on long enough to maintain dignity in the manner of my going. I spent a lot of the two months left to me answering an astonishing number of emails and letters, from both inside and outside the service, expressing outrage at what had happened. The time was full of many kindnesses and many farewells but it was far from easy. I had lost not only a job but, more importantly, a vocation, which I would never be able to practise again. There were many men and women whom I admired and cared for whom I would rarely see again. There were some who would be friends for life but now it would always be different from before.

My last day was the occasion of a police long-service medal ceremony. During these both police officers and staff are acknowledged for their twenty-two years of service in the Met. Fittingly, this took place at the Peel Centre in Hendon, where my career had begun. At the end and after warm tributes from Catherine Crawford and Paul Stephenson, my wife and I received a second standing ovation from a packed house.

During these ceremonies I always used a quotation from Theodore Roosevelt, who had not only been President of the United States of America but also had earlier been Commissioner of the New York Police Department. When I had become Deputy Commissioner my wife had had it engraved on a glass bowl which sat on my office table. When I used to read it out I altered the quotation to include women but the original reads:

It is not the critic who counts, not the one who points out how the strong man stumbled or how the doer of deeds might have done better. The credit belongs to the man who is actually in the arena, whose face is marred with sweat and dust and blood; who strives valiantly; who errs and comes short again and again; who knows the great enthusiasms, the great devotions and spends himself in a worthy cause; who, if he wins, knows the triumphs of high achievement; and who, if he fails, at least fails while daring greatly, so that his place shall never be with those cold and timid souls who know neither victory or defeat.

The arena is still there and men and women have still got to enter it and do their best. That very same day the Damian Green affair erupted, rapidly followed by the controversies over the policing of the G20 protests and the resignation of Bob Quick.

I had been in the arena and I was proud to have been there. The question is whether the rules of the arena have now been altered in a manner detrimental to effective policing. I think they have.

Blue Futures

An Afterword

I have been accused of being a supporter of the Labour party. No one knows my political allegiance. I happily worked in Surrey for a Conservative-led Police Authority. I support politics which I believe are good for the public and for policing and argue against those that I believe will be detrimental. I am not for or against proposals because they have been put forward by one political party or another.

It was in precisely that spirit that, the night before I left office, I threw a party to celebrate my time in policing. There were many old friends present and many kind speeches, together with some appalling photographs from different stages of my career. Most of the early ones showed me sporting mutton-chop sideburns and a luxuriant moustache of a type which would have been familiar to my Victorian predecessors.

The Home Secretary could not be there, as she was in Brussels, although she had spoken to me earlier in the day to express her good wishes and thanks. The main speech was therefore made by Vernon Coaker MP, by now the Policing Minister, her number two. I was determined, however, that the event should not be characterised as reflecting the kind of party-political partisanship of which I had been accused, so MPs, MPA and London Assembly members of all stripes were invited. The next day I received a courteous handwritten letter from Dominic Grieve, the Conservative Shadow Home Secretary, expressing his regret at not being able to attend (although other members of the Shadow Home Affairs team did). He ended with the words: 'As was clear from your award at Bramshill, there is widespread appreciation of the work you have done during the course of a long career to improve policing.

Should I ever become Home Secretary, I know that many of the changes you brought about in the Metropolitan Police will serve as a model for further progress.'

This is the same Dominic Grieve, who, as Shadow Attorney General, had written a letter to the Home Secretary accusing me of breaking the law in refusing the IPCC access to the scene at Stockwell (even though the relevant part of the legislation making such access compulsory had not yet been enacted) and who must have at least assented to whatever Conservative press arrangements had been responsible for this story appearing on the front page of the *Evening Standard*. Even more astonishing, this was the same Dominic Grieve, then Shadow Home Secretary, who had supported Boris Johnson's manoeuvre to force me from office, 'welcoming' the news, as the *Guardian* reported: '"We have been calling for Sir Ian to step down for almost a year," he said, criticising "a serious lack of judgment about the leadership of the most important police force in Britain"'. I do not believe that he will have seen any contradiction between any of these positions.

There is nothing particularly surprising here. Grieve's position is entirely compatible with Boris Johnson's when I met him the day after he was elected Mayor of London – and they are both compatible with the difficulties the early Commissioners faced with Melbourne and the other Whigs, after the fall of the Tory administration in which Robert Peel served as Home Secretary. Pleasant and humorous as was my first meeting with Boris, there was one discordant note. I brought up the approach he had taken to the Met during the election campaign. In particular, his use of the words 'trigger happy' to describe the Met's firearms teams was one example of how I thought he was going to have to change his language and approach to the Met now that he was the Mayor, effectively the principal budget holder and strategist for the service and soon to be Chair of the MPA. I suggested that no sensible Chief Officer of any force asks a Police Authority Chair to be uncritical, but he had to realise that he could not go on being this continuously critical of the Met. 'You will have to praise the achievements of the cops where praise is due,' I said. 'You cannot go on for long talking down the fall in crime in London which they have achieved. They need to know you care about them, which Ken made clear. That way we can work together.' He looked me straight in the face and replied, 'I agree. Look, I know that Ken, the Met and you, in particular, have a good story to tell about crime in London in these last few years – but I simply would not have been elected Mayor of London if I had admitted that.'

I have been around politicians now for the best part of fifteen years and major national politicians for nearly ten. I am no ingénu: I understand that politics is the art of the possible but the complete shamelessness of that comment was pretty staggering. But with Boris's arrival as Mayor a politician was in charge of the police who had no understanding of them nor of the delicate checks and balances by which their functions were to be controlled, nor of the history of how those checks and balances were arrived at, precisely to prevent politicians taking decisions for purely short-term political gain. The policing settlement was being casually and thoughtlessly changed back towards the conditions of the early nineteenth century.

During the early years of the Mayoralty under Ken Livingstone and of a Labour-dominated MPA, there had been mischief enough, in the way in which motions had been drafted, committee members had been appointed and the times of meetings changed and other typical tricks of the trade, but those involved had long experience of local government and indeed of the increasingly close working relationship between local authorities and the police. They did not leave politics at the door but they were aware of history and they knew operational boundaries when they saw them. Not so Boris, as he showed in his astonishing decision to speak to Damian Green MP on the telephone after his arrest. Not Boris when he popped up on Radio 4 to announce Bob Quick's resignation and the appointment of his successor, thereby pre-empting the Home Secretary or the new Commissioner from being involved in the making of the announcement – and before Bob had formally and finally agreed to step down. And not the City Hall culture that apparently seems to have facilitated the leaking of my impending resignation and the financial settlement that was subsequently agreed and the other leaks that followed.

And behind Boris was one further group, those with experience of Westminster Council, like Kit Malthouse and Simon Milton, who seem to see the police as just another potential council service. In December 2007 Milton addressed the general assembly of the Local Government Association and, on the subject of policing, stated: 'By all means tackle organised crime and national security from the centre but neighbourhood policing should be accountable to local people through their local council.' And further back behind Boris are those Tory politicians like Nick Herbert, then Shadow Minister for Police Reform, who authored the recent Conservative policy document *Policing for the People*, which first proposed breaking back policing to much smaller forces and therefore having to create the equivalent of a British FBI. Nick Herbert told me that it was in the Conservative DNA that small and local was better and he saw no barrier to turning back the clock, even reversing the 1970s amalgamations, to return to small borough and individual county forces, breaking up the Lancashires and the West Mercias, hence the need for an FBI of some sort, which he was then calling a Serious Crime Force. I countered that I knew quite a lot about DNA and it was a long, connected string. What he was proposing was entirely contrary to the DNA of the police. There is no vertical distinction in British policing. Many inquiries include both the very local and the national and international and the example of the United States, with its thousands of small forces, is not encouraging.

However, it appears quite clear that a future Conservative government will propose radical change to the policing settlement along these lines. The introduction of directly elected local police commissioners is on the front page of the Crime and Justice policy section of the Conservative Party website, 'Where We Stand', which must be the outline of their future manifesto. The detail of the thinking was most recently unveiled in November 2008, in a Private Member's Bill proposed by Douglas Carswell, Conservative MP for Harwich and Clacton. Introducing it, he said:

My Bill would abolish police authorities. Instead, a simple, effective and transparent system of local accountability should be introduced: directly elected individual justice commissioners. Justice commissioners would appoint and dismiss chief constables, set targets for the force, make their own policing plans and control their own budgets, which would be allocated as a block grant. Initially, there would be one commissioner for every one of the forty-three police forces in England and Wales, but, in time, it would make sense to bring the forces into line with local government boundaries. My Bill would enshrine in law the operational independence of chief constables.

I was glad to note that my old school teacher, also a Conservative MP, this time for Staffordshire South, Patrick Cormack, warned in response that this would introduce 'Sarah Palin'-style populist politicians. He said: 'To politicise the police in the way that has been suggested [interruption] ... Of course it would politicise the police; people would stand for election on party tickets and for populist policies. Frankly, the Bill is a prescription for anarchy and disaster, and I cannot support it.' Exactly the same point about Sarah Palin, who allegedly had fired Alaska's police chief for refusing to fire a subordinate officer who was engaged in an ugly divorce with her sister, had been made immediately after my resignation in an article in the *Guardian* by the distinguished American criminologist Larry Sherman. But there can be no doubt that Carswell is closer to current Conservative thinking than either Cormack or Sherman. Similar thinking is still obviously at play in London. Kit Malthouse gave a lengthy interview with the *Guardian* which was published on 3 September 2009 under the headline, 'We have seized control of Scotland Yard, Tories claim'. Although a number of Conservatives distanced themselves, Malthouse asserted that he and Johnson 'have their hands on the tiller of the Met' and have 'elbowed the Home Office out of the picture', so that 'Johnson's team believe the police should be answerable to elected politicians and, Malthouse said, see nothing wrong in pressing them to do things that would be electorally popular. Blair's removal by the Mayor signalled to senior officers who they would be answerable to. It is self evident there is a sanction.'

The introduction of elected Commissioners in political charge of policing currently appears likely to feature in the next Conservative manifesto and will be, in my view, a seriously flawed and historically ignorant proposal. There can be no doubt that the manner in which I left office has made the position of the most senior police officer in the land inherently more precarious than hitherto. That precariousness is a feature of American policing as is populism, which in many American jurisdictions where law-enforcement officials are elected can be extremely unpleasant. Sheriff Joe Arpaio of Maricopa County, Arizona, puts prisoners in his custody in pink underwear and refuses to use any kind of air conditioning for them in the Arizona desert. He is known as the toughest sheriff in America but, when Grady Judd, the Sheriff of Polk County in Florida, told the press in 2006 that the man who had recently killed one officer and wounded another had himself later been shot dead by police, he was not particularly reticent either. When asked why it had been necessary to shoot at the suspect 110 times, with sixty-eight bullets being found in his body afterwards, he replied, 'I suspect that the only reason that 110 rounds was all that was fired was that's all the ammunition they had', without that comment apparently raising controversy. Knowing about the Stockwell case, an American friend had alerted me to that story.

I am not suggesting that Britain would immediately or perhaps ever reach this level of lowest-common-denominator policing but the replacement of Police Authorities by single directly elected individuals has two obvious dangers. One is the danger of policing becoming subject to populist competition, what the UK-based criminologist Les Johnston has described as 'the tyranny of the majority'. The second is that a direct-line accountability of a Chief Constable to one elected individual with the power to hire and fire him or her must encourage compliance rather than competence, obedience rather than professional decision making. This would be the end of police discretion. I simply do not know how, in these circumstances, a guarantee of the long-cherished operational independence of police can be enshrined in law, as Carswell suggests. Years ago a Conservative government was forced by the House of Lords to abandon plans to give the Home Secretary the power to appoint the Chairs of Police Authorities. The great Willie Whitelaw opposed the measure from the House of Lords. This present proposal goes much further and I hope it will never see the light of day, whether introduced by the Conservatives or any other political party.

It is not certain that the ideas of Boris's inner circle and a future Cameron-appointed Home Office team will be the same but there seems little doubt that significant changes to police governance will be proposed in the Conservative manifesto for the next generation. They have consistently welcomed and built upon each new report from 'progressive Conservative' think-tanks that have proposed variations on the core idea of elected commissioners. Policy Exchange, which is known as David Cameron's favourite think-tank, the Centre for Social Justice, chaired by former police officer and now Mayor of Middlesborough, Ray Mallon, and Douglas Carswell's Direct Democracy Group have all called for an elected local commissioner. And Labour and the Liberal Democrats will seek to present competing ideas, with David Blunkett recently proposing neighbourhood referenda to settle policing priorities in a local area.

My concern is that these ideas will not sufficiently take account of the long history and painful experience which has led policing in Britain to its present form. That is not to say that the present form is immutable. As ACPO said during the debate on force restructuring led by Charles Clarke: 'We are the guardians of the service we offer, not the structures we inhabit.' Nor is it for a police officer to determine the structures of policing or of the mechanisms of democratic accountability which control it. But the fevered run-up to a General Election may not be the best time for careful thought.

There is almost nothing in the various proposals being made by the different political parties that is impossible. In other countries mixtures of politicians, police chiefs and prosecutors can work in different operational and accountability structures but each country's solution has different advantages and disadvantages, which are reflected in the balance finally arrived at. It is unlikely that a solution from one country, such as directly elected police commissioners (which I would reject) or fully elected police authorities (which I would reject), or elected prosecutors (which I might support in part for anti-social and lower level crime), or an FBI (which I would reject without a great deal of prior new thinking) or even neighbourhood referenda (which I would consider appropriate under some circumstances), can just be grafted on to an existing structure elsewhere, without making provision for the impact on existing arrangements. It is like the introduction of foreign species into an indigenous environment.

We need to pull back from making quick fixes and give our policing a wide-ranging, apolitical and dispassionate dose of fundamental scrutiny. For, although simple in some ways, policing is inherently complex and deeply connected to the mood of the times. Royal Commissions are not popular with modern governments but I am sure one is now necessary.

During the first 150 years of modern policing in Britain there were half a dozen such Commissions. It is now nearly fifty years since the 1962 Royal Commission resulted in the 1964 Police Act. It is inconceivable that those who wrote it could have imagined that what they proposed would still be the bedrock of policing generations afterwards because they could never have foreseen the political and social conditions their grandchildren would face. The model they created is out of joint. The gradual accretion of new policing structures and doctrines, the foibles of police chiefs and politicians, the making of new laws, the challenge of a new media, the erosion of the agencies and agents of social cohesion, the development of a 'postmodern' society and of a racially and religiously diverse Britain have overwhelmed the paradigm and structures devised in the early 1960s.

It is time for a further long-term view to be taken. That view can be constructed only through the mechanism of a Royal Commission. This should begin by establishing a set of principles concerning the very nature of public policing and its unique role in the state, the boundaries of its mission, its cost, the constitution and terms of engagement of its workforce, its structures for accountability to the public and the role of politicians in its control.

And those principles should begin and end with some of the ideas of David Bayley and Egon Bittner, who, with George Kelling, theoriser of 'broken windows', are the giants of late-twentieth-century American criminology. Bayley, in his 1996 article 'The Future of Policing', co-authored with Clifford Shearing, wrote:

> Modern democratic countries like the United States, Britain and Canada have reached a watershed in the evolution of their systems of crime control and law enforcement. Future generations will look back on our era as a time when one system of policing ended and another took its place. Two developments define the change – the pluralizing of policing and the search by the public police for an appropriate role.
>
> First, policing is no longer monopolized by the public police, that is, the police created by government. Policing is now being widely offered by institutions other than the state, most importantly by private companies on a commercial basis and by communities on a volunteer basis.

Bayley has spent the past two decades exploring the previously uncharted territory of the interface between public policing and both the private sector and other areas of local administration. The history of policing has always been one of shifting boundaries. For instance, in earlier times in Britain and elsewhere, the concept of policing included what would now be the preserve of environmental health or fair-trade officials, whether that be weights and measures or noise. Some of these functions have now been permanently transferred to local authority services. Equally, what was once known as Securicor began as the Night Watch Service, providing additional security patrols in London's Mayfair, and then moved into the protection of goods in transit and the securing of industrial premises, as the police withdrew from such activities. In earlier centuries the Bow Street Runners ran an effectively privatised service for the recovery of stolen goods, as did the bounty hunters of the American West. In other countries, from Brazil to South Africa, private security companies currently provide services which include not only manned guarding of premises but also armed response to alarms and armed street patrols. In a consumerist society it is possible to argue that security is a commodity to be bought and sold. Large swaths of North American cities – let alone the urban sprawls of South America – are ghettos of the rich, gated communities with their own private security patrols, into which the public police can only enter with permission or in an extreme situation. It has been estimated that some 10 per cent of greater Miami falls into this category. Gated communities have come to Britain and some commentators on the right are enthusiastic supporters of such schemes. Bayley's book dispassionately examines the implications of the gradual privatisation of policing.

I am not dispassionate. The first principle which a Royal Commission should establish is that policing should be retained in the public sector. This requirement is in a different category from discussions about various models of police structures and police accountability.

The security of the citizen should not be a commodity. Like the defence of the realm and the administration of justice, security is a fundamental part of the contract between citizen and state. Education and health have long coexisted with both private and public provision. I believe it was a mistake to allow private companies to manage prisons but even here there is a distinction: prisoners are in a controlled environment, whereas policing is the interaction between the authority of the state and citizens free in their movements, occupations, leisure and desires.

This proposition, however, forces the immediate consideration of a further principle, which is that, as presently configured, policing is simply too expensive to be provided as a purely public-sector service. The current recession and the huge sums of public debt already committed to its resolution are important but they only reinforce an argument, which I mounted during my first year as Commissioner, that ways must be found to reduce the overhead costs of policing and that neither politicians nor police chiefs should be afraid of saying so. 'Policing on the cheap' is not a pretty term but it is a legitimate aim, if we can change the noun to an adjective: 'cheaper'.

In September 2005, shortly after the London bombings, I made a speech to the national Superintendents' Association in which I laid out a view that the way to reduce costs was not merely to undertake the bonfire of bureaucracy always promised but never delivered or cut backroom costs or management overheads (all of which we should do) but to cut the costs of cops. And the way to do that is to determine how much of the police role needs the full powers of a police officer and then break the workforce up into those who have full powers, those who have limited powers and those who have none, the result of which would be a reduction in training costs and wage bills. So the question is whether we can be, as I put it:

> bold enough to explore whether certain functions can be carried out by people on short-term contracts, partially warranted only to do a certain type of the police job, whether that be surveillance, financial investigators, underwater and other specialist searchers or members of the mounted branch. This is not new. All our fingerprint staff used to be police officers. Let us take the case of firearms officers. Could we bring staff directly in from the armed services, give them a certain amount of basic training and then clear instructions as to their firearms duties, so that they would be partially warranted, on a fixed-term contract, to undertake only those duties? The question then becomes how bold we wish to be and how far we can go before we lose too much flexibility in officer deployment and make too many jobs less appealing and less interesting, which would be a mistake.

There has to be some acceptance of countervailing needs, such as the exceptional flexibility police officers provide in terms of the tasks they can undertake. Any Commissioner needs to be able, if necessary, to put tens of thousands of officers on the street at the same time. He needs them to be deployable in any way that their commanders believe appropriate and when, for instance, the President of the United States and the Countryside Alliance decide to turn up in London on the same day, he does not need people to explain that they cannot police the situation in a particular way because it is not in their job description. But there is no greater absurdity in the world of policing than the word 'civilianisation'. The whole concept that lay behind Peel's reforms was that the police were civilians in uniform. If that is the case, we need to do whatever we can to bring terms, conditions and training into sensible alignment across the whole of our workforce.

Such a change has already been proven effective. Of course, the most obvious example is Police Community Support Officers, without which Safer Neighbourhoods would not have been possible. Surrey Police undertook an experiment in which it reduced the number of detectives in a CID office and replaced them with more, lower-paid investigative assistants, with what is estimated to be a 30 per cent increase in output and a 20 per cent decrease in costs. The service needs to be high skill and high precision at one end of its spectrum of activity (use of force, deprivation of liberty, collection of evidence), and yet much more cost-effective in relation to volume activities, such as patrol, reassurance and basic crime reporting. Just as health and education have already done, the police workforce needs to be tiered to create a greater consistency between the task required and the skills, knowledge and cost of the member of staff involved.

There have been some suggestions in the current economic downturn that police officer numbers should be protected and auxilliary staff, such as PCSOs, should be cut. Nothing could be more nonsensical in the interest of attaining a more cost-effective police force in the long term.

But changes to the overall make-up of the workforce, were they to be introduced nationally, would require political courage of a major degree. For years political parties have used officer numbers to demonstrate their commitment to policing. In this chief officers have collaborated, primarily because if the increase in budget is offered in the shape of more officers or no increase at all, it is too tempting to be resisted.

But it is a logical, organisational and strategic absurdity to judge the effectiveness of policing in the United Kingdom by the number of police officers employed, just as it would be illogical to judge a health service by the number of beds or nurses or an education service by the number of schools. Policing, health and education need to be judged in terms of outcomes, not inputs.

And the outcome of policing should be reduced crime and increased public confidence in their own safety. Hence, the logical position on officer numbers should be one in which a Home Secretary could take pride in announcing that, because crime and anti-social behaviour had fallen, his or her government was able to reduce police numbers with consequent saving to the public purse. The strength of the political impossibility of that statement is its own testament.

Locking the police service into competitive political machismo around officer numbers constrains the way in which the objectives of policing can be delivered. But I cannot see any political party having the courage to make this journey alone. Only a Royal Commission will provide the kind of cover that would be needed for all parties to move away from the current situation, one which will eventually price public policing out of its monopoly over protection of the public.

There are other, less controversial but necessary ways of reducing costs which should accompany workforce reform. The alphabet soup of national policy bodies – the Association of Chief Police Officers (ACPO), the National Police Improvement Agency (NPIA) and the Chief Police Officers Staff Association (CPOSA) – needs consolidation, with ACPO shrinking back to allow its creation, NPIA, to do its job unhindered.

Charles Clarke was right to propose amalgamations among forces: the current configuration is too expensive. There can be no logical argument for forty-three forces in England and Wales (a number perilously close to the secret of the universe as revealed in *The Hitchhiker's Guide to the Galaxy*), with, for instance, the considerable resources of West Midlands Police, whose boundaries include the city of Coventry (actually part of the county of Warwickshire), sited next to the tiny Warwickshire Police force (which consequently does not police Coventry).

The logical approach is to reduce the number of forces by amalgamation. However, that is not going to happen soon, not just because its implementation would be expensive, but because the public would not see such upheaval as a priority.

Most people scarcely care which police force serves them, any more than they care about the boundaries of strategic health authorities or local education authorities. This is an argument for police professionals and accountants. People care, quite passionately, about the provision of local policing, as they do about local hospitals and schools. So those accountants and professionals have to think differently.

It is important to understand that there are elements of the policing task that have to be dealt with away from or in addition to the police's local responsibilities and we need to resolve how that should happen. Some of this is about pure economies of scale: how many forces should be allowed to run their own helicopters? Some of it is about the return on training: why should a small force with a low murder rate maintain a permanent homicide squad? Some of it is about how to respond to those organised criminal and terrorist threats which are not themselves demarcated by any existing or proposed force boundaries.

If the answer in the short term is not to be amalgamation, then the only logical answer is that police forces need to be tiered in relation to what they can be expected to deal with, in the same way as Crown Courts are tiered according to the kind of criminal cases they try. Homicide cases do not normally appear on the lists at Kingston or Aylesbury Crown Courts, whereas the Old Bailey tries an unending series of them. If there is to be a force as small as Bedfordshire Police, perhaps it should not be required to investigate stranger homicide or organised crime. Perhaps it should be required, however, to pay a levy to a nearby, larger force to do that on its behalf and that larger force should be required to come to the aid of Bedfordshire as and when needed.

Because of understandable local pride, this again will need the kind of cross-party consensus that only a Royal Commission can provide, which would also have to examine the UK's overall response to organised crime. The policing settlement arrived at in the Police Act of 1964, which followed the last Royal Commission, is primarily local and it has struggled almost ever since with criminality of a regional, national and international nature. The response was the creation of Regional Crime Squads in the 1960s, replaced in the 1990s by the unnecessarily separate National Crime Squad and National Criminal Intelligence Service, themselves replaced this century by the Serious and Organised Crime Agency. All these have been unsatisfactory and insufficiently effective, with report after report making clear that organised crime remains a potent threat to the UK economy, which is only adequately countered by the larger forces in the main conurbations. The impact of internet crime aggravates this situation and only an objective and non-partisan inquiry will be able to propose principles which can be used to balance this need against more local and therefore more obvious demands.

In a sense this is a long-standing problem which has grown but does not necessarily threaten to change the nature of the compact between police and public in Britain. But the advent of international terrorism does, and a Royal Commission should consider how terrorism should be investigated and by whom.

Peel created, and his successors and their Commissioners nurtured, a policing settlement which grew out of eighteenth-century English concerns for the rights of individual citizens. Apart from in times of war, this has evolved, steadily and fairly seamlessly, to the point where the incorporation into British policing of the concepts of late-twentieth-century Human Rights legislation was not particularly difficult. This means that while the overall task of the police is to protect the citizen from harm, a very significant emphasis is placed on individual rights. Peel, Rowan and Mayne would recognise the vast majority of the processes by which modern police forces balance their different priorities within a structure of citizens' rights.

As the story of the years since 9/11 has unfolded, however, that structure is more and more under pressure. I have made clear my distaste for the concept of the 'War on Terror'. But it needs to be understood that, but for luck, the thousands who died in the United States on 9/11 could have been joined a few years later by thousands more here in Britain. If the bombers of 21/7 had succeeded, likewise the airliner plotters, or if the Haymarket doctors had known more about the ignition of detonators, the picture of policing in Britain would be different, as would many other aspects of life in the UK. The threat faced in the past decade, particularly the past five years, has been of a kind never before encountered in the West outside warfare, characterised not just by a carelessness about human life but by an absolute determination to cause the maximum number of entirely innocent casualties, often in the most appalling way.

And the threat seems particularly acute in Britain. Because of the nature of the suspected intention of the plotters, the police have increasingly felt obliged to move away from their normal requirement for a sufficiency of evidence before arrest towards pre-emptive arrests of often unavoidably large and imprecise numbers of individuals. At the same time this very lack of precision, coupled with the difficulties of obtaining evidence caused by differences of language, encryption and the need for international inquiries, has led Britain's police to seek longer and longer terms of detention before charge. Most of those involved come from one specifically identifiable community, one under great pressure, and most of the arrests have a high media profile, as does the inevitable release of many of those who have been detained. Add to this the development of apparently secret tactics like Kratos and an argument can be mounted that the police are moving beyond the proper boundaries of their role. And, other than the government and the police, there are few other voices raised in support of the change in tactics and legislation being both introduced and sought.

There is a danger that the equivalent of the much discussed military compact between the armed forces and the public, the concept of policing by consent, is being eroded and that each further arrest of suspected terrorists makes the situation worse. And yet the risk of atrocity remains extreme. It is possible that this decade will one day be seen to have been an aberration and that the threat from Islamist-inspired terrorism will diminish. But that cannot be assumed and again a Royal Commission would be best placed to determine those principles which should set the limits of the police's mission and decide whether sufficient public will can be garnered to support the present approach to policing or whether, perhaps, some other agency must be established, with different powers, responsibilities and accountability, in order to protect the relationship between the people and their police.

I hope that this will not be necessary. The bitter rivalries between the Federal agencies in the United States and between those agencies and local police forces are unrelenting, as has been demonstrated by the failure after 9/11 to incorporate almost any part of the FBI or the CIA into the Department of Homeland Security. The acronym 'FBI' is often said by local police officers to stand for 'Famous But Ineffective'. Counter-terrorism is an essential part of policing; routine policing is an essential part of counter-terrorism; and national security depends on neighbourhood security. But not many more years can pass before this issue is fully, dispassionately and publicly considered in the UK.

In the UK, if the police should retain primacy for counter-terrorism investigation, then the Met should continue to take the national lead for the reasons I explained to Boris. However, its role needs to be enshrined in law to prevent continuous arguments over primacy and liability. Such arguments will return again and again unless straightforward legislation is introduced to distinguish between the responsibility of a local Chief Officer and that of the National Coordinator for Terrorist Investigations, working to the Commissioner of the Met.

Lastly, and particularly in the light of the way terrorism has developed, I turn to the future of accountability. Accountability for policing exists at four levels in the UK: the national, the force, the town and the neighbourhood. At the top end of policing are national institutions, including the Home Office. There is a plethora of conferences and committees but the independent voice of the citizen is missing and some form of users' council is needed, as has long existed in medicine or various arms of transport. Furthermore, it is clear that the role of the centre has grown in the years since the Tripartite Arrangement was propounded and a Royal Commission would need to consider whether the elegantly overlapping responsibilities within it need redefining.

At the next level down, every UK police force has a headquarters, combining full democratic accountability to the Police Authority and the delivery of services that require economies of scale. Police Authorities or some other form of body to which senior police officers must be accountable are a necessary part of the democratic control of policing. In terms of immediate change it will be important to recognise that to have only elected members is to risk returning to the politics of Derbyshire described in Chapter 5. The independent members introduced by the Conservatives in the early 1990s are a crucial counter-balance. The principal reform necessary is to ensure that the independent members are not chosen by the elected members. It would not be difficult to envisage a system for their selection based on Nolan principles and supervised by the Civil Service Commission or some similar body.

In London a new settlement needs to be devised which introduces representatives of the London boroughs to the Metropolitan Police Authority, probably based on the five sub-regions into which the boroughs have divided themselves, and probably at the expense of five members from the London Assembly. This would require the MPA to become, like every other Police Authority, a body which places a direct precept on the council-tax payer. Legislation also needs to be introduced to make clear the respective responsibilities for policing, in terms of subsidiarity, of the Home Secretary and the London Mayor.

Within the context of accountability, of course, any Royal Commission would have to examine and probably redefine 'operational independence'. As late as 1986, the former Chief Inspector of Constabulary, Eric St Johnston, was able to describe the concept thus: 'It has been said that, in operational matters, a Chief Constable is answerable to God, his Queen, his conscience and to no one else', showing that the Denning judgement was too wide and some police chiefs will have used that to avoid proper scrutiny. 'Operational independence' is not the equivalent of freedom from a requirement to explain operational decisions. Nonetheless, the continuing increase in target setting and the introduction of performance bonuses and annual appraisals by Police Authorities of Chief Officers have reduced the level of independence once enjoyed by earlier generations of Chief Constables and Commissioners. It is simply wrong for such a vital concept to drift and evolve without sustained, objective scrutiny.

To modernise accountability two final changes are needed which may seem but are not incompatible. First of all, it is a hangover from the Watch Committees of the tiny police forces of the past that Police Authorities should choose senior police officers other than the Chief Constable or Commissioner. What other leader of an organisation with a £100m budget would not be able to choose his or her top team, let alone the £3bn Metropolitan Police: some of the pain I described in the last chapter is because, while, as a Chief Constable and Commissioner, I could and have chosen to 'let go', as the jargon has it, some of my senior police staff colleagues, I could not do the same with a senior police officer. Police Authorities should choose the Chief, hold him or her accountable but not also saddle him or her with people that he or she does not believe to be the best available. And that availability also needs strengthening because there is just not enough geographic movement at the senior levels of the police, with too few of the best people applying for the toughest jobs and the Met, for instance, being seen as very difficult to enter at a senior level. Once someone passes through the Strategic Command Course and seeks to become a Chief Officer, they should know that their career will be, in part, centrally managed and that the Home Office and the Chief Constables and Commissioners will decide on the jobs for which they should apply (but not control who would be appointed because that would remain a matter for either the Police Authority or the Chief Officer) and reimburse them and their families for moving. In effect there would be a General Staff for the police, which would ensure that all officers at this level took a mixture of staff and line roles and the best were ruthlessly groomed for the most significant commands, which is not the case at the moment.

While other parties are searching for an alternative plan for Police Authorities to match the simplicity and potential popularity of the Conservative proposal for elected Commissioners, I am clear that while that should be avoided, any other reform of Police Authorities is not in itself enough. Nor will further tinkering with the third level of accountability below that of Police Authorities, which is the necessary, regular answerability to citizens of the man or woman in charge of a human scale chunk of policing, such as a small town or a London borough, who is responsible for the delivery of all but the most specialist of policing services. Not everyone – in fact mostly only the usual suspects but it is a crucial part of the pattern – wants to go to meetings at a town hall.

None of these will be the main way in which public involvement in policing and the development and maintenance of an appropriate contract or compact between police and public can be restored – because to think they are misunderstands how the public see policing.

These issues are important – because if they go wrong the consequences are grave. However, to most members of the public they are arcane. By all means let the politicians and the police chiefs argue over them but they are far from the main issue. And here I need to introduce Egon Bittner, born in Czechoslovakia, a Holocaust survivor and American sociologist, who has come closer than anyone else to encapsulating the nature of policing.

In his 1974 article 'Florence Nightingale in Pursuit of Willie Sutton: A Theory of the Police' Bittner wrote that 'the police officer and the police officer alone is equipped, entitled and required to deal with every exigency in which force has to be used' and he defined those exigencies as 'something that ought not to be happening and about which someone had better do something NOW'. The extraordinary title of the work needs some explanation. Willie Sutton was a notorious American bank robber, and Bittner contrasts him with Florence Nightingale to point out that only a small part of police work actually concerns crime and that more time is spent on what he defines as regulatory control and peacekeeping. Four years earlier, in an article entitled 'The Function of the Police in Modern Society', he had said, in a more academic style: 'The role of the police is to address all sorts of human problems when and insofar as their solutions do or may possibly require the use of force at the point of their occurrence.'

But I like the more immediate tone of 'Willie Sutton and Florence Nightingale' and I particularly care for three words: 'equipped', 'entitled' and 'required'. All three are important. There is one precondition for Bittner's words and that is that the police officer may be *equipped* and may be *required,* as he might be in Zimbabwe or in Myanmar, but he cannot be *entitled* in a democracy without the consent of the people, and the consent of the people will rarely be established through the work of a Police Authority or the will of government, except in outline or *in extremis*.

And that is because, while policing is delivered at four levels, the bottom one is by far the most important. What will determine the entitlement of the officer to do something, including using force, about 'something that ought not to be happening and about which someone had better do something NOW' is the absolutely vital engagement at the most local level between police and public, the level of the self-defining community of the neighbourhood.

During the days after I announced my resignation I hardly read the newspapers, most of which were full of rejoicing. However, a kind colleague drew my attention to another piece written by Martin Kettle of the *Guardian*. In assessing my achievements and demerits (with little pulling of punches there), he described me as the third key revolutionary in the modern history of the Yard (with Robert Mark and Peter Imbert) and considered my greatest contribution 'the restructuring of the Met to put neighbourhood policing at the absolute forefront of its mission'.

The reinvention of neighbourhood policing is the most important policing development of modern times. The Audit Commission study mentioned earlier, *Streetwise*, showed that the most significant boost to public confidence in policing is for a member of the public both to recognise and to know the name of his or her local officer. All other forms of accountability, most other achievements of policing and almost all other government priorities for the police pale beside the significance of local, visible and preventative policing. Safer Neighbourhoods delivered this as a possibility across the whole of London, together with wide experimentation in public consultation and engagement. The government has recently required some form of neighbourhood policing to be rolled out across every force in England and Wales. However, it remains unfinished business, ripe for further development.

This kind of very local policing is the bedrock of policing by consent and it always has been. Political parties and police chiefs should concentrate on delivering it in the best way possible. It was this kind of preventative patrol which was Peel's vision. I believe its reintroduction was the best fruit of my years of policing controversy.

I wish it well.

List of Illustrations

1. Ian Blair, 2008, (Metropolitan Police Archive).
2. Ian Blair as Claudius, photograph by Nick Bamford.
3. Hendon class photograph of 1975, (author's photograph).
4. Special course, 1978 (author's photograph).
5. Ian Blair with a Met firearms team, 2008 (author's photograph).
6. David Blunkett and Sadie, (Odd Andersen/Getty Images).
7. Ian Blair with Charles Clarke, (Metropolitan Police Archive).
8. John Reid (AFP/Getty).
9. Jacqui *Smith, (Dan Kitwood/Getty Images).*
10. *Private* Eye cover, Issue no. 1197, 9 November, 2007. Reproduced with kind permission of *Private Eye*.
11. 'I'm thinking of suing Ian Blair for racial discrimination' Cartoon by Mac, originally published in the *Daily Mail*, 12 September 2008. Reproduced with permission.
12. 'Sir Ian Blair is top cop', cartoon by Peter Brookes, first published in *The Times* 29 October, 2004, (NI Syndication).
13. 'Response to no confidence vote', cartoon by Peter Brookes, first published in *The Times*, 9 November, 2007, (NI Syndication).
14. Ian Blair with Richard Chartres, Bishop of London, (author's photograph).
15. Met Safer neighbourhood team, (Metropolitan Police Archive).
16. Ian Blair comforting mother of a fallen soldier.
17. The wreck of the Number 30 bus that exploded in Tavistock Square. (AFP/Getty Images).

18. Paul Dadge, right, helps an injured tube passenger away from Edgware Road Station. (Press Association).
19. Public viewing for the International Olympic Committee decision, Trafalgar Square. Photograph by Christopher Lee (Getty Images).
20. 7/7 memorial in Hyde Park (Press Association).
21. London car-bomb made safe by the police, 2007. Photograph by Peter Macdiarmaid (Getty Images).
22. Firefighter weeps on September 11. Photograph by Mario Tama (Getty Images).
23. The shrine in memorial to Jean Charles Menezes in Stockwell. Photograph by Max Nash (Getty Images).
24. Andy Hayman. Photograph by Scott Barbour (Getty Images).
25. Brian Paddick. Photograph by Julian Herbert (Getty Images).
26. Tarique Ghaffur. Photograph by Shaun Curry (Getty Images).
27. Cartoon by Neil Bennet (NI Syndication).
28. Boris Johnson triumphs in London Mayoral election. Photograph by Daniel Berehulak (Getty Images).

Index